THE OUTSIDER

www.**transworldbooks**.co.uk

JIMMY CONNORS

THE OUTSIDER

MY AUTOBIOGRAPHY

BANTAM PRESS

LONDON • TORONTO • SYDNEY • AUCKLAND • JOHANNESBURG

TRANSWORLD PUBLISHERS
61–63 Uxbridge Road, London W5 5SA
A Random House Group Company
www.transworldbooks.co.uk

First published in the United States
in 2013 by HarperCollins

First published in Great Britain
in 2013 by Bantam Press
an imprint of Transworld Publishers

A CIP catalogue record for this book
is available from the British Library.

ISBN 9780593069271 (cased)
9780593069288 (tpb)

All photographs are courtesy of the author unless otherwise indicated. Grateful
acknowledgment is made to Art Seitz for his photographs included in the inserts.
Photograph on page 403 by Brett Connors. Endpaper photograph © Michael Cole/
Corbis. Designed by William Ruoto.

Addresses for Random House Group Ltd companies outside the UK
can be found at: www.randomhouse.co.uk
The Random House Group Ltd Reg. No. 954009

The Random House Group Limited supports the Forest Stewardship Council® (FSC®),
the leading international forest-certification organisation. Our books carrying the FSC
label are printed on FSC®-certified paper. FSC is the only forest-certification scheme
supported by the leading environmental organisations, including Greenpeace. Our paper
procurement policy can be found at www.randomhouse.co.uk/environment

Typeset in 11.25/16.5 pt Bembo
Printed and bound in Great Britain by
CPI Group (UK) Ltd, Croydon, CR0 4YY

2 4 6 8 10 9 7 5 3 1

To Patti

CONTENTS

CONTENTS

THE OUTSIDER

1

OUT OF THE SHADOWS

'm 29 years old and for the last three years people have been telling me I'm finished, washed up, done.

That doesn't sit well with me. I'll say when I'm done and I'm not done yet. I haven't even reached my peak. Screw 'em.

It's 1981 and I lost my hold on the number one ranking in the world in the previous year, and even though I've claimed 17 titles since then, I haven't won a major tournament. There's an element of doubt creeping into my daily training: Do I still belong? Can I still compete at this level? I'm not winning. I'm being pushed onto the back burner. That's hard to take.

I'm up, I'm down. I think I'm good and then I don't win. I get up every day and do the right things, but the results aren't improving. I'm getting to the semifinals, and I'm losing matches I should win. Not good enough. Winning lesser tournaments along the way is fine, but it's not the majors and that's what I'm looking for. Anyone else in those years would have been content with my record—but not me and obviously not the media. This has been the most frustrating three years of my career.

"You're not going to reach your prime until your thirties," my mom keeps telling me. "My prime? What the hell, Mom? What was the last six or seven years about?"

"You wait," she says. "You haven't played your best tennis yet."

My wife, Patti, our two-year-old son, Brett, and I are living in

North Miami at Turnberry Isle, Florida. We moved down from Los Angeles for the tennis, but distractions are everywhere. This is a playground for the wealthy. Rich people come here from all over the world for the gambling, discos, restaurants, golf, and—I'm guessing—drugs. In the evenings I can go down to the courts and play tennis against guys who bet $5,000 a set they can beat me if I play them right-handed. Guess what? They can't. The extra cash is nice, but the fun and laughs is what it's really all about. But I have only one thing on my mind: reclaiming my position at the top of the tennis world.

I continue to work my ass off every day, practicing two and a half hours in the morning with the Turnberry Club tennis pro, Fred Stolle, a former Grand Slam champion from Australia. He stands in one corner of the court and hits the ball to the opposite corner so I have to run the whole width of the court in order to return the shot. Then he moves to the other corner and I do the same thing from the other side. Then Fred comes up to the net and stands over on the right side so that my forehand passing shots have to go up the line and my backhand has to go crosscourt. Every drill I do is designed to replicate a situation I'm going to face against my toughest opponents. I've never hit a shot in a match that I haven't practiced over and over.

Later in the day I play a couple of sets with my longtime friend David Schneider, a former top South African player, who practices with me whenever I want to fine-tune what I worked on with Fred that morning. Afterward, David and I have a Coke and relax as buddies. It's nice to let tennis go and be able to talk about other things.

It's difficult balancing tennis with family life, my friends. When I'm with my family, I feel like I'm slighting the tennis. When I'm practicing, I feel like I'm slighting my family. When I get up at 6:30 a.m., Brett is eating breakfast and watching *The Smurfs*. I want to spend time with him, but I know I have work to do on the court.

When I'm playing tennis, I feel I should be spending time at the pool with Brett and Patti. There are conflicts everywhere I turn. When friends visit, I want to go out and have fun with them, stay out late, but then I am slighting both my tennis and my family. If I go down to the restaurant for breakfast I'll see 10 people I'm obliged to say hello to and that will hold up my day.

Mom is on the phone. I talk to her at least 10 times a day. This may sound like a lot, but Mom is also my business manager. My schedule is made six months in advance, so not only is she "checking in" as a mother, mother-in-law, and grandmother; she is letting me know about commercial offers, upcoming tournaments, and all the numerous details involved in my career.

If any of the calls lasts more than a few seconds, it's because she knows I'm having problems. She's concerned about me. I have to push myself further than I want to, train harder, practice longer. I'm older and things don't come as easily now. I don't mind the physical part. It's getting into the right mental state that I find tough. I haven't been winning the way I expect to, but I have to find a way to act as if I am, so I won't talk myself out of it. I don't want to fall into that trap of saying, "Oh, shit, maybe they're right. Maybe I am finished." I have to find my self-confidence, even though I'm not sure where I left it. Things aren't working out for me, so to get myself through it I have to be twice as arrogant. That's how I'll cope. I can't go out there and just be half-assed; I've got to go all the way. I have to be prepared, I have to be in the best shape possible, and my game has to be ready.

Wembley, England. November 14, 1981.

Wembley is a big tournament at the end of the year, but it isn't a Grand Slam, and yet this isn't just another match. I'm down two sets to love, looking across the court at . . . John McEnroe.

I love playing Borg, Lendl, Nastase, Panatta, and Gerulaitis. The list of great players from my era is as long as my arm, but to play Mac is beyond the realm of just tennis. He's my gauge; I look to him to see the level I have to reach to be number one again.

Mac is the best player in the world. He's just won Wimbledon and the US Open. When McEnroe was coming up he wanted everything that I had. I was number one in the United States and he wanted that. I was number one in the world and he wanted that. Then he took it all. And now I want it back.

I'm not just going to roll over and say it's too tough, that he's too young (seven years younger to be exact). Even though Mac and I clash at every turn, we're so much alike it's scary. I'm Irish, he's Irish. I'm left-handed, he's left-handed. I've got a bad attitude, he's got a bad attitude. I've always said I would love to play myself, and Mac is as close to playing me as I'm going to get.

This McEnroe match could be my return to winning in a big way. I know my game is getting better again, and now I have a chance to prove it by beating Mac in the final.

Unfortunately, I'm down two sets to love. All I can do is to figure out how to stay out there one more minute, one more point, one more ball, one more anything to keep putting some pressure on Mac—that's all I want to do. I made my reputation on my all-out aggressive style of play and I'm going to live or die again today with that. I'm not just going to wait for something to happen. I'm going to force the action.

But, right now, I'm not in it. Mac is the show. He's doing everything right and I'm like a bit player in his future Broadway production of *Kicking Connors's Ass*. I'm getting steamrolled, but, in tennis, sometimes even the smallest thing can change the course of a match. It might be a shot, a call, an interruption from the stands, anything to relieve the pressure and the tension. Of course, that kind of small change can work against me, too. It wouldn't be the first time I let myself get sidetracked.

Mac is under what I call "confrontation time-out," which means he hasn't emptied his bucket yet, there's still more to come, and he's resting up for a second assault on the umpire. He's sitting in his chair looking up at him, and then he starts in again.

"You don't know the rules. You don't have the right to tell me anything."

I wander over to a kind, sympathetic face in the stands, a girl who looks like she's feeling sorry for me because I'm getting hammered. I suck up a few words of encouragement from her and then get back to the business at hand. That one small moment is all it takes for me to feel like I'm a part of what's going on around me. I loosen up. Now I have a chance to go inside my head and confront my demons; it's that place where I can dig up something from my past to help me push on to the win.

I look back at the way my grandfather, Pop, trained me. There was only one way to do it: his way. Anything else was unacceptable. He pushed and pushed. I could jump rope with the best of them, but Pop sometimes went too far. As a kid I'd pick up the rope and start jumping for 10 or 15 minutes. Then I'd ask, "How much do you want me to do, Pop?"

"Why don't you do five more minutes?" he'd say.

I'd be jumping rope for five more minutes and Pop would be walking back and forth in front of me, talking.

"You know, Jimmy, it might be better if you do 10 more minutes."

In that five minutes I had been jumping, I'd be trying to get the most out of that time, and I'd think, "God, now 10 more minutes?" I mean I had pushed it hard from the time I picked up the rope, so do

I keep going full-speed, or do I slow down because he might come back and say 20 more minutes?

All the time I'm jumping, I'm worrying about picking up my feet and doing it the right way, because if I miss I have to start over from the very beginning. I'm trying to concentrate and work.

"OK, Jimmy, you have 20 minutes."

At this point Pop is talking to me about nothing in particular, asking questions about school, my friends, where I want to have lunch. He's walking around, trying to get in my way, doing anything and everything to distract me and mess up my concentration.

It almost seemed like a game to him. And I would be thinking, "Son of a bitch! What's going on here? I'm exhausted!"

Looking back, I realize he was helping me build the mental and physical strength I would need to cope with the best tennis players in the world.

Pop was telling me in his way that no matter how prepared you are, there will always be something going on, either on or off the court, that will take your mind off your game. How I deal with that is down to me.

It's the beginning of the third set now and my footwork is better and I'm more prepared to hit shots. My returns become more penetrating, deeper, faster, so Mac has less time to react. I start dictating the course of play.

Once I break serve in the third set, my confidence level rises for the first time in the match. I'm hitting my groundstrokes closer to the lines, with more control and accuracy. Because of that, Mac gets to the ball late, giving him fewer opportunities to impose his game on me. Even though we're similar in some ways, our styles of play contradict each other. When one of us is really on top of his game, it detracts from the other. His strengths are serving and volleying;

mine are hitting from the back of the court and moving the ball around. So, unlike the first two sets, where Mac was serving great and coming into the net, which is his comfort zone, now he has to play the way I want him to play, from the baseline.

After I win the third set, I've turned the momentum in my favor, and even though I'm still down a set, I know that no matter what Mac plans to throw at me, I'm ready for it. Still, I want to make sure I don't get too cocky. That's still John McEnroe across the net and you can never take John McEnroe lightly. Ever.

I go up a service break in the fourth and the crowd senses a turning point. They're getting their money's worth and now they're cheering for both sides. However, the more excited the fans get the easier it is for me to get lost in their enthusiasm. So now it comes down to this: how to keep my wits about me when everyone around me is losing theirs. My job is to make the crowd go crazy, not to join them.

There's no doubt my mental game has caused me problems in the past. It seems like nothing ever runs smoothly when I'm going to play. I've even forgotten my bag or racquets because I was thinking too much about the match.

Once when I was about to play the finals of the US Open, my limo—I always had a car and driver take me to and from my matches—got rear-ended two blocks from the hotel. Now we have to go through all this crap of exchanging license numbers and names and I'm going to be late for the title match. So what do I do? Do I tell the driver to speed up and find a shortcut to the stadium? No, it's back to the hotel to start all over again. There's been a change in my routine. I have no choice.

Are you asking yourself, "Why would he do that?" It's a thing called OCD: obsessive compulsive disorder. Yup. I have it. Didn't know that, did you? Well, neither did I at the time.

When I turned pro at the age of 19, I started having what I used to call "twitches." They showed up the first time I went to Wimbledon. My first "twitch" occurs when I'm playing Centre Court and I walk over to get a Coke. I take a drink and start to put the can down, but my hand won't let go of the can.

"Time, Mr. Connors," the umpire says, noticing my bizarre behavior. "Time, Mr. Connors."

Put the damn can down and get the hell back out there, I'm telling myself. I can feel the umpire looking at me. Time is running out. But I can't let go of the can.

"Time, Mr. Connors. Time, Mr. Connors," the umpire says again.

The can doesn't feel right in my hand. For some reason, it doesn't feel solid. Twenty thousand people are watching me trying to put down a can of soda! I'm saying to myself, LET GO OF THE FUCKING CAN!

Finally, after about 25 times, the can once again feels comfortable in my hand and I'm able to put it down. I'm ready to play again.

I go to serve and now I can't stop bouncing the ball. I bounce it 30 times, trying to get the ball to feel right. Believe me, I'm not trying to throw off my opponent's game with all the bouncing, although that might be a fortunate side effect. It's just that I won't be able to stop bouncing the ball until it feels right in my hand and connected to my brain.

It was only when I was in my mid-thirties that I saw a television show on OCD, and I realized, Damn! I've got that. I thought I was just superstitious, fidgety, and nervous. Who knew they had a name for it?

I've had the symptoms of OCD since that first trip to London and throughout the rest of my career. It was exhausting. Any action— from putting something in the fridge over and over again to moving a chair to the perfect spot—could pop up at any time and totally occupy my thinking. I've probably had the symptoms of OCD since childhood, but they didn't become pronounced until the stress and excitement of my first Wimbledon.

Even now, when I let my dogs out at night before going to sleep, it happens. Long after the dogs are back in the house and in their beds, I can't get my mind off the door. Lock, unlock, repeat. Is the door closed? No, that didn't sound right. Push in the door. That doesn't feel right either. Sometimes my hand is willing but my mind isn't, and sometimes my mind is but my hand isn't. Obviously, it's not rational. If I had the answers, I'd probably have a cure.

Sometimes my kids will mess with me. I'll be in bed—comfortable, horizontal, and ready for a good night's sleep—and they'll come in and say, "Dad, I wonder if that door is locked." Now I'm up again, walking around the house six times, making sure everything is locked and locked and locked and locked and locked and locked. For the most part, though, it happens more when I'm by myself. It's embarrassing and tiring, but I've never looked at it like it was a debilitating disease. I pretty much just laughed at myself. What the hell. But if you see me when you're out to dinner, don't think I'm going to be your evening's entertainment unless I'm your waiter and you bought my book. In that case, I'll give you a show.

It's the fourth set and still tight. Mac probably thinks that if he doesn't end it now, I'll probably break his will in the fifth. After I win the fourth, I can see the change in his body language. I can sense his confidence slip.

Two sets all. Mac trips and twists his ankle. I'm not surprised; the court is a carpet laid over hardwood. It's difficult to play on. It can bunch, give a little bit, and there are dead spots. Mac walks off the pain and prepares to get back to business. He would have played me on a broken ankle. I'd have played him on a broken ankle.

Our rivalry is about respect. He's able to bring out more in me than any other player, and I hope I do the same for him. I'm fighting my ass off and so is he. There is nothing fake about our rivalry. Mac is the one player I can watch limping around the court and feel good about saying, "Fuck that guy."

The ump tells Mac to play on. So he does. He serves and takes the point. His next serve hits the lineswoman right in her stomach—it had to hurt. I look at her, grab my stomach, and double over sympathetically. She smiles, the fans laugh and then applaud. I'm loving it.

I win the game, and at the changeover there are fireworks. Mac is sitting in his chair, yelling at the ump.

"It's your stupidity. All right? It's your stupidity. That was part of my injury time. That was 20 seconds of my injury time," Mac says. "You only make it worse when you say play on when I actually hurt myself!"

He's got a point. You get 20 seconds in between points. You also get three minutes of injury time; the ump was wrong to tell Mac to play on. Mac could have called for a trainer if he wanted to, but the ump didn't seem to know the rules. When someone is the umpire in a match between Mac and me, he's sitting on a ticking bomb; in fact, he's sitting on two ticking bombs. It's just a matter of time. It's not if, but when.

So I'm hanging around on my side, thinking, "Screw him, let him fight his own battle," even though I know he's right. I've fought enough on my own.

"It doesn't have to be continuous if I hurt myself!" Mac yells at the umpire.

I'm ready to get back on the court, but at the same time I want to stay in my chair and hear the conversation. Hey, what the hell? What's another 30 seconds when some good insults might be coming from Mac? But I'm disappointed this time, because Mac says nothing as he stalks back on the court.

I'm ahead in the fifth and serving when Mac hits a backhand passing shot down the line. It's out, but it's called in. Here we go again. I'm so close and then this shit happens. I head for the umpire.

"We've been playing over three hours and I know you must be very tired," I say. "You've been doing a lot of running and everything. So just try and pay a little bit of attention." Sarcasm—the weapon of champions.

I'm playing well. The match is going my way and I can feel it. The extra work is paying off. I take the next points easily. Connors, 40-love, triple match point. Mac hits a backhand return into the net, and then it's over. I was down two sets and I battled back to win, 2-6, 3-6, 6-3, 6-4, 6-2.

This is what's it's all about. This is boxing at 90 feet. Throwing blows at each other until there's only one man left standing.

I've always said the next best thing to playing and winning is playing and losing, because at least I'm playing tennis, I'm in the game. I could never ask for anything more than that.

I've always gauged the mettle of someone's character by the way they figure out how to continue a losing fight. I always knew which guys would stay in there and battle to the end, and I knew the guys who wouldn't, and believe me there were more of those.

Those three years of criticism—hearing that I was finished, that the game was passing me by, that other players were pushing me aside—gave me a gift: They made me understand that I needed tennis. I needed to go out and win. I needed to see sold-out stadiums— the proof that I was winning. I couldn't let the critics beat me. Even if what they were saying was "Come on, Jimmy, we expect more of you." And if some of the fans were actually trying to get rid of me, I needed that motivation as well. It all made me work harder. What they didn't know was that it was the greatest compliment they could have given me. Those years were hard and frustrating, but I never once, even for a second, lost my love and passion for tennis.

My grandmother, Two-Mom, always told me to keep a little mystery about myself in life, and that's what I did during my career. As a result, there was always a lot of speculation from so-called experts and critics who thought they knew me. If they're reading this, they know what I'm talking about.

Well, now it's my turn to tell you about myself. I'm just simply telling my story, and this is the way it is and I accept full responsibility for anything and everything I ever did, have done, will do in the future.

Are we clear? OK, good. Now turn the page.

SHAPING AN ATTITUDE

'm eight years old and I'm watching a thug beat the shit out of my mother and my grandfather. There's blood on the court. I can't help them. I'm powerless. This day will transform me more than any other event in my life.

My older brother, Johnny, and I are playing tennis on the public courts in Jones Park, in East St. Louis, Illinois, with Mom and my grandmother, whom we call Two-Mom because she's like our second mom. There are five hard courts in a row and no one else is around. Two guys in their early twenties come over to hang out, and they get on the next court. They place a large transistor radio at the foot of the net post and turn it on full blast. The music is so loud we can't hear Mom giving us instructions across the net. She asks them politely to turn the music down. They ignore her. They are screwing around, yelling and swearing. Mom asks them, again, to please turn it down or move over a court. They call her a bitch. We keep playing.

My grandfather, who is chief of the parks police, comes over. Pops, as we call him, likes to watch us practice. He isn't happy with the guys next to us, but neither is he looking for trouble. We stop and watch as Pop approaches them.

"Boys, would you mind turning that down a little?"

One punk starts to bend down; I think he's going to turn off the music. Instead he throws himself at my grandfather, catches him off-guard, and tackles him to the concrete.

The punk straddles Pop, grabs him by the shirt collar, and starts banging his head into the court.

I don't even notice my mom run over to help her father. When she goes to grab the young guy by the shoulder, he whirls around and punches her right in the mouth. Her teeth go flying. Two-Mom moves toward Johnny and me, but she can't shield us from seeing our mother fall bloody onto the tennis court.

Then the punks just run away. It happens so fast that it feels like a bad dream, but it's all too real.

Two-Mom shoos everyone into the car and drives us home. Mom's friend, Booth, takes Mom into the bathroom and puts a towel on her face. At one point Mom pulls the towel away. What teeth she has left in her mouth are shoved through her lips and gums. Johnny screams, "Put it back! Put it back!" Booth gets mad and pushes Johnny out of the bathroom. Dad arrives and we take Mom and Pop to the hospital.

In the emergency room, the doctors treat Pop's head wound. Then it's Mom's turn. They pull out her last remaining teeth and she gets hundreds of stitches in her mouth.

That night we try and make Mom comfortable on the couch. Then Dad, Johnny, and I go back to the courts and search for Mom's teeth. We think maybe we should save them because they might be able to put them back or something. We just didn't know.

The next morning, Mom is resting on the couch when Johnny and I ask if she wants to go hit some tennis balls. We're too young to realize how injured she is. Yet Mom gets up and goes out into the backyard and hits balls with us. Nothing would ever keep her from playing tennis with her boys. She won't be able to pronounce any words for a month. She literally has to learn how to talk again. My mother will struggle with the injuries to her mouth until the day she dies, but she never complains or makes a big deal out of it. She never brings up the beating or uses it as an excuse.

Johnny and I talked about that day for years after it happened. We'd ask each other: Who does that? How does that even happen? How do we let something like that pass? There's no question it had a lasting psychological effect on both of us, but eventually we came to grips with it the best we could. I took my anger and used it in my tennis. Johnny dealt with it by channeling his rage in another way—by taking it to the streets.

After watching my mom get battered, the need for revenge ran strong in me, and I found I could use that emotion to achieve it. If she could hit balls the very next day after getting beat up, then I could play for one hour or five hours, no matter how bad my body ached. There's a line that Patrick Swayze has in the movie *Road House*. After he gets stabbed, the doctor, played by Kelly Lynch, asks Swayze if he enjoys pain, and he says, "Pain don't hurt." I understood that.

I could always find something to drive me, and most of the time it was those feelings of anger and rage that bubbled up from the past. My mother taught me how to harness those emotions. She called them Tiger Juices.

"Get those Tiger Juices flowing, Jimmy," she'd say to me.

Al Lynch "Pop" Thompson had been a lifeguard before he became chief of the parks police, and he was pretty famous around East St. Louis. There are still people in the area who talk about him from his police days, when he would ride around town on a huge white Harley. People knew him to be a fair man, and he wouldn't hesitate to help you if you needed it. Pop wasn't big, but he was wiry and guys knew not to mess with him, because in his younger days Pop had been a Golden Gloves middleweight boxer. He had his own style and attitude, and he built up a reputation good enough to be able to get in the ring with Joe Louis. Exhibition or not, it was still a great honor to fight the Champ.

In 1975, when I played Rod Laver in a Challenge Match at Caesars Palace, in Las Vegas, I flew Pop out to watch. This was the first
time Pop was ever on an airplane. (He used to work for the railroad,
so he always took the train.) I knew from my many visits to Caesars
Palace that Joe Louis was a member of the "Caesars family." He had
value as a sports personality and people loved being around him, so
Caesars Palace made him an official greeter. It was good for business.
He would socialize with the guests, and they, in turn, would spend
more time in the casinos.

After the match, Pop accompanied me to the post-match festivities. Try to imagine how proud I was when I saw Joe Louis at the
cocktail party, knowing that Pop had been in the ring with him. I
took Pop up to say hello to him.

"Mr. Louis, this is my grandfather, Al Lynch. He trained me,
and, at one time, he boxed with you."

Mr. Louis looked at Pop and said, "And I knocked you out,
right?"

Pop grinned, "Yeah, but you knocked everybody out."

Years later, my grandmother, Bertha, Two-Mom, told me that the
first moment she hit a tennis ball, she fell in love with the sport. She
couldn't afford lessons, but because she was a natural athlete, she was
able to teach herself how to play, figuring out on her own how to
improve her strokes and her footwork. Soon Two-Mom became an
established player in East St. Louis and the surrounding areas. She
and Pop then made a deal: He would teach her how to swim and she
would teach him how to play tennis. They went on to win several
local mixed-doubles titles, and by the late thirties and early forties
Two-Mom was one of the top-ranked women in the St. Louis district. She had a calm temperament and, like a human backboard, she
returned everything.

Two-Mom gave my mom, Gloria, her game. When my mom was a teenager, she played the Missouri Valley circuit and won district and municipal titles indoors and out. She and Two-Mom would often play doubles. In 1939, they played each other in the semifinals of the Heart of America invitational tournament, in Kansas City. Mom was 15 years old and lost 6-0, 6-0 to Two-Mom—her mother. Pretty tough lesson to learn, right?

That was the thing about growing up with these two women who loved tennis. There was no sentimentality involved. It was all about the game.

When I was old enough to play her, Mom didn't take it easy on me, either—she'd hit that ball right down my throat.

"See," she'd say. "If your own mother can do that, imagine what others will do to you."

In 1940, at 16, Mom was the youngest player in the women's Western Open tournament, in Indianapolis. By the time she was 19, she had competed twice in the US National Championships, at Forest Hills. She moved to Los Angeles, where she lived with her best friend, Pauline Betz, the great champion of her time, and played on the professional circuit. When Mom wasn't playing, she was teaching tennis to kids and coaching Hollywood celebrities like Mickey Rooney, Gilbert Roland, and Errol Flynn.

For Pop, however, and the majority of fathers in the forties, a daughter was not meant to travel all around the country playing tennis. She was supposed to get married and start a family. When he told her it was time to come home, Mom, an obedient Midwest girl with a Catholic upbringing, did just that.

Back in East St. Louis, Mom met my dad, "Big Jim" Connors, whose father, John T. Connors, was the mayor of East St. Louis. My dad had gone to Notre Dame and then served as a US Air Force second lieutenant in the Second World War, working as a bomber instructor. When he didn't return to finish his education, his father arranged for him to manage the tollbooths on the Veterans Bridge, which crossed the Mississippi River between St. Louis, Missouri, and East St. Louis, Illinois. He kept that job until the day he died, in January 1977.

After the war, Dad just wanted to have fun. He was a snappy dresser, good-looking, well built, cultured, and an all-around class act. When he proposed to Mom, she said yes immediately. The first years of their marriage were good, with a lot of friends in the area and a great social life. When my brother, Johnny, was born, in April 1951, Mom understood it was time to stay home and devote herself to the new baby, but Dad didn't see any reason to change his routine much. He liked hanging out with his friends; it was his life and he was going to live it the way he wanted.

I wasn't born to play tennis. In fact, I wasn't supposed to be born at all. (All right, I know what some of you are thinking; maybe it would have been better if I hadn't made it. Too bad.) After my mother had Johnny, she had a tubal pregnancy and a series of miscarriages and was told she couldn't—and shouldn't—get pregnant again. But she did and I was born, fragile and small. Mom said I was a little dishrag.

When Mom was pregnant with me, the family moved into a newly built house on 68th Street. A tall chain-link fence enclosed the backyard, and the whole yard was littered with debris from an ongoing construction project nearby. Mom convinced some of the workers to clean out and level the backyard for her. Then she got them to spread out a layer of concrete gravel. Two-Mom helped Mom paint white lines on the court, and they built a backboard out of two pieces of plywood. We even had a pile of gravel left over to patch up the court after it rained or after we'd used it as a bike track. People in East St. Louis didn't have tennis courts in their backyards, not even one that was makeshift, rough, uneven . . . and perfect.

I first picked up a racquet when I was three and a half. They didn't have junior racquets back then, so Pop cut down a couple racquets for Johnny and me. Johnny could just about wrap his hand around his racquet grip, but it was more difficult for me. My racquet was still too heavy, so I picked it up with both hands. Who knew that this would have such an impact on the game of tennis?

As I got a little older and a little stronger, Mom said, "Maybe we should take that hand off the racquet?" But that didn't work out, and she figured I'd give it up in a few years anyway. Back then, hardly anybody used a double-handed backhand. Sure, Pancho Segura, the great Ecuadorean tennis champion, had a two-handed forehand, but backhand? When I first started playing, people not only picked apart my style of tennis—"You can't play like that," they said—but they also considered me too small to ever make it. Really?

The two-handed backhand has some obvious downsides: You have to move quicker to get to the ball, because you don't have as much reach, and your footwork has to be more precise to get in position to use it correctly. The upside is once you get to the ball, you have the extra hand for power and direction. Unwilling to conform to other people's thinking, I stayed with what I thought could work. When Chris Evert and I came on the scene, the game of tennis changed. We both had two-handed backhands and we were winning everything. The two-handed backhand became the fashion and almost everyone started copying us. And players are still using it today.

I was the only lefty on either side of my family. When I was five years old, my mom wanted to make sure I was naturally left-handed, because I could play baseball and hit a golf ball right-handed.

"Let's try something new," she said one day. "Put your left hand behind your back and try and play right-handed."

I did as I was told, but my left hand immediately shot out without my even thinking about it and grabbed the racquet. Mom looked at me for a moment.

"OK. I guess that's the way it's going to be," she said.

In the beginning, Mom and Two-Mom would bounce balls to me and I'd try and hit them back. It was always casual and easy, never forced down my throat. It was good to have that court in the backyard, but make no mistake, it was there for a reason—so my mom could teach lessons for five bucks an hour during the summer and supplement the family income. If I didn't want to play, I didn't have to. If I wanted to ride my bike or play baseball, it was no big deal. Mom would say, "Be home by five o'clock." When I came home she'd ask if I wanted to hit a few balls. If I did, she'd put dinner on the back burner. If I didn't, we'd sit down to eat. No pressure.

Of course, back then nothing was ever a big deal. Our every moment wasn't scheduled like it is with kids today. My Mom, Two-Mom, and Pop had a way of educating me so that I didn't even realize it was happening. I watched them working hard and taking care of business. I could see, without having them say anything, that you did your job before you did anything else, and sometimes it took sacrifices, but in the end your hard work earned you rewards.

We weren't looked after every second of the day; as children we were allowed to make mistakes and take responsibility for ourselves under the guidance of our parents and grandparents. If we wanted to learn to ice-skate, well, there's the ice. Go skate. If we wanted to shoot BB guns, OK. Pop set up a rifle range in his backyard. Go shoot BB guns. I could play tennis and then grab my dog, Pepper, my miniature schnauzer, to go horse around with my friends. I wasn't a kid that needed to be entertained all the time. I liked riding my bike to my grandparents' house, which was about 10 minutes away, having some ice cream, and hanging with Pepper. Back then we had only four channels on TV, and one of the highlights was Friday night at the movies. The movie went on at eight o'clock, and instead of going out, I would stay home, pop some popcorn, lay on the floor with Pepper, and that was my evening.

But in those early years, it wasn't really tennis that I took to; it was the time spent with Mom and Two-Mom. Oh, yes, I can hear all the snide comments about my being a mama's boy, but you know what you can do with that. I learned everything from them and owe all I've ever had in my life to their mutual guidance.

I liked hanging around while Mom was teaching the local kids. I'd listen to the instructions she was giving her students and hope that some of it would rub off on me. Two-Mom was the greatest ball picker-upper of all time, and when Mom was teaching, Two-Mom would have an old-fashioned apple box and go around the court doing her thing. The box was always full—she took no breaks.

In the summer, Mom would teach eight or nine hours a day. When lunchtime came around, Two-Mom would stick a sandwich through the fence so Mom didn't have to stop. After having those two as role models, was I ever going to give up? These were the kinds of lessons I learned without anyone saying a word.

As the years passed, tennis became a bigger part of my day. Along with teaching tennis, Mom also had to carve out some court time for me. You have to remember that we are talking about the 1950s and 1960s, way before indoor tennis clubs came into existence. Anywhere I could play was a privilege.

Being brought up in Illinois was no picnic. Cold winters and hot, humid summers were the norm. There were times when we had to chip ice off our backyard court so that we could practice. I remember one winter when Mom, Two-Mom, and I were going to play on a locked court. We had a bucket of balls, racquets, and a little pick to work the lock and chip off the ice, but we decided instead to just go ahead and climb over the chain-link fence. Mom, who was always worried about everyone else, said, "Come on, Two-Mom, we'll help you over. Be careful on top." Two-Mom ignored us and just flung herself up and over the fence like it was nothing. When Mom climbed up, she got her sweat pants caught on the prongs at the top, and it took both of us a while to get her untangled and down. Of course, by then, we were on one side, locked in, staring at the balls and racquets we'd left on the other side. How can you not laugh at that?

In later winters, we would go to St. Louis's National Guard armory, crossing from Illinois into Missouri. Almost every day, Mom and Two-Mom would pick me up at school at 2 p.m. Getting there was hard work; depending on traffic, it would usually take us an hour and a half to drive across the bridge and to the armory.

During my junior-tournament days, I was playing bigger and better kids my age and not winning. How did my mom keep me interested in tennis, keep me from not being bored or discouraged? She told me that I had the basics down and that, if I kept going, I would grow into my game. How did she know that? I wish she were alive today so I could ask her. I'm Irish Catholic and not the most religious guy in the world, but I still go to church every Sunday to discuss a few topics with Mom. Maybe someday I'll get some of those answers I'm looking for. One thing I do know is that, during her years of training me, Mom had that "Fuck it" attitude toward anything that interfered with her vision for me. Maybe that's where I got my own defiant attitude.

So it was easy for me to play kids a few years older and tolerate losing, because I wasn't under any pressure—yet. I wasn't supposed to win. I would just go out there swinging away and gaining experience. Mom knew that, as my game got better, the kids my own age would become my future competition.

"If you can't beat kids your own age," she'd tell me, "you can't beat anybody."

So, I ask you, how was it that a woman from East St. Louis who loved playing and teaching tennis was able to come up with a style that fit a personality like mine? Well, she was a genius. Obviously, I'm prejudiced, but I listened to her instructions and understood that if I did what I was asked to do, that there would be rewards at the end. Once I had mastered the fundamentals, I could improvise— introduce different shots, different spins, and ways of directing the ball—anything that would make me a better player.

Mom could have taught anybody. She was able to get inside the mind of anyone she was teaching and identify the right buttons to push to get maximum result. If you talked to any of her old students today, they'd tell you the same thing.

Mom also understood what it took to keep me eager to get back out on the court. Practice was measured in quality not quantity. As a young boy, practice would last under an hour, and that remained the case pretty much throughout my career unless I was deliberately pushing myself. Sometimes I'd be on a roll, thinking I had it all figured out. I couldn't wait to play more, but that's exactly when Mom would walk on the court and call it a day. We quit when she decided I'd had enough. She never let me over-practice. Some of my buddies I grew up playing against, like Vitas, Guillermo Vilas, and Brian Gottfried, would be on the practice court for two or three hours, but for me it was 45 minutes. As a result, I always looked forward to my next workout.

Mom didn't always get it right. But as a kid, if I got annoyed at her, which was rare, I kept it to myself. When I was older and more independent, there were times when I thought she was interfering in my extracurricular life. Occasionally I would get so pissed off at her when we were practicing that I would slam down my racquet and storm off the court, yelling at her, "Get out of my life!" But that didn't last long.

A lot has been written about my mom being a stage mother, so let me set the record straight. Why was it OK for Joe Montana's dad to teach his son football or Wayne Gretzky's dad to teach him hockey but it wasn't OK for Gloria Connors to teach her son tennis? Mom stepped right into a man's world and a man's game during the height of the Women's Movement in the 1970s. Up until that point, people weren't used to dealing with a woman in the business end of tennis; both men and women players had men as managers, and men organized and ran tournaments. Along comes this feisty little woman from East St. Louis whose son was proving to be a winner, and they had to deal with her. When Billie Jean King was in the forefront as the first woman athlete to enter the boardroom, Mom had already been doing exactly that behind the scenes, fighting the established tennis bureaucracy. Now, if I hadn't been winning, they could have dismissed her and it wouldn't have been a big deal. But my mom represented me. And not only represented me but was my mother, coach, and friend.

She paid the price for treading into that traditionally male-dominated territory by having some pretty aggressive criticism thrown at her by the tennis establishment and the media. They would say she wanted my success more than I did because she had never had it herself, that she hadn't been good enough so she tried to make her son good enough. They called her "domineering" and "Dragon Lady." If it got to her, I never knew about it and neither did anyone else.

3

NOTHING WOULD EVER BE THE SAME AGAIN

What people seemed to miss entirely was the real story: Mom, Two-Mom, and Pop taught me the basic fundamentals and technique. I am proud of that, because I think it has become a lost art. But they also had a plan for how they wanted me to play, and they instilled it in me from the very beginning. No compromise. The game they taught me was a woman's game, but given to a man to beat men. It was both a very simple and yet complicated way to play, and no one else played it. No one.

Before the violent attack on Mom, the concrete courts at Jones Park played a big part in my tennis education. They had these steel nets that made a cracking, *twang* sound when you'd hit the ball into them. Also, the steel net didn't catch the balls; it would shoot them right back at you. So not only did you miss the shot; the net never let you forget it. I can still hear that sound today. On the tennis court at home, the bounce was uneven and the space behind both baselines was tight, so that's where I learned to take the ball on the rise. But at Jones Park the surface was smoother and we could play longer rallies, which gave Mom a better opportunity to assess how Johnny and I were progressing.

Mom would stand behind me, watching my every move, how I set my feet, whether I moved my body into the shot or got my racquet back soon enough, and every other little detail that helped me improve. If she saw something wrong, like I was tossing the ball too far in front of me on my serve, she would stop the session immediately and explain what the issue was—and not just when I was young—that strategy continued even after I had become the best. I always looked her square in the eye as she spoke; anything less would have been unacceptable. Why did I look her square in the eye? Respect. I knew that she meant to help me and I wanted to make sure I absorbed what she was saying.

My game was simple, but here are the two key ingredients. First, preparation. That was the foundation; be ready, racquet back, straight back, just like a gate swings. No excess motion. There's a lot of wasted motion in today's tennis, but that's not how I was taught. I was told to turn, bring the racquet back, and use my body to drive the ball. Today it's all arm power and swinging away with an open stance. Maybe you've even tried this yourself. It might be easier, but to me it's not as effective. Mom never gave me negative criticism. She was always positive, even if what we were working on wasn't quite where she wanted me to be. Mom would say, "Getting better, Jimmy, but it's not quite there.

"Move those feet. On your toes. Racquet back and time the ball."

OK, OK, I got it.

"If you've got it, then do it again and show me," she'd say.

Now, here comes the second and most important part: footwork. This is what made my game what it became. This was the hard part, and believe me, I worked on it every day.

My grandpa took great interest and pride in seeing both Johnny and me play tennis. But he knew not to get involved too much when it came to giving advice on our games. The looks Mom and Two-Mom used to throw him if he offered an opinion that wasn't asked for were enough to shut him up. Instead, he took on the role of my physical trainer, working with me as if I were a boxer.

He trained me like a boxer. He was tough. There was no discussion about the best way to train. His way was the only way. Jump rope, pick up your feet, and don't miss. If you missed, you would have to start over. No margin for error.

In my early teens Pop bought me a pair of heavy boots to run in. By then we had moved to a house at the top of a steep hill in Belleville, outside East St. Louis, and Pop had me running up that slope wearing those boots and carrying a weighted bag.

"Lift those feet high as you run, Jimmy," he'd say. "This is gonna do nothing but be good for you when it counts."

Pop was also the ultimate "Don't give a shit" guy. I remember after I had just lost 7-6 to McEnroe in the fifth set of the semifinals of the 1980 US Open. It was a really long, grueling match, and I was exhausted. On my way back to Florida, I stopped to see Mom in Belleville. When I arrived, Pop was sitting at the kitchen table, leaning back like he always did, with his hands locked behind his head. I'm standing there, just off the plane with Patti, the baby, the nanny, and 15 suitcases.

"Well, Jimmy, have you had time to figure out how to beat McEnroe yet?" Pop asked.

Wait! What?! I stared blankly at Mom and Patti.

"No, Pop, I've been kind of busy, but I'll get right on that."

That was my Pop. No nonsense. You're out there doing it, so do it right. From Mom, Two-Mom, and Pop's point of view, I should never have lost. I knew my performance was a reflection on them. Mediocrity was unacceptable, and pushing my limits started at an early age.

Although Johnny and I rarely played on the tennis courts at Jones Park after Mom's attack, we still went there with Mom, Dad, Two-Mom, and Pop to enjoy the facilities all year long. During the summer we fished in the lake, messed around in rowboats, and swam in the pool. We'd meet up with our friends for games of softball, while all around us families would be enjoying picnics and afternoons out. Not after dark, though. When the sun went down, a different kind of crowd came out, and those guys were looking for trouble.

I never looked for trouble, but one day when I was about 10 years old I found it. During the winter, the lake at Jones Park would freeze over so we could go ice-skating. People would build bonfires on the shore to roast hot dogs and marshmallows, and the kids who were old enough would have their jugs of Mogen David wine. One time, I was skating toward shore to get to the bonfire when I heard CRACK! CRACK! CRACK! The ice gave way a little. I knew what it was, but I was thinking, "I can make it." Then the ice gave way a little more, but I still believed I could make it. Then, before I knew it, I was neck deep in the freezing water, looking up and thinking, "Fuck, I didn't make it."

I was wearing about 30 pounds of winter clothes and starting to sink when suddenly I felt this big hand on my head. I had a buzz cut with a little tuft of hair in the front, and Pop grabbed me by that tuft and hauled me out. That was the day I decided that I wasn't ever going to do anything that caused me great pain. Except, well, play tennis for 47 years.

Actually, the park was responsible for teaching me another lesson. Right past the tennis courts in Jones Park was a line of lady cigar trees that had these big bean pods that Johnny and I would try and smoke. They were hard to light, but when we did take a hit, I usually ended up coughing my guts up and feeling sick. Cigarettes never stood a chance with me after that.

Pop was behind one of the most thrilling and dangerous experiences of my childhood. Beyond the lady cigar trees were the railroad tracks, a stretch of the line used by freight trains and coal cars that passed through at about five miles an hour. This was too tempting for Pop.

"Come on, boys," he said one day after tennis, and that's when we learned to ride the railcars.

Pop taught us how to run alongside the railcar, grab the post, and jump up on the step. Getting off was harder. You had to hang from the ladder on the side of the car and time your jump to make a soft landing in the bushes. Many a time I ended up with an ass full of stickers. Just all part of the learning process.

Once we got on the train, we saw a different way of life. The boxcars were filled with guys trying to make it from one place to another. Back then we called them hobos. So there we were, just off the courts, dressed in pristine tennis whites—although we weren't country-club boys—and hopping into a boxcar with hobos. Can you imagine how we felt? But there was never any tension, because we were with Pop, and Pop was always "packing heat." Watch out!

We usually didn't ride farther than the St. Louis rail yard, but once we stayed on as far as Kansas City, which was about 300 miles away. I had never been farther from home in my life on the train. When we got home from riding the railcars with Pop, Two-Mom would give him grief and Pop would just laugh it off. He was good at that.

Once Johnny and I were old enough to ride the railcars on our own, it was our favorite way to travel. If Johnny had to stay after school, he would grab a train home. If we wanted to head off into the local hills, we knew a perfect spot where we could make a soft landing.

Pop was full of fun lessons. Johnny and I would usually walk or ride our bikes to school, but sometimes we drove. It sounds crazy, but it's true. Pop taught us to drive his police car in Jones Park when I was eight years old and Johnny was ten. Pop would sit shotgun and

Johnny and I would take turns cruising along the paths. Thank God we were quick learners, because not long after we got behind the wheel, we had to take Pop to the hospital. We'd been at a swimming pool where he was teaching us some new dives. He did a speed dive from the shallow end, hit the bottom, and split his forehead open. He surfaced dizzy, disoriented, and bleeding. Johnny grabbed the keys to the police car and we managed to get Pop into the backseat, where I held a towel to his head. Johnny jumped in the driver's seat and hit the gas. He weaved through traffic, laid on the horn, and sped to the hospital. By the time we made it, there was so much blood in the backseat you would have thought Pop had been shot.

Driving became no big deal for us: hopping in a car without a license or adults; you're on your own, taking full responsibility. Whenever Pop would come over we'd take his police car out around the neighborhood. We'd visit our friends, go to the store, or drive ourselves to school. Pop never minded walking over to pick it up later. Remember, this was back in the 1950s; if you did the same thing today it'd be called "breaking the law." Occasionally, someone would see us driving past, trying to peer over the dashboard, and call the cops. When we were pulled over, we'd simply explain to the officer that Al Thompson was our grandfather and we'd be off the hook.

He'd say, "All right, then. Say hi to your pop and be careful going back."

What a time we had back then.

Mom didn't mind, but Dad didn't like us driving at all. He was busy working on the bridge all day so he wouldn't be around when we took the car, but he'd hear about it later.

Dad was a straight-shooter. If we ever did anything wrong, which we did—a lot—we always had to stand up to it. There was one time we snuck off to the house of a guy who pissed us off for some reason and slashed his tires. When Dad found out what we had done, he made us go over the next morning before school to apologize and pay for the damage. We had no money, but Dad wasn't interested in excuses. So how could we pay it off? Well, it was either a job or the belt, and I preferred the job. If you were out of line, you were out of line, and you had to do something about it. Never hide from your screw-ups.

Dad might not have been as involved in my upbringing as much as Mom, but he wanted us to do well in school. Unfortunately, I was never very good at it.

Johnny and I went to St. Phillip's grade school, 20 blocks from where we lived. In first grade, Mom would drop me off at school, and every day she would stop by the grocery store to decide what to put on that night's dinner table. By the time she got home, I'd be waiting on the back porch with Pepper. That didn't sit well with her, so back in the car and back to school I went.

School was torture for me from the very beginning. By the second grade, I'd settled down a little, mainly because the headmaster, Monsignor Forney, let Johnny and me play tennis during recess on one of the two courts he had built next to the baseball diamond. It was unusual in the 1950s for a grade school to have tennis courts— and a stroke of luck that my own school was one of them—but the monsignor loved the game, and he also got to hit with us once in a while. We loved it, too, because it got us out of school. To most of our classmates, tennis wasn't a real sport. White socks and white shorts? Come on, get real. If you didn't play baseball, basketball, or football, you'd better be able to run fast.

The kids used to give me a hard time, constantly teasing and pushing me around, especially after the monsignor let me leave school early in the third grade to go play at Jones Park. Johnny looked out for me as much as he could. He was good with his fists and protected me because I was small for my age.

Even when Johnny wasn't around to help, I didn't care how the kids at school treated me. I figured I'd be leaving East St. Louis, anyway. Mom had told me tennis was my way out of there, so I put up with the bullying and got on with it.

In class, I was a clock-watcher. I'd look at it every three minutes and the day would just drag on. My attention span was nonexistent, and it was an effort for me to read. I'd read lines multiple times because I'd lose my place or keep reading the same lines over and over again. Then I would forget what I was reading and have to start all over. Like I still do today.

It wasn't until I was an adult that I discovered I had something called an ocular-motor sensory deficit. That's the new, twenty-first-century version of you can't read. My eyesight was good, but my eyes didn't have the ability to work together. If I could have read with just one eye, I probably would have done OK, but I couldn't track the words using the two of them. No wonder I also had a short attention span and had trouble with reading comprehension.

Looking back, I have no idea how I was able to play tennis at all, but on the court I had perfect vision. I was able to see the ball quickly when it came off my opponent's racquet and track it into my hitting zone, trying to keep my eye on the ball until I made contact. Not bad for a guy who couldn't follow words on a printed page.

This eye problem was the reason why I always insisted on three-paragraph contracts in business. You tell me what you want me to do, I'll do it, and you'll pay me. I couldn't read 20 pages of a contract. I had no interest in the small print.

It wasn't until I turned 45 and got reading glasses that I was able to see clearly. It only took 30 years. On a flight from California to New York, my wife, Patti, will finish an entire book while I can read only about 60 pages. When I play tennis these days, I don't wear my glasses; it's too uncomfortable, because I wear progressive lenses.

It's better for me to see the ball come off my opponent's racquet, because I have a feel for where it's going. Once it crosses the net, I lose sight of it, so that by the time the ball gets close to me, it's a blur. Basically, I make my contact with the ball by memory. After playing for so many years, it's funny how that works.

So all you guys on the Senior Tour didn't know you were playing Mr. Magoo, did you? Funny what you'll do to keep playing a game you love.

In many ways, I guess we were a pretty regular 1950s American family in those early days. I say pretty regular because some interesting characters used to visit our house from time to time.

My dad's father, John T. Connors, passed away before I was born, and I'm sorry I never got to know him. My brother was named for him. John T. had been the police commissioner before he was elected mayor. There was a lot going on in City Hall during those years. Because of its river, railroad, and stockyards, East St. Louis was closely connected to Chicago. Back in 1947, Grandpa Connors was among 19 officials indicted for malfeasance for ignoring evidence of gambling and election irregularities. For my grandfather to have survived as mayor for as long as he did, he must have been strong-willed and one hell of a mover and a shaker. I sometimes wondered how many of his character traits I ended up inheriting. As time went on, I discovered more than a few.

One of my grandfather's friends, who was also close to my parents, was Frank "Buster" Wortman. Buster owned the Paddock lounge, in East St. Louis, where our family would go for dinner on occasion. One night, when Johnny and I were about eight and six years old, respectively, we were in the restaurant when a group of men burst through the front door. They looked around, rushed over to a corner of the room, and started shooting at four guys who were halfway out of their seats. A bunch of Buster's men surrounded our table and rushed us all into the kitchen. It turns out that Buster was the target and the shooters got the wrong table. I don't remember seeing him much after that. It was only years later that I found out that Buster had been a bootlegger, a gambler, and a member of the Shelton Brothers Gang during Prohibition. He then went on to take over St. Louis's illegal gambling operations in Southwest Illinois.

After my dad got out of the service, as a favor to my grandfather, Mayor John T., Buster offered to let my dad open up all the gambling for him in Granite City, a steel town near our home. Dad started doing that, but then Grandma Connors found out and put a stop to it. That was when Dad became the general manager of the Veterans Bridge, where he pulled in $10,000 a year. Talk about a life-changing decision.

But not every character from Mayor John T.'s interesting past got us caught up in the middle of a gunfight. One night, right around Christmas in the early 1980s, I had just come back to visit my family in Belleville after a full year on the road playing tennis. We decided to go meet Johnny at Charlie Gitto's Italian Restaurant, in downtown St. Louis. The owner, Charlie, had been at Johnny's wedding, and he was glad to see Mom and me and made a fuss whenever we'd come in for dinner. Two of Charlie's more colorful friends, Ralph "Shorty" Caleca, and his driver, Joe, were in the restaurant, and Johnny invited them to join us for dinner. Shorty had been one of the top bosses of organized crime in St. Louis in the 1940s, and he still held a great deal of power.

Let me back up for a second. From the time Johnny and I were little kids, Mom would sing a jingle to Dad just before the holidays: *"All I want for Christmas is a gray cashmere sweater with a white fox collar."* We'd hear it every year, and the joke was that she never got the sweater. For some reason, that night at dinner, we got to talking about that jingle. Shorty, who was in his late seventies at the time, suddenly growled:

"What'd she say? What'd she want?"

Johnny gets a call the next day from Charlie saying that Shorty wants to see him. So Johnny goes to the restaurant and there's a box with Mom's name on it.

"This is from Shorty. He says Merry Christmas to your Mom," says Charlie.

Johnny brings the box home and we put it under the Christmas tree. The next morning, Mom opens the box and I think you can guess what was in it.

I played my first junior event when I was seven years old. Mom drove Johnny and me a hundred miles to Flora for the Southern Illinois tournament. It was my first real tennis competition that was part of a circuit, and it was a big deal for me. Johnny won the event, and I was happy for him. I saw what it was like to walk off with the trophy.

I always looked up to Johnny, and it was right around this time that he started becoming interested in other things besides tennis. We would be practicing, and Johnny's shots would suddenly go flying over the back fence. Mom knew he wanted to be somewhere else, and she let him go. I wasn't like that. If I was on the court, I was there for the duration, trying to do the right thing.

The following year, Mom and I went back to Flora and I won my first-ever competition. I'd spent the year playing small events around the district, gaining experience and learning what it took to win. Johnny didn't go with us, because by that time he was a confident ten-year-old helping Dad out at the Veterans Bridge tollbooth. He worked on the bridge through high school and always seemed to come home with a pocket full of dimes and quarters. He had a knack for that.

As we got older, Mom could see we needed more than just the backyard or Jones Park to hit balls or play doubles against other kids. However, finding a better place for us proved to be a challenge.

The Knights of Columbus building on State Street, East St. Louis, was a Catholic social club that had a small basketball court behind a huge set of wooden doors that were locked but not very secure. There was a gap at the bottom of the doors that was just large enough for Johnny, Two-Mom, Mom, and me to squeeze through on our stomachs. There we could practice, uninterrupted, against the wall and on the hard wooden floor. After we finished, we'd play basketball with Mom and Two-Mom.

It was at the Knights of Columbus basketball court that I began to refine a technique that Mom had been drilling into both Johnny and me from our very first lessons in the backyard: hitting the ball flat and early. On those floorboards, if you didn't attack the ball, it would fly past you before you had time to set yourself. I sometimes wonder if Mom was aware of the progression from the backyard court to Jones Park to the Knights of Columbus and then on to the armory. Had Mom planned it or was she just seizing opportunities as they came her way?

Mom first took us to the National Guard armory in 1963, and I couldn't believe how big the place was. Its heavy steel doors looked large enough to drive a tank through. Above the doors was the military crest with words carved into the stonework: ARMORY, 138TH INFANTRY, MISSOURI NATIONAL GUARD.

Inside the armory's huge gymnasium, tennis courts were marked out on the highly polished floorboards. The armory was the only indoor tennis facility in St. Louis, and I was from the wrong side of the Mississippi River. Finding a game was hard, I was small, my mother was my coach, and I wasn't a member of the clique of kids from the good side of the river. In their eyes, I was an outsider, taking up valuable court time. But Mom figured out a way to make them accept us. She offered to coach some of the kids if they would hit with me. I would hang around all day on weekends and during vacations, if there was a latecomer or a no-show, I'd be out there like a shot, offering to play with anyone. That sense of being an outsider has never left me.

If I laid the foundation of my game at the Knights of Columbus, I took it to a new level at the armory. Balls came off that surface like lightning and would be gone before you knew it. There was no time to stay back and let the ball come to you. You had to move to the ball, meet it on the rise, and attack it. The three years I played at the armory set me apart from a lot of the other players of my generation. Many of them, like Borg, sat back, waiting for a mistake. I took the game to them, looking to be the aggressor.

For the first few months we played at the armory, Johnny would come with us, but he soon lost interest. After Mom and I finished practice, I would go look for my brother. I usually found him climbing all around the armory roof trying to hit passing cars with the crab apples that grew from the trees near the entrance. That was on his good days.

One day I couldn't find Johnny anywhere, so I sat on the steps of the armory and waited for Mom to finish coaching the other kids. I heard Johnny calling my name and looked over at the compound for military vehicles. Johnny was sitting behind the wheel of an Army jeep, driving in a circle.

"Come on, Jimmy, I opened the gate. Jump in."

When and where had Johnny learned to pick locks and hot-wire cars? I still haven't figured that out. I ran through the gate and jumped into the jeep with Johnny. The tanks and armored vehicles parked in rows made for a perfect racetrack.

"You do know how to stop this thing, right?"

"No idea," Johnny replied.

It was at that point that Johnny slammed the jeep into a big green truck.

"Let's get out of here," said Johnny. "We don't want to get court-martialed."

Johnny and I loved watching westerns on TV and playing cowboys and Indians with our friends. One night, when I was 11, we were lying in bed talking about how great it would be to be out there riding the range like the real thing.

"Let's get a horse!" Johnny said.

"Yeah, OK," I said. If Johnny thought it was a good idea, then so did I.

Growing up, I'd have given my left nut to be part of whatever he was doing. I loved tennis, but when I came home after practice I just wanted to hang around with my brother. He was always good about that, but in later years, when he was involved in riskier activities, he became protective of me and wouldn't let me tag along. And thank goodness for that.

We told Dad we wanted a horse and he thought we were crazy.

"OK, you want a horse, you buy it yourselves."

Buy it ourselves? Horses and boarding cost real money. But then Johnny had his stash from collecting tolls on the bridge, and with it we bought a riding quarter horse. Johnny paid my half, and my down payment was cleaning out the stall the first few weeks. Dad soon began to share our interest in riding and eventually bought his own horse, as well as one for me, a two-year-old palomino named Peaches. Boy, was she a handful, and I went flying over her pretty head countless times.

We used to jump a train that led to a low trestle bridge spanning a creek by our home and take the horses along the levee and into the hills to look for arrowheads. There, we would make corrals for the horses from fallen trees and camp out overnight. It was a lot of fun, but making believe we were living in the days of the Old West turned out not to be my thing; I liked the comforts of home—no furry creatures in my bed, thank you.

Within the year, Dad sank his own money into the stables we used, and it turned into a business. At one time we had about 50 quarter horses there, with bloodlines, starting gates, and roping.

Right around the time that Johnny bought his horse and started working with Dad on the Veterans Bridge, Mom knew that Johnny wasn't going to dedicate himself to tennis. She basically told him to go ahead and do what he thought was right. The implication was: "I'm going to devote myself to Jimmy now."

Most of my summers were spent traveling with Mom. On the junior circuit, you advanced in stages, gaining experience and confidence along the way. First you played a local district tournament, then a USTA section, and if you were good enough, you went on to the nationals. I began to play the Missouri Valley Section events of the US Tennis Association tournaments, which covered Illinois, Kansas, Missouri, and Iowa. As I improved, I would come home between tournaments for only a day or two before leaving again.

In 1963 I made the first of four visits with Mom and Two-Mom to the Manker Patten Tennis Club, in Chattanooga, Tennessee, for the national championships—first for boys 12 and under, then 14 and under. I didn't win any of them. I made the quarters on the first trip and the semis a year later, where I was beaten by Brian Gottfried, who would end up becoming a friend and competitor throughout my career on the professional circuit.

My junior record was good enough to qualify for the tournaments I wanted to enter, but it wasn't spectacular. By the end of my junior career, I made the US top ten for my age group, but I was far from being the best. Gottfried, Dick Stockton, and Eddie Dibbs were considered better than me, and they were.

Mom's biggest challenge with me during my junior years was trying to rein me in. I hated losing. I wanted to practice more, to play more, to travel more so that I could start winning, and when I couldn't do that I would become discouraged and frustrated. But Mom always seemed to figure out a way to lift my spirits.

"Don't worry, Jimmy, you're just not big enough yet. That's the only reason you aren't winning. It's going to happen, trust me. Keep working hard, do the right things, and the wins will follow."

When I was on the junior circuit Mom knew that winning or losing was just one part of the process. She wanted to see me improve, to lock in new shots, and to move better. Rushing things didn't make sense to her. She always looked at the big picture. But what was the big picture? There was no money in tennis, so my career beyond the juniors was important only in that it could lead to a tennis scholarship to a top university and allow me to experience life beyond East St. Louis.

When I first traveled to the tournaments where I had to sleep overnight, I stayed in a room with a few of my tennis buddies. Someone always had to sack out on the floor—usually me. Early on in my junior career I told Mom that living like that was just not my thing, and she arranged different accommodations away from everyone else. You can guess how that's been interpreted over the years.

Gloria Connors drove a wedge between her son and his
    peers.
Gloria Connors thought her son was better than everyone
    else of his generation.

Gloria Connors refused to let her son become friends with
    the other boys.
Gloria Connors forced her son to view other kids as the
    enemy.

Bullshit. I separated myself because I wanted to and because I hated feeling crowded. I wanted to concentrate on my tennis. This wasn't a vacation for me. It was a time to play the best I could. That's all I cared about.

We're in Miami at the Orange Bowl in 1964, walking by the practice courts. A small crowd is watching a couple of guys practicing on the court nearby, and Mom and I go over to see what's happening. I hear this weird noise as the ball flies off the strings of a racquet. It's not the normal sound I'm used to and it gets my attention. The racquet the guy is holding is silver, with two prongs at the top of the handle. Even the head looks different. It turns out to be a demonstration by Wilson Sporting Goods of a new prototype racquet they're calling the T2000. It's cool, and I really want one. Mom happens to know the Wilson rep, Jack Staton, who is running the event, and she asks him if we can get a T2000. He tells her it's a one-off but says he'll see what he can do.

A few weeks later, a package comes to the house addressed to me. Inside, wrapped in plastic, are four T2000 racquets and a note: "Jimmy, let me know what you think. Enjoy the racquets. Jack, the Wilson Tennis Company."

The racquets were sent unstrung. Two-Mom looks at them and makes a face. "There aren't any holes. I don't see how to string that thing."

Pop picks up one of the racquets and turns it over in his hands. "I don't know, either, but we'll figure it out."

For an hour they hunch over the kitchen table with a pick and awl. Instead of pushing the strings through holes and tying them off, with the T2000 you have to weave them in and out of the frame.

"There you go, Jimmy. Go try it out with your mom," says Pop.

Mom hits a soft ball to me. I take an easy swing, just to get the feel of the new racquet. Whoa, what happened there? It felt like an electric shock. The racquet jerks out of my hand and the ball flies a mile over the back fence. Over the afternoon I manage to feel comfortable, then, suddenly, ZING, the next one shoots off incredibly fast, as if off a trampoline. It takes me four or five months to master that racquet, in which time I lose to virtually everyone I play. It doesn't matter; I know I have something special in my hands. That first T2000 takes a beating over the weeks and months as my frustration gets the better of me, but I'm determined to stick it out.

Because of the open throat on the racquet, there is little wind resistance when the ball comes off the strings. Once I get used to the speed I can generate, I realize I can make shots I found impossible before. And because it's strung with more tension than my wooden racquets, I can hit with more power. It fits in my hand like it's molded to my fingers, and I also like the way it looks: silver and modern, different from the rest. What was it about me, even back then, that didn't want to be like everybody else?

For a while I was the only kid in any of the tournaments who showed up with the T2000. Slowly, other guys started to give it a try. I liked watching them and knowing they would never have the patience to master that racquet. And I wasn't about to give away any secrets. I loved that racquet so much that I slept with it. Seriously.

In 1965, we moved to a nicer neighborhood in Belleville. Some of my dad's contacts in the construction business built us a house on Gerold Lane. It was OK with Mom; her gravel court had done its job and sentiment had no role to play in the decision.

For me, the move brought a new set of friends. Johnny and I spent a lot of time at the Dorchester Swim Club, swimming, playing Ping-Pong, and eating the best fried-fish sandwiches I've ever tasted. The place attracted a big group of kids and sometimes there would be some trouble. Nothing too serious, a smashed window, a few fights, the usual mischief.

On the road to East St. Louis from Belleville, near our old grade school, there was a viaduct known as the "rat hole." Johnny and his friends would meet guys from different areas and, as Johnny used to say, "there were a lot of broken noses." Johnny used to enjoy that kind of thing, and he was good at it.

"I can take a punch," Johnny used to say to me. "After seeing what Mom went through, nothing scares me and nothing hurts. They can hit me with a baseball bat and I know it can't be as bad as what she endured. I can get back up."

He built up quite a reputation for himself as a guy who loved to fight, which sometimes came in handy for me.

Now, you have to understand, looking for trouble back then was not a high priority, even though that may have changed later on in my life. But, at the time, I had all the tension I could handle just fighting with myself while I was playing tennis.

I had already made a bit of a name for myself in grade school and high school by winning tournaments and getting written up in the papers. I was at a high school dance and some guy decided to start giving me a hard time. He was talking shit and shoving me when suddenly Johnny turns up. He gives the guy a look.

"I understand you want to take my brother outside," Johnny says to him. "You know, I've never had respect for a guy who wanted to go outside."

He shut right up; Johnny's reputation had preceded him.

Johnny turned to me. "Jimmy, now haul off and let him have it."

I looked at Johnny like he was nuts.

"Jimmy, if you don't let him have it, I'm going to beat his ass," Johnny said. "Then I'm going to beat your ass for not punching him."

What choice did I have? So we went at it. What the hell. It wasn't as bad as I thought. That wasn't the last time I ever mixed it up.

I didn't have as much freedom as Johnny during that time. When we moved to Gerold Lane, it took another half an hour, depending on the traffic, to get to the armory. Since we were still seen as outsiders, the only court time we could book would be first thing in the morning or just before they closed, which meant going to bed early on Friday night so we could be up by 6 the next morning. It was an early lesson in discipline. If I wanted to spend time with my friends I still had to get up at dawn and play tennis. After that, the rest of the day was mine to do what I wanted.

Once we moved, Mom had to find a way to supplement our income. Traveling to tournaments and staying at hotels didn't come cheap, and the lessons she gave at the armory didn't cover it. She found a job coaching at the Triple A Club, in Forest Park, St. Louis, where her hours were flexible enough during the summer so that she could still come on the road with me.

I was 15 when I won a set from my mom for the first time.

We're in Kalamazoo, Michigan, for the boys' under-16 national championship. I'm playing a practice set with Mom, playing like we always do; she never gives an inch and I never want her to. Today the Tiger Juices are flowing hard. It's a tight set, match point to me, and I make a passing shot that Mom can't reach. I win.

Upset, I run to the net, crying, "I'm sorry! I'm sorry!"

Mom smiles.

"This is the moment I've been waiting for," she says. "Now I know you're ready to move on."

My childhood in tennis is over. I win my first major title at that tournament in Kalamazoo, to become the best player in my age group. Yet the one set that sticks in my mind is the set I took from Mom.

I had been away from home for a few weeks leading up to the nationals, so when the tournament was over I headed back to Belleville straight from Michigan. I telephoned Johnny from the airport to find out if he would be home. He congratulated me and told me to meet him at a bar to celebrate. He said they had a new game they called foosball and he wanted me to come and watch him play.

When I got to the bar, Johnny was at the foosball table with his friend Mike and they were destroying these two guys who were getting really pissed. I could tell things were about to turn ugly. When Johnny scored the goal to win yet another game, one of the guys got up in his face.

"You're a fucking cheater, you little shit. You lifted the table."

"Fuck you. It's bolted to the floor. Who do you think I am, Hercules? Or are you too stupid to know who that is?"

The punches started to fly. It was crazy in there and not someplace I wanted to be. I hit the floor and crawled out, leaving Johnny in his element. He'd chosen his path and I had chosen mine.

Mom knew she had taken my game as far as she could for now and decided it was time for me to take the next step in my tennis education. When the professional circuit came to St. Louis, Mom and Two-Mom took me to meet one of its stars, Pancho Segura. Mom knew Pancho from her days playing tennis back in the 1940s. According to Pancho, he had tried to "romance" Mom. In fact, he'd had a rival at the time, Jimmy Evert, Chrissie's father, but neither guy had any success with her. My mom was a good Catholic girl, barely in her twenties, and had no interest in a relationship, but

Pancho later told me he'd gotten pretty close during a tournament in Mexico City. There was a group of players in a hotel room and Pancho thought Mom might be giving in to his charms. Just then, they heard noises coming from the next room, where the actor Gilbert Roland was getting busy with some young woman. It spooked Mom and that was it for Pancho. His romantic hopes crashed and burned then and there.

Mom had always admired Pancho's game. In the pre-Open days of the 1940s and '50s, Pancho was one of the best players of his generation. Throughout his professional career, he was never out of the world's top five, claiming the number one spot in 1952, the year I was born.

Pancho should never have made it as a tennis player. He was only 5'6", slender, with bowed legs from a bout of rickets he had suffered as a child. He was brought up in extreme poverty in Ecuador, the oldest of nine kids living on an annual income of $2,000 that their father brought in from his job as a caretaker of a tennis club. Pancho earned a handful of change as a ball boy at the club, then fought his way to the very top of the professional game in the United States, winning the US Pro Tennis Championships for three years running. In 1950, he beat Jack Kramer in the semis, followed by Frank Kovacs, and then in the finals in 1951 and 1952, he overcame Pancho Gonzales, one of the greatest players of all time.

When I first met Pancho Segura, he had been retired from the circuit for several years, and was coaching at the Beverly Hills Tennis Club, in LA, but he still made appearances in professional tournaments from time to time, which was why he was in St. Louis in 1967.

We met on a hotel balcony, where Pancho was doing a photo shoot. I barely said a word as Mom and Two-Mom discussed my future with him.

"Pancho, my son has some talent. I want you to take a look at him."

I remember peering out from behind Two-Mom and seeing Pancho roll his eyes. He'd heard it all before, many times. But this was Gloria Thompson and he would do anything for her.

"OK, if you want to send your son to train with me, that's fine. Let's see what he's got."

Later that day, Mom asked me what I thought about living in California. Since I hated my high school, Assumption High, a Catholic school run by a bunch of tough Brothers I couldn't relate to—I'll leave it at that—I took about two seconds to answer.

"California? Sure, Mom."

"If that's what you want, then let's go for it."

What was it that Pancho saw in me? Why did he agree to take me on? I wasn't even going to be the highest-ranked kid he worked with. I was number four in the country, which was pretty good, but Pancho already had the number one, 18-year-old Erik Van Dillen. Why did he think I'd outplay all those other guys? I've asked him about this many times over the years, over many beers. His answer is always the same.

"Jimbo, I loved your pride. You were born to be a champion. I could see you had big balls. And you were coachable."

Pride mattered to Pancho. He had fought hard to get to where he was. I think he also saw something of himself in me.

"You were like a deer running around that court, Jimbo, reacting fast, chasing down every ball, a showman who would excite people. You made me smile."

At 15 years old, my game was still raw, but Pancho identified two shots that he believed were better than anything he'd seen before.

"Your first-serve return, no one saw it but me. I knew as you grew stronger it would become the best in tennis. But your backhand—

that was the difference. It barely cleared the net with pace, and by the time the other guy had a chance to react, it was too late. That draws a short ball, which is the secret of the game."

Mom and I went to Beverly Hills and I hit a few tennis balls with Pancho. In the summer of 1968, I moved to California for good. And nothing would ever be the same again.

4

LOSE LIKE A MAN,
WIN LIKE A MAN

want to go home.

It's late summer and I'm a million miles from East St. Louis, not even 16 years old, and I feel completely out of my element. At home I was seen as a little weird, running around in white tennis shorts, playing a game that was still reserved for rich kids with country-club backgrounds, but at least I knew the place and the people. Now Mom, Two-Mom, Pop, and I are sitting in Ships, a diner on Wilshire Boulevard in Los Angeles. I open the menu and the first thing I see is a veggie burger and a soy smoothie. I don't think we're in East St. Louis any more, Toto. Do I really belong here?

Mom and I, arrived in the morning from St. Louis. We had taken a taxi from the airport to the Del Capri hotel, but Two-Mom and Pop had driven all the way from Illinois in my 1967 maroon Corvette. For years afterward they'd talk about how they arrived in LA with the top down, like Hollywood stars. Man, they loved that.

I'd bought that used 'Vette earlier in the summer for $2,600, money I had saved from helping Johnny out in the tollbooth and part-time jobs I picked up whenever I had time. I spent a couple of winters at a gas station and did other odd jobs: shoveling snow, raking leaves, and mowing lawns. I'd do anything to put money toward that car.

"Why don't you want to stay, Jimmy?" Mom asks.

"I miss my dog. I miss Johnny. I don't think I can do this."

"All right, I understand," she says. "We can arrange a flight home, but since we're here, why don't you and Pop take the car and go exploring." Mom always knew how to play me.

She takes a map out of her purse and spreads it on the table.

"Look," she says, pointing, "that's the LA Tennis Club, and here's the Beverly Hills Tennis Club, where Pancho teaches. Why don't you and Pop go take a look if you feel like it?"

What Mom understands—and what I don't—is that in Los Angeles and Beverly Hills, unlike in East St. Louis, tennis is hot.

Pop and I were gone most of the day. We just got in the car and drove. We were looking for the tennis clubs but got distracted by Grauman's Chinese Theatre, the Hollywood sign, and Sunset Boulevard, sights I knew only from the local news in East St. Louis. By the end of the day we'd put some miles on the car and become familiar with my new stomping grounds. I had told Mom we'd be back by dark, in time for dinner, and when we got to the hotel, Mom and Two-Mom were excited to hear about how our day went.

"I'm not leaving," I announced. "No way. I'm staying."

And that's how my life changed forever.

We stayed at the hotel for three days, cruising around the city and having fun. Then Pop went back home on the train and Mom, Two-Mom, and I looked around for an apartment. The plan was for them to stay with me and help me settle in; they would then go back to Belleville and leave me on my own for a while. Every now and then one or both of them would come back for a week to make sure I was under control. Never a problem, of course, for a 16-year-old living on his own in LA . . . I mean, what could possibly go wrong?

My first apartment was clean, cheap, and on the third floor. We realized the mistake after the first week; I came in one day and saw

Two-Mom leaning against the wall on the second-floor landing, wheezing. I'd never seen that before.

"You OK, Two-Mom?" I asked.

She looked a little embarrassed. "It's nothing, Jimbo." (She was the only one who could call me Jimbo without permission.) "Just a little out of breath from walking up those stairs too fast. I'm fine."

As we took the last flight of stairs together I noticed Two-Mom gently rubbing her chest. I didn't think much of it at the time. I wish I had.

We managed to get out of the apartment lease and find a new place on Wilshire Boulevard, a two-bedroom on the ground floor that was five minutes from Rexford High, my new school, five minutes from the Beverly Hills Tennis Club and five minutes from the courts at UCLA. The only problem was the rent, $400 a month.

"We'll manage, Jimmy," Mom said. And somehow we did. When Mom was in LA, she coached tennis and waited tables at Nibblers Restaurant, on Wilshire. To help us out, Pop would send me $20 from his Social Security check every month. But I knew I'd have to find a way to make some money with tennis.

Pancho got me enrolled in Rexford High School in the same class as his son Spencer, who was my age. It was as far away as you could get from Assumption High in East St. Louis. The kids at Rexford were either really rich, like the Hiltons, or showbiz prodigies, like David Cassidy.

Los Angeles in the late 1960s was a hotbed for sex, drugs, and rock and roll. If you wanted it, you could have it—whatever it was.

"What's that shit?" I asked Spencer the first time I saw a table lined with white powder at a high school party. "Sugar?"

Cocaine was pretty tame compared with the other stuff that was going around. Back home, my buddies might sneak some Ripple or Mogen David grape (my favorite wine), but here guys were smoking, and snorting God knows what.

I was growing up fast. Some of the lessons I learned were pretty harsh. One day a guy in school OD'd right in front of me, in the school parking lot, at 10:15 in the morning. I don't know what he was on—LSD? heroin?—but he just collapsed and went into convulsions. I watched him flopping around like a fish and foaming at the mouth, and that told me all I needed to know about drugs. I didn't want any part of them. I got in my car and took off for the tennis courts. Mom had worked too hard to provide me with opportunities that didn't exist in East St. Louis. It might lead to a career or to college, I didn't know, but I wasn't going to screw things up.

I knew I had two choices. I could take advantage of everything that was offered to me and get as much out of it as possible, or I could be a half-assed prick and end up back in Illinois. I wasn't going back. The other kids could get their highs from drugs, but I would find mine on the court.

Spencer Segura felt the same way. In the beginning he must've thought of me as a redneck pushed on him by his father—a kid straight out of the Midwest with a corncob up his butt. In fact, his friends used to call me "cornpone," but soon Spencer and I became like brothers. When Mom or Two-Mom weren't around, Spencer and Pancho were my family. Before I even got to California, Pancho had told Spencer that he thought I was going to be "the next great player." I don't know how I would've reacted to this if I had been Spencer, but it didn't seem to bother him. He was a good player in his own right and would join the professional tennis circuit in the 1970s, but he never saw me as a rival. We had the same goals, the same attitudes, and the same work ethic. We both had hardworking fathers who weren't around much when we were young, and although we had a lot of fun with other friends at school, we always knew we were different. And best of all, Spencer knew the LA scene and helped me adjust to my new life.

I had four classes a semester and the arrangement was that I'd go to school from 8:15 a.m. until the nutrition break at 10:15, when I would escape to the Beverly Hills Tennis Club. As for getting through school, let's just say I got there. I graduated, even with my reading issues and attention-deficit problems. I could play five hours of tennis without losing my concentration, but I still couldn't read five pages of a schoolbook.

Pancho and I had a good relationship from the very beginning.

"All I ask," Pancho said, "is that you believe in yourself. No negative thoughts, no excuses. Lose like a man and win like a man. If you're injured, don't play; if you play, you're not injured. Always give one hundred percent and I'll be happy."

Those words stuck with me throughout my career.

Mom had handed me over to Pancho so that he could take me to the next level of competition. The only thing she told him was "Leave Jimmy's game alone. I don't want you to change that. You provide whatever else is necessary."

Pancho was no angel. He helped me to gain experience off the court as well as on it, and that was just as important to him as the tennis. He took Spencer and me out to restaurants and taught us that having a drink with dinner was no big deal. He showed us how to handle ourselves early on, at 16 years old. If you think that's all he taught us, well, use your imagination.

Pancho kept on top of my schoolwork, too. If Spencer and I missed class or walked on the court too tired to take care of business, then we answered to Pancho, a no-nonsense guy even down to the smallest detail. One day Spencer and I decided that our buzz-cut haircuts were out of style and it was time to make a change, so we told the barber to let the rest of our hair grow as long as the tuft in front. Afterward we went to the tennis club to hit a few balls, and Pancho walked straight onto the court.

"I thought you guys were going to get your hair cut," he said.

"Yeah, we did. It's the new look."

We were soon on our way back to the barber. The buzz cut was suddenly back in style.

We had more freedom on weekends. On Friday nights, Pancho would ask us if we had practiced our tennis and we'd say yes. He would ask us if we had done our homework and I'd say, "Why would we want to do that?" Even though that was my attitude toward school, it wasn't Spencer's. He went on to graduate college and to become a successful lawyer, so school was an important part of his life. But on Friday nights, even Pancho would relax a bit and tell us it was time to go out and have some fun. And we did.

The Beverly Hills Tennis Club had been founded by Fred Perry and Ellsworth Vines, along with Golden Age movie star Fredric March, and it was only two minutes from Rodeo Drive. It was like a Hollywood club, and all the big names would be there, taking lessons from Pancho and other pros, playing on one of the five courts or just socializing. Burt Bacharach, Anthony Newley, Kirk Douglas, Julie Andrews, Lloyd Bridges, and countless other celebrities were attracted by Pancho's personality and reputation. He even did a little matchmaking by introducing a girl he knew, Candy, to Aaron Spelling; they ended up married for almost 40 years, until his death.

Baseball legend Hank Greenberg was another regular at the club, and we played a few matches together. He was in his late fifties, so I played right-handed. It seemed only fair. Hank had been a first baseman for the Detroit Tigers in the 1930s and '40s and one of the premier sluggers of his generation, smashing 58 home runs in 1938. One time I asked him what was so difficult about being a power hitter, and he said, "You have a round ball, you're trying to hit it with a round bat, and you're trying to hit it square. Nothing like finding the sweet spot." When I wasn't working on my tennis, I loved hanging around Mr. Greenberg, hearing his stories and gambling on backgammon.

Spencer and I were good friends with Desi Arnaz Jr. and Dino Martin Jr., Dean Martin's son. When I first met Dino Jr., he was already a rock star and regularly on the cover of teen magazines, but what he really wanted to be was a top tennis player. He took lessons from Pancho and was naturally athletic, but he had just come to the game a little too late to excel. Spencer and I spent a lot of time with Dino, up at his father's house, where there was a tennis court, and also in nightclubs where all Dino had to do was wink and through the doors we went.

I remember watching Spencer and Dino from the bar that overlooked the court at the Martins' palatial home on Mountain Drive, in Beverly Hills, waiting my turn to play. All of a sudden, Dino's father, the great Dean Martin, came up to me and introduced himself, all laid back and smooth, as he was in those Rat Pack movies. He asked me if I wanted a drink. Did he know I was only 16? I looked at him in amazement—a man I'd seen only on TV—and thought, sure, what the hell.

All of the TV and movie stars wanted to hit with the best young tennis players around, and they respected our ability on the court. Spencer and I decided maybe we could make a few bucks while we were at it. We'd play doubles for $20 a set, which was our gas money for the week. We gave our opponents a 4-0 lead, just to be fair. Talk about pressure. But I'll tell you what—you don't lose a match like that when you've only got $5 in your pocket. Pretty soon we began to win a bit too often, so we mixed it up a little, me playing with the weaker celebrity against Spencer and the better guy.

Bob Evans, the movie producer who went on to make *The God-*

father with Francis Ford Coppola, was a regular partner of mine. In one match, Spencer almost took his head off with a vicious overhead. He was pretty annoyed by the aggressive tactics and started complaining that Spencer and I were colluding with each other. Now really, do you think I would ever do that? He claims to have played over 40 matches with me as his partner and never won a set. We are still friends today, and he'll never let me live that down.

With Spencer and Dino's connections around town, we didn't have any trouble spending our weekends in the hottest bars and restaurants in LA. The Daisy Club, where my friend George was the bartender, was one of my favorites. George was a champion surfer—no wave was too big for him—but tennis was his real passion. He also happened to mix the best whiskey sours in town. It was during one of those nights out that I first met Frank Sinatra. By then, Spencer and I were 18 and having dinner with a girl we knew from high school who worked for Eileen Ford, then the top modeling agency in the world. Mr. Sinatra was at a table across from us and he came over to talk to Spencer.

"Hey, you're Pancho's son, right? You guys want to see a show? Settle up and follow me."

Mr. Sinatra took us next door to a studio where we watched as he recorded three songs for the upcoming Jerry Lewis telethon. It was just the Chairman of the Board, the sound engineers, and us. People would pay a fortune to be in the room when Sinatra sang, and here we were, a couple of kids, having a once-in-a-lifetime show for free.

Pancho once told me a story about Jack Kramer, who had been the world's best tennis player in his day and who would go on to found the players' union. Jack thought Pancho was crazy when he told him I was going to be better than Stan Smith. This was the age of tall players—Smith was 6'4", Dick Stockton 6'2", Brian Gottfried and Erik Van Dillen were both 6'0". I was 5'9", skinny, and had a double-handed backhand. What chance did I have? Jack thought. Erik Van Dillen even refused to play a match with me once at the LA Tennis Club, saying, "Why? He's too small." Pancho's reply was typical. "Don't give me that shit. He's going to kick your ass."

That was the kind of thing Pancho saw as his challenge—and mine. He told me not to worry about what anyone else said. "They're tall, Jimbo"—it was OK if Pancho called me that—"but they move like turtles with broken legs. Listen to me, and I can help you be a champion. You have a choice: You fight to be the best, or you settle for being one of many with all the others." That was a big moment for me. It was then that I fully realized I wasn't in California just to escape East St. Louis. With Pancho's help, I was there to be number one.

I worked hard with Pancho, but it wasn't any less fun. He'd run Spencer and me all over the court from corner to corner. We'd be exhausted and he'd be laughing his ass off because he knew we never wanted him to think we weren't up to the task, no matter what he threw at us.

"Boys, you've got to understand this is what you're going to face when you take on the best." There was always a purpose.

Pancho's methods were similar to Mom's. If I made a mistake in practice, like not staying low enough on a backhand down the line, he would stop the session, explain the problem, and show me exactly what I'd been doing wrong and how to fix it. If I would miss a backhand down the line, he would actually come onto the court and show me how to do it. I was a visual learner, so being able to see how it was done correctly was important for me. Pancho didn't want bad habits creeping into my game, like not moving my feet properly or not getting my racquet back soon enough. If I messed up in a match, he would wait a day or two before telling me what the problem was. I remember a match against Roy Emerson at the LA Tennis Club during which I didn't take the ball early enough and move forward at the right time. Pancho said nothing for 24 hours. Then he took me back on the court and demonstrated how I *should* have played Emerson.

He was, and remains, my mentor, along with Mom. Without the two of them, I would never have become a champion. What Pancho taught me during those years at the Beverly Hills Tennis Club would fill 10 volumes if I tried to compile the lessons. But it really comes down to three words: confidence, aggression, and strategy.

When I started up with Pancho, my groundstrokes were already in place. Running down every ball came naturally, and my concentration and footwork were probably as good as anyone's. Thanks to Pop's training I could reach the ball quickly, which gave me extra seconds to decide where I was going to hit my return. Pancho's training added a layer of sophistication to my game.

His first step was to make me more aggressive. I had always been a traditional baseliner, keeping the ball in play and slugging it out in long rallies. Pancho taught me to put my opponents on their heels, forcing them to place shots inside my service line.

Pancho called that area of the court the "winning zone." "If you have the ball there," he would say, "you control the point, you have options—short, deep, volley." Pancho showed me how to put my opponent in a defensive situation and bury him. My killer instinct took over as my confidence grew.

"Coach," I used to say to Pancho before a match, "I'm going to make that guy walk bowlegged like you." He loved that.

If I took a chance and missed, that was OK, because I knew I'd get better. I had no fear, especially on the big points, the ones that make a difference in the match. You can be in the best shape of your life, hitting the ball great, but if you can't come through when it counts, you ain't walking away with the trophy. That's where Tiger Juices come in.

A huge part of my tennis education with Pancho was on the mental side of the game. It's a given that every professional can hit the ball well, but the difference between the 100th best player in the world and the number one is minuscule, and it isn't found on the court. It's in your head and guts. They didn't call Pancho "Sneaky" for nothing. He was brilliant at messing with your head. He would do the opposite of what you expected. If you moved in to cover a drop shot, he'd lob you; if you stayed back to force a rally, he'd come up with an angled volley. Pancho always knew the right shot to play, because he used the score to his advantage.

We used to sit at one of the tables in the club snack bar and Pancho would draw diagrams on cocktail napkins to illustrate how to play key points. The strategy would depend on the match situation. If you're ahead, you do one thing; if you're behind, you do something else. At 30-15, you can force the next point, move in quickly on your return, and put your opponent under immediate pressure. If you're down 30-40, you have to nail your first serve, and make sure you pull your opponent out of position, then keep him pinned back with deep balls to prevent him from attacking. It sounds simple, yet making it happen is anything but.

Before my matches, Pancho would pull out those cocktail napkins again to show me the strengths and weaknesses of my opponent and how I could combat their particular approach to the game. He would create these scenarios, like it's 30-30 on the other guy's second serve, then explain how the guy would probably play the point. When these moments came up in a real match, I could anticipate them and get the edge. Or he would notice certain traits, like how to tell from the angle of my opponent's racquet if his shot was going to be short. Or the way an opponent tossed the ball up on his serve might indicate whether it was coming down the center or out wide.

Pancho didn't have to keep hammering any of this into my head. I ate it up. I devoured every word. Tennis isn't rocket science, but Pancho simplified things in a way that made perfect sense. Because I trusted him, I wasn't afraid to incorporate his instructions into matches, no matter how high the stakes. I never, ever thought I had reached the point where I knew everything about the game. I worked hard every day. There was nothing else in the world I would rather have been doing.

All the top juniors in Southern California found their way to the Beverly Hills Tennis Club. The competition back then was the best in the country, and not only between young players. On any given day you might see Arthur Ashe or Stan Smith hitting balls on the back courts. The world's best players would come to us, or we'd find them at UCLA or USC.

Almost every guy I played would have a different weapon, a different skill—big serve, baseline, power, net game, height, speed, topspin, you name it—and I faced these variations on a regular basis. Nothing I came across in the world's major tournaments ever surprised me.

Tennis never became a drag, because we never played in the same place two days in a row. If we weren't at the Beverly Hills Tennis Club or over at one of the LA colleges, we might be up in Bel Air playing at Bobby Kreiss's court, in the garden behind his house. Spencer and I would sit around having a Coke, watching Bobby's father put his three sons through their paces, and after a while we'd join in. We were all friends, so there was more to practice than just the tennis; it was a chance to be with our buddies while we worked.

Some of Pancho's pals—like Bobby Riggs, Pancho Gonzales, Charlie Pasarell, Rod Laver, Ken Rosewall, and Roy Emerson— would stop in to see him when they were passing through Los Angeles. Any time these guys were hanging around and talking, Spencer and I would be in the corner, soaking up as much information as possible. We never spoke ourselves; we just listened. At the end of the day, Gonzales might say to me, "Come on, kid, and hit some balls with me." Me? Play with Pancho Gonzales? Hell, yes!

Gonzales wasn't an easy guy to get to know—he could be moody and difficult—but after a while he seemed to accept me, and I loved watching him play. For a big man he was surprisingly elegant, moving about the court with agility and finesse. And he could do things with his racquet that I'd never seen before, particularly when he was at net, where he angled his volleys with deadly precision. I learned a lot, not just by studying his game but by seeing the kind of killer instinct he brought to every match. "The great champions were always vicious competitors," I remember him saying. "You never lose respect for a man who is a vicious competitor, and you never hate a man you respect." That seemed a pretty good code to live by.

One afternoon, I'd been watching Gonzales play for about an hour. After every couple of games, he walked to the back of the court and beat his Spalding Smasher against the concrete wall.

"Excuse me, Mr. Gonzales, but with all due respect, what the hell are you doing?"

"Kid, look here. The top of my racquet is out of shape now. I want to see how the ball reacts when I hit it off the strings there. Maybe I can find a new shot. I don't know, but I'm going to try and figure it out."

"See this tape around the rim? It's lead," he continued. "It makes the racquet heavier so I can let the racquet do some of the work. Here, take some and try it yourself."

That proved to be a huge part of my success with the T2000, because it added the extra weight that I needed to be able to keep that racquet under control. If I was tired, I would take the lead tape off. If I was feeling good, I would add a little more for increased power.

During my first year in Beverly Hills, I went with Spencer, Dino, and the two Panchos to Phoenix for a pro-am tournament. We flew there on a plane owned by Kirk Kerkorian, a businessman who helped make Las Vegas into what it is today. No one loved playing or being around tennis more than Mr. Kerkorian. I was buzzing before we even got to the airport. Private jet?! Oh, yeah.

I played Gonzales in a singles exhibition. It was sweltering in Phoenix, and during one of the changeovers Pancho paused to give me a piece of advice.

"Kid, I want you to drink some orange juice. It's hot and you need the fluid."

I wasn't really an OJ guy, but this was Pancho Gonzales, so I said, "OK."

"Just take a couple of sips," he warned me. "Too much and you'll cramp."

At the next changeover, he told me to do the same thing again, and the next, and pretty soon I started to stagger. He had been giving me screwdrivers in that heat! You know, vodka and orange juice. You'd think at 16 years old I would have noticed. I could barely hit a ball and the two Panchos couldn't stop laughing. They taught me a good lesson: Tennis and alcohol don't mix—not on the court, anyway.

At the time I saw it as a sign that I had been accepted, but, more than that, the two Panchos were showing me that it was OK to have some fun and to entertain the fans while you were playing.

At some point during that trip I called the landlord of my apartment to ask him to check up on my car. The Corvette had become like a pet to me, since I didn't have my dog.

"Yeah, about your car," the landlord said, "your friend came and picked it up. I gave him the spare keys you left. Next time you probably should tell me things like that before you leave."

What?! "I didn't have someone come to take my car," I told him. "What the hell?"

"Well, he knew all about you and he had a set of keys to your apartment. He said you must've forgotten to say something about it."

"Someone is screwing with you. Call the cops and tell them my car has been stolen."

I gave him the phone number at my hotel and when I came back later that evening, there was a message for me to get in touch with the police station.

"No, Mr. Connors, we don't actually have your car, but we did find it. It was pulled over this afternoon with three men in it. We spoke to the driver and everything checked out, so we let them go."

"What do you mean, it checked out? I never said anyone could take my car. Who was driving?"

"Your brother, John Connors."

That figured.

I should've guessed it was Johnny and his buddies taking some time off from Belleville. Sure, guys, come to LA, we'll go to the beach and drive up and down Sunset Boulevard in my brother's convertible. I had to laugh. Sort of.

Not long after the trip to Phoenix, I watched Pancho Gonzales at the Pan Pacific tournament. He missed an easy shot, and in frustration he spun around and threw his racquet toward the back curtain, just barely missing the line judge's head. Gonzales didn't blink; he just walked over, picked up the racquet, and went back to playing. The crowd started shouting and booing, while Gonzales acted as if nothing had happened, going on to win the match. It was clear he couldn't care less if they were for him or against him; he just played the way he wanted to. I liked that.

People used to say Pancho Segura encouraged me to act up on

court, but that's not true. It wasn't one person in particular but the environment in which I learned the game. Those old pros knew how to entertain, they understood what people wanted, and in the same way that I absorbed parts of their games and made them my own, I also took on their attitudes. Tennis in those days was struggling to find its place in the sports landscape, so something had to be done to attract larger crowds. The guys today don't seem to see tennis in the same light; it's all business to them. I understand that; they all play great tennis, but I've got to ask: Where is the show?

If Pancho Segura didn't encourage my theatrics on the court, neither did he discourage them. It used to make him laugh when I would turn to the line judges and suggest, for example, that they "eat me." I used to ask myself: Just what does that mean? And what kind of sick fuck comes up with that?

But Pancho always had a word of warning. "Jimbo, remember it's all about timing. Don't let anything get in the way of your tennis. Just make sure after you act up, you get your concentration and your head back into the game."

Let's just say I couldn't follow every single piece of advice he gave me.

5

THE MAIN LOCKER ROOM

've been a gambling man all my life.

As a kid I'd bet on anything: a game of pool or the football or basketball game playing on TV. Hell, I'd throw quarters against the wall just to see which side turned over, heads or tails. Pop said gambling ran in our blood, and I never was a boy to disappoint him. The riverboat casinos that popped up on the Mississippi in the early 1990s only seemed to confirm the truth of Pop's statement, as you'll find out later. Whether it was tossing quarters against the wall or starting a riverboat gaming company, it was all the same to me.

The truth is, I formed bad habits. If I win three games, I want to win five; if I win five games, I want to win six. I play until I can't anymore. Excuse me, sir, know where I can find a hot meal?

At the Beverly Hills Tennis Club, we'd sit by the pool and play backgammon whenever we weren't practicing. When Pancho and Bobby Riggs were around, they might try to get some action going. Come nine o'clock at night we usually had a live one, maybe Spencer versus Riggs's son, Larry, or me against some guys from UCLA who thought they could make a little extra spending money. It was never any kind of formal agreement—too much pressure, right?— but we all knew where we stood. If I was playing I didn't mind putting down some cash on myself, and Pancho once staked $10,000 of his own money on a match between me and Erik Van Dillen, the top under-18 in the country. To hear Pancho tell the story today, adjusted for inflation, it was a million bucks. But no one, he said, would take the bet. Too bad. I would have won Pancho a shitload of money.

How could I not love hanging around that world of Segura and Riggs? Seeing how they operated, and their passion for the game, made a big impression on me. I learned all the little things from them, like playing fair, staying friends after a match, and being able to make a deal on a handshake, things that became a part of my life throughout my whole career. All the downtime I spent talking with Pancho elevated our relationship to the level of more than just mentor and protégé. He became like a father.

Two-Mom introduced me to Bill Riordan, a brash, cigar-smoking maverick and a promoter who ran his own circuit around the United States. He would come to play a huge role in my life throughout the first half of the 1970s. He'd slip me a few bucks under the table for expenses when I played for him as an amateur, which was the first time I felt like I was being paid for playing tennis.

Two-Mom had recommended Bill because she thought he was someone who could make things happen. She was right. He was Barnum & Bailey rolled into one, a promoter's promoter who could carry on a conversation with three different people at once, on three different subjects, and never miss a beat. When he swaggered into the room, you knew something good was going down. He was a big character—flamboyant, fun to be around. Bill never minced words. He once sent Donald Dell, a co-founder of the Association of Tennis Professionals (ATP) and a very influential figure in tennis, a telegram that read, "Dear Donald. Fuck you. Stronger message to follow."

The Riordan circuit, which he named the Independent Players circuit, gave me a place to hone my skills, and to gain confidence in my game. The first tournament I played on Bill's tour was the

National Indoor Championship, held in a gymnasium in Salisbury, Maryland. And it was there that I met Himself. Mr. Ilie Nastase.

It's February 1969. I'm 16 years old and Nastase has just beaten me 7-5 in the third set. The minute I get into the locker room I start throwing my racquets around. I had opportunities on the court and I blew them. I'm about as pissed as I've ever been, and now I have to get on a plane and go back to high school. Then Nastase walks in. He doesn't speak much English but somehow communicates that we should go out and get some dinner. Despite the language barrier, we manage that night to start a friendship that has lasted to this day.

"Nasty," as he liked to be called, was already famous when I met him. In fact, he was the first international tennis star planet Earth had ever known. He was plenty big in the States, but around the world he stopped traffic. You couldn't walk down the street with Nasty anywhere overseas without being mobbed. His vice was women, and they loved his good looks, his charm, and his floppy jet-black hair. Hanging around with him could flat wear you out.

He was the ultimate player—practically born in a pair of tennis shorts. He had the game, and when he played it he made everyone else look like Skippy the Punk, me included. The way he played, his imagination on the court, was unequaled. Nasty's only shortcoming, if you can even call it that, was his mental capacity to handle pressure. If he had something on his mind, he couldn't shake it. He'd hang on to it game after game after game. His emotions would get the better of him and end up costing him matches.

In a lot of ways, Nasty was my second mentor after Pancho. I liked his attitude, his style, and his flair. I was less impressed by his work ethic; he didn't bother practicing. He felt, because of all his talent, he didn't need to. I, on the other hand, had to work for everything I got.

In May 1970 I reached the finals of the Southern California men's tournament, where I lost to Pancho Gonzales. He was 42 years old but still one of the best players in the world. I was a few months shy of my 18th birthday. Anyway, the match would soon pay some dividends.

A month later, I beat Bobby Kreiss in straight sets, 6–4, 6–2, to win the Southern California juniors tournament, and in September that year I played my first Grand Slam. I qualified to make the first round of the US Open only to lose to Britain's Mark Cox, on grass. Grass? As far as I was concerned that surface was for cows, not tennis.

You would've thought that making the main draw of my first Grand Slam would've been a big deal for me, but it wasn't; it just felt like the next step in a natural progression. Believe it or not, I had other things on my mind, like playing doubles with Pancho Gonzales. Segura had asked Gonzales to enter us in the US Open doubles. He wouldn't give other players the time of day and he's going to play doubles with me? Holy shit!

Gonzales could have had anyone as his partner, but he agreed to play with me, perhaps because he saw my potential in the Southern Cal final.

We made it through to the quarters, a pretty decent achievement, given my lack of experience on grass. We beat some good teams, probably solely based on how intimidating Gonzales was. Whenever we came to a major point in a match, like 4–4 in a best-of-nine tiebreaker, and we could pick who faced the serve, Gonzales would say, "You take it."

What?

"Uh, are you sure, Pancho?"

He would smile, "You take it, kid. Don't be afraid. Trust yourself. And don't miss!"

Pancho knew I was young and inexperienced, and he also knew that putting me under pressure would show him whether I could handle it or not. He only encouraged me, pushing me to the limit he thought I could handle. Deep down he had a soft heart, but because he was such a fierce competitor, he couldn't let just anyone see it. His excitement when we won was never extreme, because he knew we had another match to play, but I will never forget how he treated me after our loss. It wasn't a big deal and he would explain to me why we'd lost and what we probably should have done to win the match. He was proud of the way I handled the pressure and felt that, if I continued playing, I could take my place among the best. His faith in me was no small thing and helped push me to the next level.

The Pacific Southwest Championships was held in Los Angeles right after the US Open and attracted a star-studded field. It was a massive opportunity for me to show again that I could play with the big boys. I won five qualifying matches to get to the main draw and a match against the great Australian, Roy Emerson. Roy had come into town after a defeat in the doubles finals at the US Open and a fourth-round singles loss to Stan Smith. I'm sure he wasn't looking forward to facing an 18-year-old who had something to prove.

When we walked onto the court, there was hardly anyone in the stands other than Pancho, Spencer, and a few of my other good friends.

Pancho had used up half a dozen cocktail napkins briefing me on Emerson's game. He told me to hit the ball low to his forehand and keep him away from the net.

"Whenever you can, Jimbo, play to that. Attack him hard. Don't let him settle."

The historic LA Tennis Club has seen all the legends, but this match on the poolside court turns out to be one that will be remembered for a long time. After I take the first set on a tiebreaker, word starts to spread and spectators start filtering over. The standing-room-only area for the fans quickly fills up.

I lose the second set in a tiebreaker and feel the match slipping away. Then I start to remember everything Mom and Pancho have told me. Don't be afraid of the big points. Trust yourself. Be aggressive. Don't let up. No fear.

I have a break point early in the third set. Now I'm dealing with my first opportunity for a major win. Don't get ahead of yourself. Relax. Don't think, just play; all the hard work and preparation have been done. I remember Pancho's advice to hit deep to his forehand, and when Emerson gives me a short reply, I hit a high forehand volley into the open court for a winner. Game, set, match, Connors.

When I shook hands with Emerson at the net, I couldn't believe what had just happened. Despite my outward confidence, it wasn't until I actually beat one of the world's best players that I really started to believe I could play at that level.

I was in shock as I made my way off the court. Pancho and Spencer were the first ones to congratulate me. I think Pancho was prouder of me then I was of myself, and to celebrate he said he was going to take us out for a dinner at my favorite restaurant, the Steak Pit, on Melrose in West LA.

"Give me a minute and I'll be ready," I told Pancho and Spencer on my way to the locker room.

There were two locker rooms at the LA Tennis Club, and before the match I had been given a place in the second one, designated for juniors. Now it was a different story. As I walked down the hallway, an official came up to me and said, "Excuse me, Mr. Connors—your clothes have been moved into the main locker room. Please follow me."

He showed me where they had put my bag, and it was right next to Gonzales's locker. I realized as I stood in that hallowed space that I had finally reached the big-time.

I left the club with Pancho and Spencer and made sure I was out of sight before I went berserk. It finally sunk in. Once I got to the restaurant I called my mom to let her know the result of the match. There was dead silence on the other end of the line. "Mom? You there?"

She was speechless.

My run didn't end there. I defeated the South African, Ray Moore, in the next round, before losing to Clark Graebner, one of the highest-ranked players in the United States at the time, in the quarterfinals. Even though the loss bothered me, beating Emerson had just made my young career.

After graduating from high school, in 1970, I won a tennis scholarship to UCLA. At the time I thought if things didn't work out for me in tennis, I might become a lawyer. Maybe I should've stayed with that plan, because over the years lawyers have screwed me over more than anyone else. I'm sure I would've made a decent defense attorney, because I never would have allowed my clients to be steamrolled.

There was just one flaw in my early legal ambitions, and that was my academic issues. Unable to concentrate on reading, my mind was always somewhere else. I'm not someone who can juggle a lot of conflicting thoughts. That's why tennis works for me—when the ball is in play, that's all I need to think about.

Still, I had to figure out a way to get through college. So I paid a senior to help me out—$20 for every term paper. I didn't do it out of disrespect for the teachers; there just weren't enough hours in my day to deal with studying. I'd get in from playing tennis at eight o'clock in the evening and I'd be too tired to hit the books.

As far as I could see, this "extra help" was the only solution. The senior would Xerox "my" paper and give it to me to put in my own handwriting. It worked for a while, until even the chore of copying over the assignments got to be too much and I made the mistake of handing in one of the Xeroxed pages. The professor wasn't impressed and called me out in front of the whole class. What could I say? I was busted.

It was the best one year of college I ever attended.

I had decided to go to UCLA after Coach Glenn Bassett told me that if I would come to UCLA he wouldn't recruit anyone else that year. He was an excellent motivator and worked hard with me on my conditioning. He left my game alone and focused on my fitness and strength, with sprints and long-distance runs as well as lots of hitting during our four-hour practice sessions. With his guidance, and the experience I was getting from playing tons of matches against older, more seasoned players from other schools, my game took another step forward.

Given that I was a freshman often pitted against juniors and seniors, I struggled in some matches but grew stronger as the season went on, and I felt I had a legitimate shot to win an NCAA title in singles. I faced my old friend and nemesis Roscoe Tanner in the final and knew I was in for a dogfight. Roscoe had a huge serve that he used to keep his opponents on their heels. But I was able to return most of his rockets, and I caused him problems with my groundstrokes. Ultimately, I simply refused to lose and my fierce desire got me through. Not only did I take the singles title on my own; I became the first freshman to win the NCAA championship—but I also helped UCLA blow away the opposition in the team standings. All in all, not a bad way to cap off my college career.

After winning the NCAA, I was supposed to jump on a plane to

London to play my first Wimbledon, but I had injured my shoulder from playing so much tennis and I had to take some time off. Once my shoulder felt stronger, I went to Louisville to practice with Nasty for a couple of days before my next event. Arriving at the tournament, I made my way to the locker room and there's Eddie Dibbs in the process of painting Nasty black. What the hell? I knew Nasty and Arthur Ashe were playing doubles, and I also knew their relationship was strained at best, even if deep down they had affection for each other. But this?

"Are you sure you want to do this, you crazy motherfucker?" I said.

"Oh, yeah, he's got to do it, Connors," said Eddie, who has always been a lovable maniac. "This is going to be great."

So there I was in Louisville, Kentucky, helping Dibbs put blackface on Nasty to play doubles with Arthur Ashe, a black man. We weren't all that bright back then, to say the least.

Once everyone else is on the court and the crowd has taken their seats, Nasty makes his grand entrance as if nothing is out of the ordinary. Except that with the sun beating down on the court, the black paint is starting to melt on his face. I can only groan, "Oh, my God! Oh, my God!" The people in the stands just sit there in horrified silence. Ashe, however, starts to laugh. He laughs so hard, in fact, that he can't begin to play for like five minutes. Nasty doesn't break character and plays his normal game as the black makeup drips off his face and onto the court. Only Nasty could have gotten away with a stunt like this. Who won? Does it really matter? The important thing is that we got out of there alive.

Having witnessed Nasty's latest circus act, Riordan suggested I partner with him in doubles. Bill was no dummy. He knew if he was going to pull in the crowds that he craved for his independent tour, he would need more than just Nasty, and he immediately picked up on the chemistry between the two of us. It takes a strong, focused personality to be a singles player, and Nasty and I possessed that gene in spades. At the same time, we weren't above having some fun on the court. We talked a lot during matches, often about the important issues of the day, like what hot restaurant we would be going to that night, and with whom.

Then there were the women, always the women. Nasty was out of control. When he was on court, he'd spend every free minute scanning the crowd for prospects. If I was watching the match, he'd send me up in the stands to tell whatever pretty girl he had picked out that the Great Nastase would like to invite her to dinner and, oh, yeah, bring along your attractive friend in the next seat. Once they accepted, that would be the last I'd see of Nasty for a week.

Nasty speaks six languages, and he's written several books in French. When he retired, in 1985, he went through a bout of depression as he tried to figure out the next act in his life. As he was coming out of his funk, he wrote and recorded a song called "Globetrotter Lover," which I'm sure you're all familiar with. But it actually made it to the number two spot on the French charts. *Mon Dieu!*

It was tough for me to play against Nasty, because we were such good friends. We also practiced together, which meant he knew my game better than anyone. He beat me 10 times in a row, and I remember telling Mom, "Nasty has my number."

"Well, I have news for you," Mom said. "You guys aren't going to be friends for very long, because he's losing respect for you. He's beating you and laughing at you while he's doing it."

Mom was a master of psychology—at least mine. I went on to beat Nasty something like 26 consecutive times. He didn't seem to mind it too much. Nasty was the kind of guy who would always say, "It's OK, it's OK," when someone else came out on top, and then he'd go have a ham sandwich and a Coke. My buddy was easy to please; all he really wanted was a blonde and a bite to eat.

I figured that if I had been able to accept all my prize money in the summer of '71, I probably would have made around $50,000. In anyone's world, that's a lot of money; for a college student, it was beyond belief, and I couldn't take a penny.

"Jeez, mom, I can't keep on giving up all this money."

"That's OK, Jimmy. Just go back to school and get your education. You never know how long you're going to be playing tennis or what will happen in the future. You need a fallback."

I tried pushing the issue, but she insisted that I had to finish college before making any decisions. I entered my sophomore year in the fall of 1971, and the following January I played another of Bill's tournaments in Baltimore, where once again I lost to Nasty in the finals. After that match, I remembered a conversation I had with the actor Lloyd Bridges. Mr. Bridges was one of the regulars at the Beverly Hills Tennis Club; he loved the game and was quite a decent player. He also happened to be the father of Cindy, the girl I was dating. I had been over at his house, talking about my future and how as an amateur I hadn't been able to accept any of the prize money. I told him how frustrating it was for me that my mother insisted I finish college. He said something then that would snap my head back.

"I understand what your mom is saying, Jimmy, but think of it this way: You may never get this chance again. You've got to strike while the iron is hot."

After the Baltimore defeat, I called home.

"Mom, I'm sorry, but I can't do it anymore. I just played this great tournament and lost in the final to Nasty in three sets. I'm playing too well now. I've got to take my chance. I'm turning pro. I promise I'll go back to college once I've given this a try and made some money."

OK, so I lied.

Her reaction surprised me. "You do what you think is best, Jimmy."

I quit school, turned pro, entered the first tournament possible, on the hard indoor floors of Jacksonville, and won. I made something like $1,500.

Then I got drafted.

6

NASTY ENTERTAINMENT

T he Vietnam War still had a year to go before the official cease-
fire, and the draft was ordering up troops through the lottery
system. I should've been in the lottery the year before, but I
had a student exemption. Turning pro cost me the exemption, and
because I had a low number I'd be near the front of the line when
the call came. My brother, Johnny, would've picked up his bags, his
gun, and his uniform and been out the door before they even finished saying his name, but—and I'm not ashamed to tell you this—I
was terrified. Now, let's get one thing straight: I had and will always
have the utmost respect and gratitude for the men and women who
serve our country and keep us safe. As scared as I was, when it came
right down to it I was willing to do my duty.

I went through all the physicals and was mentally prepared to
go, when suddenly I was told I was no longer needed. To this day I
don't know why, and to be honest, back then I didn't ask too many
questions. But I promised myself that I wasn't going to waste the gift
of time that had just been handed to me.

OK, a little history lesson, Connors style.

When I turned professional, in January 1972, I had some big
decisions to make. I had to figure out what tournaments I wanted to
play because there were so many options.

Grand Slam events, which are also called the majors, are the ones where you make your reputation, then as now. They have the most ranking points, the most prize money, and they attract the most attention. Winning the Grand Slam means winning all four of the majors—the Australian Open, the French Open, Wimbledon, and the US Open—in the same year. Rod Laver is still the last man to have accomplished that feat, and he did it twice, in 1962 and 1969. Before 1968, only amateurs could play in the majors, but that year was the beginning of the Open Era, so professional players could compete as well.

And there went the neighborhood. Two-Mom always said, "Beware of open tennis." I didn't know what she meant, but I soon found out.

Suddenly there was a whole load of money to be made in tennis and a whole lot of people were fighting for a piece of the action.

On one side you had the central governing authority, the International Lawn Tennis Federation (ILTF), allied with a bunch of national associations, including the United States Lawn Tennis Association (USLTA). The ILTF sanctioned the most important world tournaments, including the four Slams.

On the other side was the World Championship of Tennis (WCT), dreamed up by the legendary sports promoter Lamar Hunt, the first guy to put players under contract. The WCT sanctioned its own circuit and controlled which players could participate. It's too bad that when things spiraled out of control, and too many rival promoters muddied the waters, Hunt decided to take his expertise—and considerable resources—to other sports. He could have owned tennis, because he gave players a way to earn a living. He made the game more popular by increasing prize money and giving the players a choice of where they wanted to play. But in the end, Hunt refused to get caught in the petty politics between the different factions, which ultimately proved detrimental to the game. Basically, the World Championship of Tennis threatened to overtake the Grand Prix circuit, organized by the ILTF. And they didn't like it.

Both sides dug in their heels until it all came to a head, in July 1971, over an impossible clash of schedules. This resulted in the ILTF voting to prohibit WCT players from participating in its events for the following year.

The power struggle was eventually solved by carving up the tennis schedule like a Thanksgiving turkey. The WCT pulled back from staging tournaments in the summer and fall and became the popular circuit for the first four months of the year, before the main Slams in Paris, London, and New York. Just to make things more interesting, Bill Riordan started his own circuit, the Independent Players Association (IPA), which was a direct rival to the WCT and where I played from January through April.

Then, in 1972, to further complicate things, along comes the Association of Tennis Professionals (ATP), headed by Jack Kramer, Donald Dell, Arthur Ashe, and the South African Cliff Drysdale. Even though players had to pay a fee to join the ATP, by the end of 1974 it had 125 members, including 99 of the top 100 players. Guess who the exception was? And the title of this book is?

Tennis became one big bowl of alphabet soup, and, for better and for worse, we were all swimming in it.

Pressure was coming from all sides to declare your allegiance and pick your poison, but as always, the outsider in me dictated my choice. I was open to all events, but I wasn't under contract to anybody. I just wanted to play tennis. Some people have said I was afraid to play the other circuits, but nothing could be further from the truth. I went with Bill because he had looked after me over the years, inviting me to tournaments and—as I said—slipping me expense money under the table. I also knew that on the IPA tour I could hold my own and still compete against some top players. My choice was not only controversial; it brought criticism from the press and players alike.

In Bill's camp were guys like Nastase, Ion Tiriac, Jan Kodes, Roger Taylor, and Vitas Gerulaitis, and by playing them on a regular basis I could hone my game and gain more experience. After the Riordan events concluded in the spring, the Grand Prix circuit schedule took over, pitting me against the rest of the world's best players, like Laver and Ken Rosewall, John Newcombe, Ashe, and Stan Smith. It was no big deal. I'd be ready for them.

A lot of other young guys were getting thrown into the mix straightaway and losing week after week. What good would that do? I wasn't in a hurry. By biding my time and traveling with Bill to out-of-the-way places, I felt like I could keep an air of mystery around me, just as Two-Mom had advised. The Grand Slam champions—those supposed powerhouses of the sport—were barely aware of my game in the early days, which definitely worked to my advantage.

Bill was taking tennis where it had never been before. While the ILTF and WCT were staging tournaments in major cities, we found ourselves in more intimate venues where we could sell out the stadiums. Initially, Bill faced restrictions in terms of the prize money he could offer, or else he would be in breach of the agreement brokered between the ILTF and the WCT, which had granted Bill limited subsidiary rights. If he ignored these financial limits, his players faced possible exclusion from all the major events in the summer. But Bill, being Bill, always found ways to entice players to his tournaments. He'd invite major corporations to sponsor bonus pools that would go to the winners of the most events. And, let's face it, who couldn't use a little extra cash at the end of a long, hard season?

Bill laid out the situation in simple terms. I could join the other bandwagons like the WCT and be one of the herd, or I could go with him. Together we'd make some noise and I'd end up earning a shitload of money and become famous. That doesn't sound bad. Where do I sign?

Bill used to tell me that just winning wasn't enough; we had to entertain, to put on a show. It was in his blood. His father had financial interests in several prizefighters, and Bill had spent his youth ringside at Madison Square Garden, soaking up the showbiz atmosphere. Boxing had a big influence on his vision for the future of tennis. He also believed in the appeal of the Eastern European contingent of Nastase, Tiriac, and Kodes. With their talent and theatrical personalities, the Riordan circuit stoked interest and created controversy, and Bill milked it for all it was worth. He encouraged his players to kick up the energy in arenas like the Coliseum in Hampton, Virginia, where eight or nine thousand people would scream and shout as if they were watching a heavyweight bout.

It was loud and it was in your face, but it wasn't just about the spectacle. Riordan also knew his tennis. Back in the late 1950s, in his home state of Maryland, he formed the Salisbury Tennis Association and ran clinics in the local parks that produced a string of high-quality junior players. He also coached his local high school team to great success, promoted the United States national men's indoor tennis championships in Salisbury and, in 1964, had even joined the enemy, the USLTA, as an official delegate—until the power struggles brought on by the Open Era pushed him out and forced him to set up his show.

Bill had no fear of going mano a mano with anyone, slugging it out like the street fighter he was. Mostly this worked in my favor, but it could also backfire, when he went after people he felt had done him wrong, like that time he sued Ashe and the ATP. Hell, he even sued me once. All in all, Bill had a huge impact on the game of tennis. This was boom time, the gold rush, and he was at the heart of it. Pretty soon the moneymen caught on, and big holiday resorts started giving up expensive real estate to build courts for their guests to play on. My timing could not have been better.

Since Nastase and I were already friends when I turned professional, the fact that he was a part of the Riordan circuit was a giant lure.

Nasty was the big name in the IPA ranks in 1972, but Bill also knew he needed someone else who would represent all that his tour stood for—taking tennis to the heartland, playing in front of real sports fans. When he signed me he got exactly that: a young, brash, hard-hitting American. A maverick. An outsider.

He made me the star of the show. As I won more and more tournaments, Bill used to schedule my matches for Wednesday, rather than Monday, so that I could spend the early part of each week meeting sponsors and local dignitaries, shaking hands, making small talk, playing exhibition matches. I didn't mind one bit. I understood that this was part of Bill's master plan to ride me to the top.

Bill would introduce me at cocktail parties with the words "The one and only Jimmy Connors," even though I hardly deserved the title. After that kind of buildup, you can't just sit there with your thumb up your ass. You have to jump in, schmooze the money guys, and give the fans what they want—the kind of show that will keep them coming back. It didn't matter if I was tired or in a crappy mood; when I was on, I was on, and I got to be pretty good at it.

I wonder sometimes how I learned in those first couple of years to speak in public without making a fool of myself. Of course, some people might think I never learned that lesson, but this is my book; I can write what I want. I wasn't really looking for star billing, and I honestly don't know how it all happened. It just did. Playing tennis was my thing, but I eventually got a Ph.D. in marketing and promotion from Riordan University.

I remember reading, years later, an interview in *Sports Illustrated* where Bill said, "With Jimmy, sometimes it was like leading a symphony. And I don't believe anyone could have done it like Connors. He never deviated from the script I wrote him. Even today, at his press conferences, some of my best lines surface."

Attaboy, Bill.

Life on the tennis circuit has a reputation for being all about glamour and parties, first-class travel and five-star accommodations. Let me tell you, it wasn't, not back in the early 1970s. Mom or Bill would organize my travel, but it was still a pain in the ass, sorting out a flight from, say, Paramus, New Jersey, to Roanoke, Virginia. I'd be on standby most of the time, kicking around a string of departure lounges, drinking sodas and staring into space, trying to save money. I played two years on the circuit before I could afford to buy a first-class ticket anywhere.

The truth is, in the beginning I was bored out of my mind most of the time. My regimen went as follows: practice a little in the morning (on the one court available in many of Riordan's venues), then go for a walk to kill some time, return to the hotel to rest and watch television—westerns, whenever I could find them, but also daytime soap operas. Life didn't get much better than a doubleheader of *As the World Turns* and *The Guiding Light*. I went out only after my matches, usually late at night to find a place to eat, and misbehave with Nasty. As you can imagine, life in Salisbury, Maryland, was kickin'.

There is a big difference between a pretender and a weekender. The guys who were knocked out in the first or second rounds could spend their lives hanging around the bars, playing the tennis-pro card to pick up girls. I couldn't do that. Staying out until 3 a.m. doesn't catch up with you the next day—with me, it usually took three or four days, which is when I was playing in the semis and finals and needed all my energy and focus. I'll say it again: Tennis is all about timing.

On those few occasions when I stepped over the line, the one that Pancho had drawn for me, I became sluggish, my reactions slowed and my intensity level hard to maintain. Normally, I would happily stay out on the court for as long as it took to win, but when I felt tired, my mind began to play tricks on me. *He's too good for you, Jimmy. Give it up. You don't have what it takes. You're humiliating yourself.* I was strong enough physically to play through exhaustion, but it was those momentary lapses of mental toughness that would drag me down.

That was unacceptable. It went against everything Mom, Pancho, Two-Mom, and Pop had taught me. So I was careful and saved most of my nighttime adventures for when I was back home in Los Angeles.

The fans, however, made it all worthwhile. They came out in the thousands in places like Little Rock, Arkansas, and Shreveport, Louisiana, places better known for football.

At the beginning it was only the country-club set that came to watch, but that quickly changed as word spread about some of the antics that Nasty and I brought to the party. We talked to the fans, shouted, laughed, cursed, and made rude gestures, but they came back the next day to see more. The noise, the abuse, the language—it was wild. Who wouldn't enjoy that? That's how the transition occurred; the country-clubbers remained, appreciating the quality of the tennis, but they were joined by new fans, who came for the show.

As the rivalries intensified—Nasty and me, Vitas and me, Nasty and Tiriac—it became more like Ali vs. Frazier than Laver vs. Emerson. Those guys were definitely tennis royalty, but we were the new generation, blue-collar stars, always at each other's throats.

Once my reputation and my notoriety spread, the agents came calling. It happened pretty much immediately following that first victory in Jacksonville, right after I turned pro. I was happy to let Mom handle the business end of it, allowing me to concentrate on my game. I trusted her judgment completely. Even though she was criticized for it, Mom wasn't shy about being a manager. Mark Mc-Cormack, the fabled founder of IMG, the biggest sports agency in the world, went to her and asked me to join his stable of players. When that didn't work out, he paid a visit to the La Costa club in Carlsbad, California, where Pancho was now the head pro. McCormack tried his best to persuade Pancho that I'd be much better off with IMG than with Riordan. Pancho took McCormack's offer to Mom but recommended against it.

"Gloria," he explained, "if Jimbo signs with McCormack, he'll just be one of 10 other guys, and when opportunities come along they'll be ahead of him. He has got to be somewhere where he is number one. You and Bill, you're doing a good job. Stick with it."

It wasn't a big surprise that I got a call in March 1972 to join the US Davis Cup squad for a tie in Kingston, Jamaica. I had practiced with the team the previous fall, so I knew the setup and the captain, Dennis Ralston. I was happy to go and looking forward to representing my country.

The team that met up in the Caribbean consisted of Ralston, Erik Van Dillen, Tom Gorman, Stan Smith, and me—a strong lineup, but not so strong that I thought I would be squeezed out of the singles. Yet that's exactly what happened: Ralston threw Van Dillen in ahead of me, and I was left to slice the oranges.

I was pissed because as far as I was concerned, I had earned and deserved an opportunity to play. I felt that if I wasn't there to compete, then I shouldn't be there at all. As it turned out, none of that mattered. Before practice one afternoon, I got a call in my hotel room. Mom was on the line from Los Angeles, where she was staying in my apartment.

"Jimmy, we have a problem. I'd like for you to come home."

I didn't even question her. I took the first flight out.

I had to wait through the night, and then I caught a plane from Kingston to Miami, then from Miami to LA, only to have to stop in Houston on the last leg, due to a storm. The whole way, I tried not to let my fears take hold and think the worst—that maybe Two-Mom had just fallen and injured herself.

I called Mom from Houston to let her know my flight had been delayed.

"Is it Two-Mom?"

"Yes," she replied, her voice quavering. "She's gone."

How could Two-Mom, the woman who had done so much for me, who had made me laugh, chased after my stray tennis balls, cooked and cleaned for me, treated me to ice cream and soda—how could she not be here anymore? How was it possible that she would never see me walk onto Centre Court at Wimbledon, play for my country, win the US Open five times, or any of the things we had dreamed about together? She would never know what became of me. I would never feel her hand on my shoulder and have that feeling of comfort, the sense that "everything will be OK." We'd been through so much hard work together—in the East St. Louis backyard, in Jones Park, the armory, on the junior circuit—and now, just as everything was beginning to pay off, just as things were starting to get good, she had left us. It wasn't fair.

Did I cry? Not in public.

Mom had been with Two-Mom when it happened; the two of them were inseparable. They had traveled to Beverly Hills from East St. Louis to enjoy the early-spring sunshine and help me prepare for my first professional summer, once I had returned from Jamaica.

Mom was in the kitchen, making something to eat, when Two-Mom came in from her bedroom. She had a strange look on her face, like some big revelation had suddenly come to her.

"Gloria, I know why they . . ."

That was her last breath. She collapsed, suffering a massive heart attack, and died instantly. Mom watched her own mother die in front of her. The thought of that, and of Mom having to remember that moment for the rest of her life, was like a punch in my gut.

Looking back, I should probably have paid more attention to the hints of Two-Mom's decline. Coming across her on that landing in my first apartment in LA, when she was wheezing and rubbing her chest, was certainly a sign that she wasn't in the best of health, but the idea that indestructible Two-Mom might have a weakness was just unthinkable. Her passing shook all of us—me, Johnny, Pop, my dad, and Mom most of all.

I've often wondered who the "they" were that Two-Mom was talking about in her final words on earth and also how the sentence ended. I know why they are giving Jimmy a hard time? I know why they don't want Jimmy to play? She wanted to tell Mom something important, but she never got the chance.

On the flight to LA I had been thinking of two things that Two-Mom taught me, which remain the foundations of how I live my life still: "Take care of your business" and "If you can't afford it, don't buy it." Her instructions were elementary, just five or six fundamentals, but that is all you ever really need. As for my tennis, it's simple: I would not be where I am without the love and hard work of my grandmother.

Throughout my career I carried notes from her in my socks, and I read them before every match and if I ever found myself in trouble while playing. I wasn't ever embarrassed to pull out those slips of paper. At any time, I don't care who you are, you have to be able to go back to the basics.

Don't forget to take the ball early.
Don't forget to keep your eye on the ball.
Don't forget to reach up on your serve.

Mom and I arranged for Two-Mom to be taken back to Belleville for a private funeral. Pop said that's what she would have wanted. She was popular in the local area and it could have been a big public event, but when it came down to it, as Pop explained, Two-Mom cared about family above everything else.

As I stood by her graveside on that March morning, I looked across at my father, my brother, Mom, and Pop, all of us wrapped up in heavy coats against the chill, united in our grief. For the first time in many years we felt like a family, the thing that mattered most to Two-Mom. But she was gone. It made me wonder, had tennis already done too much damage, or was there more to come?

Back at the house, I took Mom to one side.

"I'm done," I told her. "I'm quitting. Everything that we put into this, all the work, and now just as things are starting to pay off, this happens. I'm out."

I was serious. I wanted to walk away.

"I'll go back to school for you, Mom. I'll get that education you always wanted me to have. I'll figure something out."

"Jimmy, that's your choice. But Two-Mom loved tennis; it was a huge part of her life. She dedicated herself to it so that you could become the best you could be. Do you really want to walk away from all of that?"

I needed time to think, which is something I did best while walking my dog. For years, it had been Pepper by my side, but when he passed on, my schnauzer Charlie took over as my wingman. Walking with Charlie after talking to Mom, I had a vision of Two-Mom standing by the fence in our backyard, slightly crouched, the handbag she always carried clutched to her side, looking intently at me through her wing-tipped glasses, watching me serve, making mental notes to discuss with Mom later. Could I really let her down, after everything she had done for me?

"You're right," I told my mom when Charlie and I returned. "I can't walk away."

And it was never talked about again. And I still miss Two-Mom every day.

By the summer of 1972, the battle lines had been drawn. Everyone knew that Riordan, my mom, and I were a force to be reckoned with. As for the so-called tennis establishment, screw 'em. It's no different from how I had been brought up. Us against them, Jimmy, us against them.

The French Open that year was an emotional minefield. My nerves were still raw from losing Two-Mom, and it was only the second time in my life that I had traveled outside the United States. I had always fantasized about walking onto the red clay of Roland Garros and looking up into the stands and seeing Mom and Two-Mom sitting there. Now that was never going to happen and it hit me hard.

I arrived in Paris with a strong reputation on the strength of my two pro-tournament wins, but my concentration wasn't where it needed to be for me to perform at my best, and I lost in the second round to Harold Solomon in straight sets. I had grown up with Harold, and we were friends, but he was also my nemesis throughout the course of my career. He was an amazing player, like a human backboard—there seemed to be no shot that he couldn't return—and that ability to keep the ball in play for endless rallies would give me and a lot of other guys fits.

I could rationalize the defeat as the result of my grief over Two-Mom, but I could feel the pressure building, and it was pressure I was putting on myself. I was desperate to show the world that the game Two-Mom had worked so hard to give me was good enough to compete with the best.

A month later, I'm on the grass of the Queens Club, in London.

Bounce, bounce, bounce, bounce, bounce, bounce, bounce.

Jimmy, you've got to serve. Jimmy, serve. Serve.

Bounce, bounce, bounce, bounce.

Toss it up, Jimmy. Toss it up. Serve.

I can't. I need to count. That's 10, no, 11. Start again. Bounce. One bounce. Two times, six times, no, eight.

I'm facing the veteran Australian Neale Fraser and struggling to find my rhythm. The umpire threatens to default me if I don't speed things up, but it feels beyond me. I need to bounce the ball a certain number of times before I serve, and if I lose track I have to start over again. It was kind of like jumping rope when Pop was training me.

It's my first match in London, in freakish 100-degree heat, and I can't stop bouncing the ball. I've bounced it 42 times and finally someone in the stands yells out, "Come on, Connors, serve already!"

"I can't," I answer sheepishly, and just a little pathetically.

Bounce, bounce, bounce, and JUST TOSS THE DAMN THING! And I do.

Thank God, now I can play.

I went back to the hotel that night and actually practiced bouncing the ball and letting it go. Can you imagine how restful that evening was? What I didn't realize then was that what was going on with me actually had a name: obsessive compulsive disorder. I began to feel obliged to check at least 10 times that every door in my apartment was locked, every window closed, before I could go to bed for the night. I had trouble sleeping, worrying that I had overlooked something; I would drag myself out of bed repeatedly, test everything once again, return to bed, and immediately become convinced I had probably miscounted. Even getting out of the apartment could be a chore. I'd be at the point of leaving when it would hit me. Check again, check again, and check again. You've got to be sure. Living with OCD was a pain in the ass.

It took a physical toll on me—sometimes I found myself passing out from exhaustion—but I didn't realize that I needed to get help. How could I go to a doctor and tell him I couldn't leave my own house? I had to beat this on my own.

At major tournaments like Wimbledon and the US Open, signs of my OCD went way beyond my relentless ball bouncing. I insisted on being driven to the stadiums by exactly the same route every day, or acute anxiety would set in. Weirdly, I had no trouble sleeping in hotel rooms because there was only one door, but at home it was a different matter. The constant need to be sure everything was OK brought on new compulsions. To turn on lights I had to flick the switch three times first; before taking a drink I'd tap my glass four times; at traffic lights and stop signs I had to tap on the brakes four times. (Aren't you glad you weren't behind me?)

I ultimately managed to control the ball-bouncing—sort of. I'd allow myself four bounces, but if that didn't feel right, I'd have to keep at it until it did, releasing the ball only on an even number. Over the last 30 years I've gotten a handle on most of my various rituals. I'll say it again: I hate being beaten more than I like to win. OCD has always been a part of my life, but I don't dwell on it. It only makes it worse. I've had three hip operations, and I need an even number. How do you live with that?

If only I had been able to talk to Two-Mom about the OCD. Of course she would have said, "Oh, get over it. There's no such thing. What do you want for dinner?"

7

LOVE GAME

A week before the Queen's Club tournament in June 1972, I attended an official dinner to celebrate the US team's victory in the Wightman Cup. They had defeated the British 5-2 in a contest played that year at Wimbledon. One of the US team members was Wendy Overton, a friend of mine and a top-10 doubles player, who needed a date for the dinner and asked if I could go.

I probably wasn't very good company for Wendy that evening, though, because all through the meal I couldn't take my eyes off cute, young Chris Evert across the way. I knew who she was—Mom and I had caught a ride to Coral Gables with Chris and her parents back in 1965—and I wanted to get to know her better. I would glance over at her table and see her smiling at me, or I would try and catch her eye when she was in mid-conversation with the Wightman Cup team coach, Bill Graves.

When dinner was finished, I walked over and introduced myself. It was a nice opening to take the conversation to another level.

I was always told that you should always leave a party with the girl you came with, so at the end of the festivities, I made sure to take Wendy back to her hotel. It didn't take me long, though, to find out just what room Chrissie was staying in.

For the first time that year, the Queen's Club was also hosting the ladies' Rothmans grass-court championship, which was the warm-up tournament for Wimbledon, so it wasn't hard to make sure I ran into Chrissie again. The dining-room area of the club was small, and one day when Chrissie was sitting there before one of her matches, I pulled up a chair next to her at lunch and turned on the charm faucet! I wasn't looking for a steady girlfriend. But I thought we could have some fun together.

Later in the week, I called her at her hotel and asked her to dinner.

We went to the famous Rib Room, at the Carlton Tower Hotel. Then we moved on to what had become my favorite stop in London, the Playboy Club, a haven for every vice I ever had. It had great food, was full of beautiful women, and upstairs there were blackjack and craps tables. Does life get any better than that? Not for me, it doesn't. But that night I can honestly say I just wanted to be with Chrissie. We had a lot in common—the same anxieties and pressures, the same expectations and hopes. Chrissie could be serious-minded and dedicated, but when she relaxed she was easy to be around, and I could make her laugh. That night we ran around London, acting like kids in high school—which, by the way, she still was.

Some things stay private. Or as Two-Mom always told me, "Keep a little mystery about yourself." On the way back to our hotel, we kissed for the first time. I know this will take a lot of you by surprise, but I played the gentleman and said goodnight.

Chrissie and I both won at Queen's, taking my year's total to three victories—and then it was on to Wimbledon, where the press caught on to us as a couple. They constantly snapped photographs as we walked around the grounds or when we hit the town after our matches. She was only 17, but Chrissie was already making a name for herself in tennis—she had reached the semis of the US Open the previous year, losing to Billie Jean King—and I wasn't fooling myself which one of us the papers were interested in. It really didn't bother me; I just thought the whole thing was fun, running away from photographers and ducking behind cars. We were just kids having a good time.

When the draw for Wimbledon was announced, it was clear that I wouldn't be able to ease my way into the tournament under the radar. Instead, I was scheduled to play the second match on Centre Court, on opening day, against seventh-seeded Bob Hewitt. Playing on Centre Court in my first match at my first Wimbledon was something I had dreamed about my whole life. What the hell. There was no more exciting place to launch a career.

I had heard many stories about the whole Wimbledon experience from some of the older American players, like Charlie Pasarell and Stan Smith, but nothing impressed me more than the Rolls-Royce, which I was told would pick you up and take you to the grounds. Wow! Nineteen years old, and I'm going to be riding in a Rolls? Yeah, I've arrived. So you can imagine my disappointment when I walked out of my hotel and saw that my ride was not a Rolls—they had cut that out the year before—but instead just a regular old taxi. And just when I thought I was hot shit.

As it was my first Wimbledon, Bill Riordan, Pancho, and Mom were all there. Mom always watched my matches; we never thought anything about it, and I don't think too many people really paid much attention to her. Not until that Monday afternoon of my opening match on Centre Court, that is. There, as I faced Hewitt, the myth of Gloria Connors, the pushy stage mom who never let her son out of her sight, was born.

"Come on, Jimmy," Mom called out, midway through the second set.

That's all she said. She called out three words of encouragement to her son at a crucial stage in the match. Jeez, given the press reaction the next day, you would have thought she had run onto the court like a streaker and incited a riot. Overnight, she became the loud-mouthed American woman who didn't understand, or didn't care, about the sacred traditions of the All-England Club. Come on, what's that all about? I guess they didn't like it that the new generation, the one I represented, was pushing out the old. Mom was an easy target. We found the whole thing pretty funny, especially when a tabloid cartoon showed me holding hands with a giant gorilla as I walked onto Centre Court and stood looking up at the referee. The caption read, "Sorry, everyone, Mom couldn't make it today."

Those British hacks: Oh, what a sense of humor they have.

I caused a major upset by defeating Hewitt, who had arrived on the back of wins at two prestigious tournaments staged in England in those days, the Bristol Open and the British Hard Court Championships, in Bournemouth.

When I walked off Centre Court, I discovered that my clothes had been moved from the junior locker room, or Locker Room 2, into Locker Room 1 with the rest of the big boys. I had arrived, and it didn't take long.

I beat my good friend and lifelong rival, the great Adriano Panatta, of Italy, in the third round before losing in the quarters to Nasty, the second seed, in straight sets. It wasn't bad for my first visit to Wimbledon, and Chrissie, on her debut, made it through to the semis, where she lost to Evonne Goolagong, the young Australian champion, in a much-anticipated match.

I may not have won the tournament, but I did leave London with a girlfriend.

I gave a less than dazzling display on the grass of the 1972 US Open, losing in the first round to Tom Gorman in five sets (Nasty went on to win his first Slam, beating Ashe in the finals), but that major disappointment was offset by three more tournament victories, in Columbus, Cincinnati, and Albany, taking my career total to six by the end of the year. They were pretty decent results and more than justified my decision to turn pro. If only Two-Mom had been there to see it.

The new year then brought a string of wins on the Riordan circuit, which I was determined to use as a springboard for my second trip to Europe. Unfortunately, things didn't work out the way I wanted, especially not in Paris. If it hadn't been for the doubles, I'd have been on a boat back across the English Channel straight after my first-round loss to the unseeded Mexican Raúl Ramírez, a defeat I marked by hurling a couple of racquets across my hotel room in disgust. I'd given a lousy performance. In one respect I was lucky: My aim hadn't improved from earlier in the day. If it had, I'd have been adding the cost of a new lamp to my hotel bill.

Nasty and I made it through to the doubles finals, where we lost to Tom Okker and John Newcombe in a tight five-set match. Given that Nasty also had the singles final to play (he defeated Niki Pilic, of Yugoslavia, in straight sets), it was no great surprise that we ran out of steam. In fact, Nasty didn't drop a set the entire tournament, except when he was playing with me. I'm not reading anything into that. Well, not much.

The contractual dispute between the WCT and the ILTF had resulted in several players being barred from taking their place at Wimbledon the previous year, and in 1973, matters deteriorated further still. At the center of the controversy this time was Nasty's opponent in the French finals, Pilic. It wasn't clear whether he had refused to play in a Davis Cup tie or wasn't allowed to play, but the consequences were that his national authority suspended him. The ITLF backed the decision, and Pilic was dropped from the Wimbledon draw. In protest, most of the ATP members withdrew from the tournament, leaving just a few top players like Nasty, Jan Kodes, and Roger Taylor, of England. This watered-down field played a part in my promotion to sixth seed, and my target was a place in the semis, if not the finals.

I coasted through the first four rounds, dropping only one set, on the way to a meeting with Alex Metreveli, of the Soviet Union, in the quarterfinals. There, I ran smack into an Iron Curtain. Bang! I was gone, but at least Nasty and I were alive in the doubles.

Nasty, the number one seed, had gotten dumped from the singles in the fourth round by American Sandy Mayer, and afterward he called me at my hotel.

"Jimmy, Nikki wants to leave. She's had enough." His wife, Dominique, didn't want to hang around for what she saw as the sideshow of the doubles.

"I get it, Nasty, don't worry. If you don't want to play, no big deal. It's not worth it."

Maybe he didn't want to let me down—after all, it was only my second Wimbledon—or maybe he didn't want anyone to think he was giving in to Dominique too easily, I don't know, but Nasty decided to stick around.

We laughed and joked our way to the finals, where we faced the Australians, John Cooper and Neale Fraser. We decided that every chance we got, whenever Cooper and Fraser got anywhere near the net, we'd hit lobs, over and over again, and no one played like that on grass. They were quality players who probably didn't think this was nearly as funny as Nasty and I did, and they fought hard, taking us all the way to the fifth set before we eventually won. It was my first Grand Slam title, and although it was only in doubles, I couldn't wait for the formal presentation in front of the Centre Court crowd.

But by the time the officials were ready to present, it was no longer us, only me. Dominique had eventually had her way and told Nasty he couldn't hang out after our victory. The crowd applauded when I walked, alone, out onto the sacred grass, with an awkward grin on my face, and as I held up the twin trophies, I imagined Nasty laughing as he sipped his first drink on the flight home to Romania.

Not long after, Spencer Segura and I went to Romania ourselves, for an exhibition match in Bucharest. I've never seen anything like it in my life. Remember, Romania during this time was behind the Iron Curtain, yet when we arrived, even as two young Americans, we didn't have to clear customs. We were treated as VIPs because we were with Mr. Nastase, and normal rules did not apply.

Driving from the airport to the hotel meant passing through numerous military checkpoints. Normally, this would have meant having our papers scrutinized, or maybe even a search of the car, but not for us. Each time we approached one of those security posts, the officers in charge would recognize Nasty's car and immediately raise the barrier and move off to one side, standing stiff and proper in their huge gray coats, saluting as we passed. All Nasty could do was smile.

We weren't kidding ourselves that we were seeing the real country, however. This was Romania for the 1 percent, and Nasty was their superstar. He took his responsibilities to his countrymen seriously. He didn't hide himself away. He walked the streets, waving to the crowds and talking to anyone who approached him. The only glimpse Spencer and I ever had of the real Romania was at the airport, when we were leaving. Waiting at the gate to board our flight back to London, we were surrounded by a group of locals, pleading for help.

"You are American, you help us get on the plane, please?"

"Here, take this piece of paper. It has my name and address.

Please, when you are back at home, arrange a visa for me to leave here."

"Can you buy me an American passport? Please, I must have one."

It upset me that we couldn't do anything to help. Once we were on board, I looked out of the window across the runway, where a dozen men were clearing the snow off the tarmac with brooms. By one of the hangars I could see airport workers huddled around the flames of a fire they had lit in an old oil drum. Away from the glamour of Nasty's Bucharest, Romania reminded me of those old black-and-white newsreels of the Great Depression, where people lost everything and yet still kept going.

Nasty had the language and the temper of the devil but a face that plenty of women loved. At the same time, he recognized the important position he held, representing Romanian culture and promoting his country as best as he could. He was charming, funny, and caring. He loved to party and stay out late, but drinking and gambling were not his thing, and I never saw him take drugs. As I said, for Nasty, it was all about the women, scores of them, each more beautiful than the next. Nasty claimed in his autobiography that he'd slept with over 2,500 women. I couldn't tell you if he was exaggerating, since I was only around for 1,500 of them. His strength and stamina both on and off the court were impressive, to say the least.

Once, when Spencer and I were in London, Nasty wanted to go out with us. You know this is only going to lead to trouble. As always, Nasty attracted a gorgeous woman, and he couldn't keep his hands to himself. So back to the hotel we went, where Nasty stashed his handful in my room, which was right next door to the room he was sharing with his wife, Nikki. Spencer and I played checkers in the corner (two out of three of us were losers), and now all of a sudden Nasty's trying to be quiet since he remembered that his, um . . . wife was next door. He opens the door to walk out into the hallway, tells us goodnight, turns, and is face to face with Nikki. How he got himself out of that I'll never know. Oh, and I forgot about that one. Make it 1,501.

I wasn't a bad doubles player, but playing with Nasty helped show me where I needed to improve. The quick-fire rallies sharpened my volleys, and each set was like a master class in the art of the topspin lob.

I didn't have his natural topspin, but that didn't keep me from trying to figure out a way to incorporate some of it into my game. Topspinners use a Western-style grip, with their palm under the handle, allowing them to roll the racquet easier. My hand fits more comfortably toward the side of the handle, which is great for hitting the ball flat. If I tried to copy Nasty's stroke, I would have blown out my wrist in a second, but studying his technique did give me another weapon in my arsenal.

Nasty and I continued to play doubles together through 1975, when we won the US Open. After that I was pretty much done. I was playing in too many singles matches by then, and I didn't want to hang around stadiums all day long waiting for the late-night doubles. Other players took an opposite view; John McEnroe, for instance, viewed doubles as good practice, and his partnership with Peter Fleming brought him countless Grand Slam doubles titles, but I didn't need that. I was wary of burning myself out with too much tennis. I thrived on staying hungry.

I was young and impressionable, and a lot of what I saw from Nasty rubbed off on me. The good the bad and the truly ugly. On the court he could be completely out of control, like the time in 1976 when he called the German player Hans-Jürgen Pohmann "Hitler." That was one of the more controversial matches in US Open history. Sometimes I'd watch him swearing at umpires, throwing his racquet, giving the finger to a line judge, or threatening to smash photographers' cameras and I would cringe. Then two tournaments later, I'd be doing exactly the same thing. But I would also watch the way Nasty moved, gliding across the court in anticipation of the next shot. The way he played tennis made him the best show in town, and whatever else you got was just an added bonus. That's why every time he played, the stadium was packed—you never knew what you were going to get.

I matched my Wimbledon performance by reaching the quarterfinals of the US Open in September 1973, with a significant win against Tom Okker in the fourth round. Tom had been in the world's top 10 for years and was lightning-fast around the court. As always, Pancho had been analyzing my opponents and devised a strategy for me to follow.

"He can volley, Jimmy, and he rushes the net very fast. Hit the ball flat and keep it low, and when you see him coming to the net, make sure you mix up your passing shots. Don't forget the lob; that will catch even Okker off guard."

The lessons I learned on the doubles courts with Nasty came in handy in that match, especially my improved lob. I had Tom confused, reluctant to commit himself to the net but unable to contend with my groundstrokes when it came to battling it out from the baseline. It took him out of his comfort zone, and a 6-3, 6-2, 6-4 victory set up my first meeting with the great John Newcombe in the quarters. Although I was beaten in straight sets, it was tight. I lost tiebreakers in the second and the third, and while I was disappointed, I knew the distance between me and the man who was to become that year's champion was getting increasingly closer. I respected him, but I didn't fear him.

My big breakthrough as a singles player came in the fall of 1973, at the US Pro championships, at the Longwood Cricket Club, in Boston. Longwood was full of talented players. This is my opportunity to move to the next stage, I thought. Bring it on.

Be careful what you wish for.

In the first round, I was drawn against world number one and top seed Stan Smith. I attacked him with my groundstrokes—I don't think he knew what hit him—and won in straight sets. I then beat Ray Moore, Dick Stockton, and Cliff Richey to reach the finals, where number two seed Arthur Ashe stood in my way.

Pancho knew Ashe well—they were friends from his days at Beverly Hills—and he had plenty to say to me just before the match.

"Jimbo, he's good, but you are better. He plays quiet, confident, so rattle him. Attack his serve from the start by returning hard and deep down the middle. Cut off his angles and be aggressive."

I followed Pancho's advice, jumping on Arthur's serve at every opportunity. I had to, because the match would hinge on the ability of one of us to come up with something out of the ordinary. I kept at it, never letting him settle into a rhythm, and it paid off. We battled for three hours before I won, 6-3, 4-6, 6-4, 3-6, 6-2. That first big win not only felt overdue but good—really good.

Before that triumph, I had heard whispers from certain members of the press that I was just Chris Evert's boyfriend. It seemed that our relationship was getting more attention than the tournaments I was winning. What the hell? It was just another distraction I had to deal with. I was the US Pro champion now. Screw 'em. I was starting to make my own name now.

Chrissie and I tried to see as much of each other as possible, but it was hard with our separate tour commitments. When we were together, everything was good, but long-distance relationships are tough. When you're 5,000 miles apart, doubt enters your mind, and things can be taken out of context. We'd disagree about the little stuff that didn't really matter and we'd end up blowing it out of proportion. When that happens, there's only one place for the conversation to go, and that's downhill. We'd end up arguing and then all kinds of accusations would fly, and I would think, "Really? Is that good for a relationship?" Better to hang up before things get out of hand.

I know I strayed, several times, over the two years we were together, both at home in California and on tour. I was young, hanging out with buddies like Nasty, Spencer, Dino Martin, David Schneider, and Vitas Gerulaitis. What do you think happened? After every match, we'd be surrounded by women, Chrissie would be in a different state or country, and the two of us might have had another fight on the phone. It happened. I'm not proud of it, but that's what I did.

Attitudes toward sex had changed. It was after the pill (and before AIDS), and women were enjoying their sexual freedom. If they wanted to chase you, they would, and sometimes I didn't run very fast. One-night stands were common on tour, and I had my fair share. That shy, laid-back approach worked pretty well for me.

Chrissie might not want to admit it, but America's Sweetheart was no angel, either. It's hard to keep secrets in the tennis world.

I wanted to make it work between us, and I'm sure she did too, but I guess we both saw our relationship as a temporary thing, two kids sowing their wild oats before settling down. Last I checked, that wasn't a crime.

The reality was that if I wanted to see Chrissie, I had to get on a plane, so I'd call Bill Riordan and ask him to arrange a flight to wherever she was that week. I was doing all of the running around, and it began to have a detrimental effect on my game.

To remedy the situation, we decided to play some mixed doubles. We'd competed at the US Open in 1972 and had done pretty well, reaching the quarterfinals. Over the next two years in New York, we went one better each time, getting to the semis in 1973 and the finals in 1974. We also paired up at Wimbledon, where we reached the quarterfinals in 1973 and the third round in 1974, before withdrawing because of our singles commitments.

It wasn't a bad record, but that really wasn't the point as far as I was concerned. Although for me mixed doubles was about having some fun with Chrissie, she took it very seriously, finding it almost impossible to rein in her competitive spirit. I certainly understood, but there's a point where you have to let go. Mixed doubles just didn't matter enough in my world, and I didn't think it should have in Chrissie's, not compared with her success in singles. Still, who was I to make that decision? Chrissie saw things differently. It was as though she felt that losing was a sign of weakness, which could give her rivals on the tour an advantage in future tournaments.

Now, everything I'm saying on these pages is obviously my opinion, and Chrissie may have a different take on things, but this is how I feel. Our different attitudes would clash on the court. In mixed doubles, no matter what tournament it is, who I'm playing against, or what round it is, I've always refused to blast the ball at my female opponent, even if the other guy is aiming at my partner. When that happened, I'd give the guy some shit, but I would never take my anger out on his teammate. Chrissie wasn't particularly happy about that and said she thought I should go ahead and bury the other woman. I would just shrug and get on with the game, and that made her even madder.

Everyone has his or her insecurities; I had mine and Chrissie had hers. In the often claustrophobic, intense world of tennis, you can feel as though everything revolves around you, and her need to be the center of attention at all times became too much.

Believe it or not, there were moments when the spotlight didn't belong to either one of us, and I relished those. Remember how much I loved westerns as a kid? Well, having a chance to meet and spend time with John Wayne was an opportunity I just couldn't let pass.

Lornie Kuhle is one of my oldest friends, going back to when we were just youngsters playing tournaments in Illinois. When we hooked up again, after I moved to Beverly Hills, Lornie was married to John Wayne's daughter Aissa, and Chrissie and I went to Mr. Wayne's house on a number of occasions.

The Duke enjoyed his tennis, and we'd play at one of his local clubs in Newport Beach. In the evening, after dinner, there was usually some betting action on the backgammon board, and he talked just like he did in the movies. Whenever he took a pip off the board, he would say in that slow drawl, "Let's get that guy on outta here." I loved that! John Fuckin' Wayne! Are you kidding me? Backgammon with John Wayne! But Chrissie always seemed to want to go home early, no matter how much fun I was having, and, as I recall, she usually got her way. All the Duke could do was wink at me and say, "Well, good luck, pilgrim."

A phrase I used to hear a lot—not from Chrissie but from the people around her—was "We've got to do what's right for Chris." I got the point, but I had enough on my hands taking care of my own business. When you have two people in a relationship who both want to be number one, it's tough. The math doesn't work. You both expect to be treated in a certain way, and that's impossible, because someone has to concede. For most of our relationship, it felt like that person tended to be me.

In another attempt to see more of Chrissie (and because I was on the road all the time, anyway), I even moved to a hotel in Florida near her house. We would hit balls together whenever I was there, and I saw it as a positive move, but Mom disagreed, probably with good reason. Choosing Chrissie over, say, Spencer for practice sessions was a one-sided deal. Chrissie's game improved while mine didn't. Hitting with me was good for her—the pace of my shots helped quicken her reactions—but not me. Before a tournament, I'd have to take a few extra days to practice with the guys and get used to the speed and power again. Mom found that hard to deal with and made little attempt to hide her feelings, causing yet more tension between Chrissie and me, which we really didn't need.

In November 1974, Chrissie and I both won the singles at the South African Open, in Johannesburg. This was during the apartheid regime, and because Arthur Ashe was the first black athlete to be given a visa to play in the country, the press interest in him was insane. They followed him everywhere, shoving microphones in his face and demanding a comment on every political issue. Arthur stayed cool throughout the whole tournament, but how he managed to concentrate on tennis I'll never know.

Understandably, Arthur was desperate to win in South Africa, maybe more so than in any other tournament. I later read that he had identified the weaknesses in my game that he intended to exploit. They were as follows:

My serve. (I'll give him that—it was only as good as it
  needed to be.)
My forehand. (Only in comparison with my backhand,
  which was only the best in the game. Quiet—this is my
  book.)

Shots with no pace. (People always said that, but I never saw
  it as a weakness.)
My overhead. (Just because I'm short? I resent that.)

Ashe's mistake was to underestimate my groundstrokes, just as
he had in Boston, and I blew him away in three straight sets for my
17th tournament win. With so many weaknesses, I sure won a lot.

That South African trip was important to me for another reason.
There was no better place in the world to buy a diamond engagement ring. Of course, back then we didn't know anything about
blood diamonds.

I'd been thinking about proposing to Chrissie for a few weeks.
Yeah, I know, with both of us finding it hard to be in the same place
for more than five minutes, and with our extracurricular activities, it
hardly sounds like a good way to start a life together. But I honestly
felt that once we were engaged, things would be different. I was so
naïve.

There were obvious problems. As a married couple, we couldn't
keep doing what we had been doing, letting tennis dominate our
lives. And what if we started a family? Would Chrissie keep playing?
How would I feel about that? Something or someone had to give. I
am old-school now and I was old-school then, and in my eyes, I had
to be the principal breadwinner in our household. But was that fair
to Chrissie? I'm not quitting, I told myself, so why should she? I was
trying to look out for both of our interests. One of us had to. But
in South Africa, I managed to forget about all those issues. After all,
despite everything, she was "The One." We would spend the rest of
our lives together, and somehow we would work it out.

We kept our engagement a secret because I still had to ask Chrissie's father for permission to marry his daughter. I knew it was a
done deal, but I was still nervous as hell when I went down to see

him in Fort Lauderdale. Mr. Evert and I spoke for a few minutes behind the closed doors of the Holiday Park Tennis Center pro shop (I didn't want to wander too far from my comfort zone), and he was very cool about it. I don't know how happy he was, and I'm pretty sure he was thinking, "Well, this will never happen," but he gave us his blessing anyway. I was 21 and about to get married.

It's crazy when I think about it now. Why didn't we wait a while? Well, why would we? We were in love and we told ourselves that this was the right thing to do.

Throughout the fall of 1973, Pancho had been bombarded with requests—there was even talk of possible inducements such as first-class airline tickets—for me to enter the Australian Open, in December. Frank Sedgman, who played out of Melbourne and had been one of the world's greatest players in the late 1940s and early 1950s, even lobbied his old buddy Pancho to try to persuade me to go Down Under. With their crazy scheduling—a tournament on the other side of the world over Christmas and New Year's—the organizers struggled to attract top-class players and had identified me as a valuable draw.

Of course they had. I had 11 titles to my name for the year, I was one half of the most famous couple in tennis, and I was about to be named the number three player in the world, based on the new ATP computer-ranking system. When Pancho explained how much they wanted me there, I thought, why not? Especially since I knew Chrissie had already entered. Christmas in the sunshine with my new fiancée sounded like a good deal.

Australia in December is stupid hot and at times the weather matched my mood. The facilities were basic, to say the least—the Kooyong Stadium had a tiny locker room with a single shower and one toilet cubicle—but that didn't bother me. I'd been in worse places on the Riordan circuit. No, what pissed me off was the partisan crowd, screaming approval at every hometown player and abuse at every foreigner. Guess who was their main target?

I took the brunt of it; three of the five matches I played to reach my first Grand Slam final were against Aussies. Every time I beat a local hero, the fans roared their disapproval. Who was this upstart American brat hell-bent on ruining their party? Hearing the crowd booing was one thing, but what the hell was the deal with those flies? Where were they breeding those things anyway? They looked like B-52s coming down on me.

Spencer and Chrissie did their best to calm me down, and I know that without them I would have imploded and been on my way home long before I met another Australian, Phil Dent, in the finals. But even Chrissie was getting on my nerves. Nobody was safe. With the organizers usually scheduling me on the court after Chrissie, I would go along to support her, sometimes bringing a sandwich and Pepsi for my lunch. Chrissie didn't seem to like that one little bit. If she noticed me eating and not paying attention during her match, she would throw me a look, which wasn't hard for me to read: "If you're not going to watch me play, then get out of here." That pissed me off even more than the hostile Australian fans, because it was embarrassing; I thought everyone in the stadium could see what was going on. Run along, Jimmy, do what you're told.

We were not even married yet and the tension was already building. I was in Chrissie's corner, rooting for her, but I felt she was treating me like some sort of, well, househusband. You know how it is, guys: You can't do anything right. I needed to eat before my matches and I wanted to see her play. What was I supposed to do? Stay back at the hotel and miss her match altogether? I'm sure that would have gone down really well.

Chrissie's mood swings could drive anyone crazy, but that didn't change the fact that I loved her. No one is perfect, I told myself. I was no prize, either; she had to put up with a lot, too. Did I just say that? The question was, could my patience, which was thin at the best of times, cope with so much drama? I convinced myself it could.

Phil Dent took the full force of the frustration and aggression that had been building in me from the first day of the tournament. Fortunately, I managed to channel it into my game. The super-dry, well-worn grass of Kooyong reminded me of the armory floorboards, and I adopted the approach Mom had taught me back in St. Louis, moving forward, taking the ball early, blasting it down the lines and across the court. Even with the crowd cheering their countryman on, he didn't stand a chance. I took the first two sets, and although he managed to rally in the third set, taking it 6-4 and putting on a show for his fans, it was just a momentary setback. I regrouped, ignored the lynch mob in the stands, and won the fourth, 6-3, to capture my first Grand Slam title.

I was ecstatic, even if, to be brutally honest, the Australian Open in the 1970s didn't draw the number of top players that it should have. The long flight and the unfortunate timing of the tournament limited the field. But it was still a Grand Slam and an important win in anybody's book.

If the scheduling had been like it is today, I would have gone to Australia more often. But I played the Australian Open only twice in my career, winning it in 1974 and losing to John Newcombe in the finals the following year, and I thought that was good enough. I don't regret any of the decisions I made, but who knows; if I had played the Australian a few more times, would I have won more majors? Your guess is as good as mine.

Between 1974 and 1979, I also didn't play in the French Open— we'll come to that in a minute—so there was a long period of time when I was competing only in Wimbledon and the US Open. So get this—in my career I won eight Slams and was in the finals of seven others, basically playing only two majors a year. Take it for what it's worth.

Getting that first win in the Australian Open was huge. That victory did set me up perfectly for what was to become the most extraordinary single year of my career: I would win 15 tournaments and lose only four matches out of 103. I also saw it as a launchpad that would catapult me toward the French Open and Wimbledon.

I was partially correct.

8

TWIN PEAKS

Nothing could stop me in 1974. My body finally filled out, the last of my puppy fat disappeared, and I felt stronger than ever. I had the confidence of a first-time Grand Slam winner and I was ready to rip the heart out of anyone who stood in my way.

After a run of seven tournament wins through March—in Roanoke, Little Rock, Birmingham, Salisbury, Hampton (Virginia), Salt Lake City, and Tempe—I was steaming toward the remaining three Slams of the year. Throw in a couple of doubles victories (one with Frew McMillan, one with Vitas Gerulaitis) and it seemed like I couldn't lose.

As I made my way across the country, from big cities to small towns, I would walk into restaurants with Nasty and it was like a couple of movie stars had entered the room. Television had made us more recognizable, and the popularity of tennis was hitting new heights. One evening, people even started clapping as soon as we came through the doors. Thinking the applause was for Nasty, I waited for him to pass in front of me, but he held back.

"No, Connors boy," he said fondly, "this is for you."

Just as American tennis, and tennis in general, was on the rise, along came the French Tennis Federation and its president, Philippe Chatrier, to pull a power play.

But first another history lesson. World Team Tennis, created in

114 / JIMMY CONNORS

1973 by Jordan Kaiser, Dennis Murphy, Fred Barman, and Larry King (Billie Jean's husband at the time), took its cue from football, baseball, and basketball. They aligned a sports team with a major city and franchised it, just when tennis was becoming more and more accessible to regular sports fans. The WTT was innovative; it allowed on-court coaching, substitutions, and featured mixed male and female teams. There was crowd participation, guaranteed payments to players, and deep-rooted interstate rivalries. Matches were decided on the basis of total number of games won during one set each of men's singles, women's singles, men's doubles, women's doubles, and mixed doubles. Were these guys crazy? No way; it was a shot in tennis's arm. I was all for it and I signed with the Baltimore Banners for the 1974 season. This was going to be both fun and profitable.

The establishment (the ILTF, in essence) was spooked by the WTT organization, because they thought its version of the sport was too extreme. I've always suspected that the single element that riled the establishment the most was the salaries over and above prize money, because that was something really out of the ordinary. Why they couldn't work together, I'll never know. The ILTF feared the WTT would undermine the privileged position of their major tournaments. The U.S.-based Team Tennis was obviously a threat to the European tour, I guess because of the summer schedule and the French Open in particular—and the WTT had to be dealt a blow.

Chatrier decided that anyone who signed with WTT would be denied access to Roland Garros, the site of the French Open, and the ATP supported that decision. That left Evonne Goolagong and me, both winners of the Australian Open earlier in the year, dripping wet and hung out to dry. Paris at the very end of May is beautiful, and I should've been in a good mood despite my less-than-stunning results at Roland Garros over the past two years. The problem was I was in a court, not on one.

Bill Riordan had filed a claim to have my ban from the French Open overturned, and although this was the last place I wanted to be (you know how I feel about lawyers), I knew this was important. Fair enough, I thought. As Bill saw it, the establishment was unlawfully standing in the way of my opportunity to have a crack at the calendar Grand Slam. In doing so, it was depriving me of the chance to collect an incentive payment that I had been offered by a perfume company, if I managed to win all four majors in a single season—a sum equal to my Baltimore Banners salary. The judge wasn't impressed, and our action was dismissed.

Fuck it. Move on.

That was the end of the dispute, as far as I was concerned. I wasn't bitter. I was disappointed, especially since Chrissie had been allowed to play in Paris, beating Olga Morozova in the finals to win her first major. But would I make the long trip to Australia a second time to give myself another chance at a Slam? That's what I was thinking about as I made my way to London and on up to Manchester for a grass-court warm-up tournament—and another victory. Back to business.

So it came as a huge surprise, the night before Wimbledon began, to read in the newspapers that I had decided to raise the stakes. Apparently, I was taking out a lawsuit against Jack Kramer (the ATP CEO), Donald Dell (the ATP legal counsel), and Commercial Union Assurance (the sponsors of the ILTF's Grand Prix circuit) for restraint of trade. The lawsuit basically said that Kramer and Dell, supported by Commercial Union, had used their influence to have me banned from the French Open.

For good measure, Riordan also threw in claims that their actions amounted to an unfair monopoly over world tennis, and their insistence on controlling TV deals—plus the balls, towels, and programs used at tournaments—was anti-competitive. This all meant, basically, that I couldn't pursue my chosen career. The combined total of these claims? A mere $30 million.

The headlines said that Jimmy Connors was suing his fellow players—and Arthur Ashe in particular, in his role as president of the ATP—for the sum of $10 million, the amount allocated to the restraint-of-trade part of the lawsuit, and that was the first I heard of it. I had been completely in the dark. It was Bill Riordan, the ultimate shit-stirrer, up to his old tricks. To make matters worse, when Mom heard the news, she was as surprised as I was. It was one of the very few occasions in my career when she wasn't in control of what was going on.

Riordan didn't seem at all concerned or embarrassed when I demanded to know what the hell he'd done. I think it's fair to say that he had a score to settle with the people he felt were trying to squeeze him out of the game with their scheduling carve-up in 1972.

"Jimmy, leave it to me. Those guys, they're frauds. You stick to tennis, and I'll beat the rest. And don't forget, any publicity is good publicity."

Despite his assurances, I wasn't convinced that this was a good move or good publicity. Even though I was being used as a pawn, overnight I became the most hated player on the circuit. The ATP had to use its membership fees to defend the case, which brought a load of antagonism my way. Why weigh yourself down with needless baggage? Why provide your opponents with an added incentive to beat you? Why did I let Bill continue with the lawsuit? I honestly don't know, because all it was to me was a pain in the ass.

The atmosphere was tense, and it became very personal. During Wimbledon, and throughout the rest of the year, whenever I walked into a locker room, every player would turn his back on me. You can guess how well I reacted to that. They don't care about me, so I don't give a fuck about them. Just protecting myself. Even so, it wasn't exactly comfortable sitting there getting ready to play, knowing that out of the 40 guys in the room, 39 were against you. Arthur Ashe later wrote that whenever he walked past me during Wimbledon in 1974 he wanted to smack me in the mouth. Oh, Arthur, settle down.

In some ways those experiences helped mold my attitude over the rest of my career. I didn't start the fight, and I couldn't end the fight. I was simply in the middle of a nasty power struggle and being cast as the villain. Well, screw you. I'll use the aggravation to motivate myself.

Whenever I was in London, I liked to stay at a hotel called the Inn on the Park, right on Hyde Park Corner, near Downing Street, Buckingham Palace, and the Hard Rock Cafe. I didn't really care about being close to the All-England Club. After matches, I needed to escape the tennis scene and do my own thing. Plus, at the time, there was only one restaurant in Wimbledon Village, and central London had so much more to offer . . . the Playboy Club, for starters. In 1974, Chrissie was booked into the same hotel, too. (OK, so she was with her mother, but then when wasn't she?) Mrs. Evert seemed to go everywhere with Chrissie, all summer long, right across Europe, and I guess rightfully so—Chrissie was a teenager, after all. But whenever I turned around, Mrs. Evert was there, watching. It was almost like she didn't trust me.

Crazy, I know. America's Sweetheart and the most hated guy in tennis. What could possibly go wrong there?

My mom traveled with me, too, but she wasn't interested in my nighttime activities. I wasn't her daughter. She understood that boys would be boys. Provided nothing got in the way of my tennis, she didn't really mind.

"When you work, you work, Jimmy. When you play, you play. And you should put just as much effort into that as you do your tennis."

I didn't disappoint her on the court, so I couldn't disappoint her off of it.

The situation with Chrissie and her mom was different. I got that. It just meant we had to be a little smarter in order to spend some time alone together.

Some months earlier, I had played against a young South African guy named David Schneider. It was a tight match, and halfway through he started rolling his shoulders to help him relax.

"What's that you got there—chicken wings?!" I shouted over the net.

"Fuck you, Connors. At least I ain't some mommy's boy."

I knew right then he was my kind of guy. I liked the way he played and I liked his attitude. I thought he was an asshole and he thought I was a prick. We were perfect for each other. As we were walking to the locker room after the match, I asked David if he would practice with me the next day.

"Yeah, sure. Give me a call."

"Bring your chicken wings. We'll give it a go."

At five o'clock the next morning I called him.

"Connors, what the hell are you doing? It's the middle of the night, man."

"Come on, get up. You said you'd practice with me. I've got a court booked at 6 a.m. Let's go."

We've been best friends ever since.

David was sharing his room with a bunch of other South African players. They went everywhere together like a unit, which was something that just didn't happen in US tennis (or maybe it did, just not with me). They had grown up together, traveling across South Africa to tournaments in the backs of trucks and camping out overnight to save money. They watched each other's backs, supported each other whenever necessary. I liked that. Even though I would have hated living in those conditions, there was something about their loyalty that appealed to me.

Schneider didn't need me as a friend—he had enough of those already—and he wasn't looking for anything in return, so I knew he would be someone I could trust. And it's true; he's never once let me down. Two-Mom told me when I was growing up that if you could count your good friends on one hand, then you'd be lucky. David Schneider is one of those guys. He was then and he is now.

David was playing at Wimbledon, and was in London with his girlfriend, Laurie, who happened to be friendly with Chrissie. That gave us the perfect cover. Chrissie would tell her mom that she was meeting up with Laurie, who would pick Chrissie up from the hotel. I would be nowhere in sight, usually already sitting with David two blocks away at the bar of the Playboy Club.

As I think I've made clear, I loved the Playboy Club, and it was always my first stop the day I arrived in London. You could never tell who would be there, but usually some combination of Nasty, Spencer, John Lloyd, or Gerulaitis would show up. No fun gambling alone.

The club had a carving buffet, where you lined up for thick slices of roast pork, beef, or turkey. That could take you an hour on a busy night, but you didn't care because the scenery was never boring. After dinner you could either hit the craps or blackjack tables upstairs or the disco in the basement. I didn't spend every night at the club when I was in town, just most of them, with or without Chrissie. And I would always have a good time in one way or another.

Chrissie and I spent a lot of time together with Schneider and his girlfriend over those two weeks at Wimbledon in 1974, but we also enjoyed the occasional night out on our own. Mrs. Evert was OK with that, as long as Chrissie didn't have a match the next day. When we were out together, the British tabloid newspapers went into a full-out frenzy, way beyond what had ever happened to us before.

That year's Wimbledon had been dubbed the Love Double by the press, because Chrissie and I were both strong contenders for the championships, and the media craze about our relationship had long since gone over the top. On our first night out as a couple, we emerged from the Playboy Club to find 40 photographers waiting for us. We felt like the Beatles, having to run through the streets of London to escape the paparazzi. It was nuts, especially when Chrissie outran me! But we didn't mind; it was all one big adventure.

Even when we didn't stay out late, neither of us managed to get much rest, particularly during the nights after Chrissie had been playing her singles matches. What can I say? Sometimes passion won out over tennis. We were young and we could cope, although Pancho, seeing me sluggish in the morning, wasn't very happy. Pancho used to wait for me in the lobby after Laurie had dropped Chrissie off. He would then accompany me to my room to make sure that Chrissie wasn't waiting for me there. He would even look in on me from time to time during the night just to make sure I was alone and sleeping. I guess Chrissie's mom probably did the same thing, so there was a lot of hallway sneaking required, and I can tell you we got pretty good at it.

No matter how much sleep I got, if I had a match the next day, I liked to be up at nine in the morning, grab breakfast, and be out of the hotel by 11 for some practice. There were courts available at Wimbledon, but I liked to keep my distance as much as possible. The fact that no one was talking to me didn't make any difference. Some guys loved being part of that scene, hanging around all day. Not me. If I was supposed to be on court at 2 p.m., I would roll through the gates of the grounds at 1:40. Why be any earlier?

Since I wasn't using the courts at the All-England Club, I had to find somewhere else to practice in London, and that wasn't easy. During the two weeks of Wimbledon it seemed as though every single weekend warrior came out to play. The courts were there—London is a big city, after all—but you just had to be Sherlock Holmes to find them.

The year before, I'd discovered a sports club, by the River Thames near Chiswick Bridge, a few miles from Wimbledon. Spencer and I drove up to the clubhouse; we could see about 20 courts in pretty good shape, and they were all empty. It looked perfect. We asked the guy in charge if it would be OK if we used a court to practice.

"Well, I don't know about that," he said. "I'll have to check if we have any free."

OK, I thought, I'm willing to play that game.

After five minutes of looking through pieces of paper in his tiny office, he came back and pointed to a court way out in the back, with ruts and bare patches in the grass. After checking it out, we considered ourselves lucky to have lines and a net.

"What are you charging?" I asked.

"Twelve pounds an hour."

I paid, we played, and I told the guy that we'd be back around the same time tomorrow.

"I'll see what I can sort out for you, sir," he said.

By the next day, I think he had realized who we were and directed us toward a better court—one that I knew wasn't going to cost us just 12 pounds.

"Thank you. How much?" I asked.

"This one is premium rate. One hundred pounds an hour, sir."

What a surprise. Did he think he could take advantage of me

because I only had an eighth-grade education? I wasn't that stupid. But we didn't have much choice. We shook hands on the deal, and after our practice, we talked to him again.

"OK, buddy, let's get one thing straight here. I plan on being around for a while, but I'm not coming back if it's going to cost a hundred pounds an hour. Can we figure out a price for the rest of my stay?"

"The problem is, sir, with the way you two play, you're tearing up the grass, and it's very expensive to repair."

"Fair enough. How about this: We agree on a daily rate right now that covers everything. That way, if we do screw up the surface a little, you won't be bitching at us."

We settled on 75 pounds. How generous . . . of both of us.

On our third visit it was raining, but not enough to stop us. We went out to practice and after an hour the court had turned to mud. We knew the guy was going to go nuts when he saw the state of the grass, so we made a quick exit, poking our heads into his office on our way out to the car: "Thank you, see you next year."

He must have known something was up, because by the time we were driving out of the parking lot, he was chasing after us, cursing at us in a Cockney accent the likes of which we'd never heard.

"If I catch you out 'ere again, you short-assed Yankee twat, I'll shove that girlie racquet of yours so far up that little poof's arse of yours, you won't know whether you're shitting or playing mixed fucking doubles."

Needless to say, we didn't return to that club in 1974. We came across some courts by accident in the nice residential area of Holland Park. Schneider and I had been given directions at our hotel desk to a place that could string my racquets, but we got lost. All the streets seemed to look identical and have the same name, but as we drove around we spotted a small club hidden away behind some trees. It had four private courts, for local residents only. We pleaded our case, and from then on, Holland Park became the perfect place for me to practice during Wimbledon.

Wimbledon and Jimmy Connors wasn't exactly a match made in tennis heaven. Over the years we clashed more than once over what I saw as their stiff, old-fashioned rules. The crowds at Wimbledon took a long time to warm to me. To them I was an arrogant, crude American kid who had no respect for the traditions of their tournament, and they were right. But we eventually came to an understanding and even grew to appreciate each other.

Although Wimbledon wasn't my "cup of tea," there were a lot of elements of the tournament that I enjoyed. Centre Court was a wonderful theater for tennis, despite the unpredictable bounce of the grass, and I loved walking around the outside courts and mingling with the fans, who took so much pride in feeling a part of the championships.

But it came at a price. As well as all that grass, there were more than two miles of hedges at the All-England Club, acres of flowerbeds and trees, and for me that added up to one thing during an English summer: pollen.

Ivan Lendl once said he couldn't play Wimbledon because he was allergic to grass. Maybe he was, and maybe that's why he never won the tournament, but it's strange how it didn't seem to affect him on a golf course. I get serious hay fever, but I never used it as an excuse. I wasn't looking for an alibi and I didn't need one.

When I was young and training with Pop, he taught me how to breathe through my nose. As an ex-boxer, he knew that opening your mouth to take a breath was not only dangerous (because your jaw is a lot more vulnerable if it isn't closed); it was also an indication of fatigue, and you don't want to give your opponent any sort of boost by thinking that you're tired. Breathing through your nose increases your mobility, because once you've mastered it, you can take constant breaths, drawing oxygen at a steady level. If you breathe through your mouth, you tend to hold your breath when you're tense, which slows you down.

Pop worked hard with me on this part of my training. It's common practice today, but back then it was almost unheard of. During long rallies I breathed in and out through my nose to maintain my energy levels. When I needed to explode into a shot, I exhaled sharply through my mouth. This produced a well-known side effect: the grunt. It's been said that I was the first tennis player to grunt—I don't know if that's true or not—but I sure was the highest-profile player at the time to do it. I wasn't consciously trying to put anyone off; it was just a byproduct of how I had been taught to breathe.

The trouble with breathing through my nose was that it caused my allergy symptoms to increase tenfold. It was brutal. I eventually found a steroid shot which worked for me, but for a long time I had to use spray to clear my sinuses. It's crazy how an innocent thing like that can be turned into something really outrageous. One guy wrote a book on tennis in which he insinuated that I was doing cocaine at Wimbledon in 1980; he said that my nose spray, which I used at the changeovers, contained more than a decongestant.

Total bullshit. I have never taken cocaine in my life. That guy is a prick and he knows who he is.

That summer at Wimbledon I had a far-from-easy ride through to the finals. The truth is that the surface didn't really suit my game, and I was still learning how different playing on grass could be. I knew I had to change my game, at least a little, if I was going to win Wimbledon. Many of my opponents were more experienced on grass. I was still predominantly a baseliner; I was more aggressive than I had been as a teenager but still happy to rely on my ground-strokes.

To counteract Wimbledon's uneven bounces, I adopted the high-risk tactic of volleying three quarters of the way back from the net, in an area tennis coaches call "no man's land." Playing in "no man's land" on grass means putting yourself in a tough spot—you're more vulnerable to passing shots—but by taking the ball out of the air, I was being more assertive. I also mixed up my game in a way that surprised many people, coming to the net more often, just as Pancho had taught me.

"Go for their ankles with your returns, Jimbo, and when you see them out of position, move in for the kill."

It paid off in 1974, but sometimes only barely. My second-round opponent, Phil Dent, was out for revenge after Melbourne, and at Wimbledon we went the distance over two days before I eventually won 10-8 in the fifth. In the quarters I faced the defending champion, Jan Kodes, who also pushed me to five sets; and in the semis, Dick Stockton won the first set 6-4 before I pulled my game together to win in four.

The day before my final against Ken Rosewall, the first half of the Love Double was completed when Chrissie again beat Olga Morozova, 6-0, 6-4 this time. She was thrilled—we both were—and she wanted to celebrate, but Pancho put his foot down. The weather forecast for the finals was for temperatures in the nineties, and Pancho was determined that nothing was going to sap my stamina. He was no fool, and that night he slept on a chair in my hotel room, keeping a watchful eye on me, so I would be ready for my final.

Pancho later told me that Chrissie had come to my room that night.

"Darling Chrissie," he explained, "you have just won the tournament, but Jimmy, he still has to play. He needs his rest. After he beats Rosewall, you can have him on toast."

Pancho has such a way with words.

I didn't think for a moment that I could lose that final, even though it seemed as though almost the entire tennis world was against me. I was a spoiler and no one likes a spoiler, especially one who causes a lot of trouble.

Ken Rosewall was the epitome of the gentleman player, and he was a great one at that. He was very popular, and he was in his fourth and probably his last Wimbledon final, the only Slam that he hadn't won. All the fans on Centre Court were rooting for Rosewall; except maybe for Pancho, Bill, Mom, and Chrissie, who I was pretty sure were on my side. I understood Rosewall's emotional relationship with the crowd, but I had to take my chance. What if I never got another opportunity to win Wimbledon?

The match itself is a blur. Everything fell into place. I got on top early and never felt under threat, and it seemed like I had all the time in the world. In fact, I reached a state close to tennis nirvana that day. That's how I felt about the match then, and it's how I feel now. Incredibly, the same thing occurred a couple of months later, when I played Rosewall again, in New York, in the finals of the US Open.

Being able to play almost perfect tennis for an entire match is incredible, make no mistake about it. I've also been on the receiving end, when an opponent attained the same level. Take a look at the list of the shortest Wimbledon finals ever: I think I'm on top in the Open Era. It only took McEnroe 80 minutes to beat me in 1984: 6-1, 6-1, 6-2.

On the championship point against Rosewall at Wimbledon, I served deep, and he couldn't handle the return. It was over, I had done it, although I had no understanding of what that really meant at the time. When I jumped over the net to shake hands with Ken, I was in an ecstatic fog. Even with that famous trophy in my hands, I didn't really grasp what I had done. I was crazy happy, but the fact that my life had just changed forever did not register with me at the time. Winning Wimbledon and the US Open were the reasons why I became a tennis professional.

Try to imagine what it was like in those moments directly after my first Wimbledon victory. I was in a daze, and I was told what to do, where to go, and whom to speak to. It was Wimbledon and they had their protocols and commitments.

"Walk over there, Mr. Connors, to the photographers."

"Now walk around the court, present the cup to the crowd."

"Over here, Mr. Connors. The BBC has to interview you."

"When that's over, you'll speak to these newspaper reporters here."

During the chaos, my dad called to congratulate me. I didn't know about it until afterward, and a lot has been made about that phone call over the years by my critics in the press, about how I couldn't be bothered to talk to my dad after winning Wimbledon. It didn't happen like that at all.

I loved my dad, even though we weren't as close as we might have been under different circumstances. Tennis wasn't one of his interests, and although he approved of my dedication, he had nothing to contribute to my training in the way Mom, Two-Mom, and Pop did. What my dad did give me was the freedom to follow my dream, and he worked his whole life to help support that. No matter what, he was always proud of me.

We spoke later, and he told me that he'd watched the finals and was happy about how all my hard work had paid off. I was glad he called, and those people who read more into it should mind their own business and fuck off.

In the car on the way back to the Inn on the Park to change for the Champions Ball, at the Grosvenor House hotel, it finally hit me. I had just won Wimbledon. This was different from any other tournament. This was life-changing. All those questions that had been asked, that I had asked myself—*Could Connors do it on the biggest stage? Was he good enough?*—had been answered. At the same time, it felt like the show was suddenly over. It was a strange sensation, the letdown. I had the Wimbledon trophy in my hands, but within a day or two I would have to start to work on getting the only other one that really mattered to me, the US Open.

The Champions Ball was nice, if a little stuffy. Chrissie and I danced some, but where we really wanted to be was out on the town. After the Playboy Club, we moved on to Annabel's nightclub, and Chrissie called it a night long before I did. I knew a lot of people in London after hanging around town over the past two years with Pancho, Spencer, and Nasty. It was time to catch up with my friends and have some fun.

My plan was to go straight home after London and catch up on some sleep in order to be fully rested and prepared for Team Tennis. A lot of the top guys were playing in it, and I saw it as a good way to practice before the US Open.

Riordan had other plans: "You have an appointment in New York, Jimmy."

At JFK, Bill had a car waiting. It dropped us outside of a Midtown hospital, at the children's cancer ward. I went from thinking I was on a pedestal, after winning Wimbledon, back down to earth in less than a second. This was going to be a reality check, and if I'm being honest, at first I was annoyed.

"Come on, Bill, could we have waited a day or so to do this?"

Then I walked through those doors and I understood. Right in front of me, in row upon row of beds, was the fragility of life and a real demonstration of how lucky I was. This was a stark reminder to me to be grateful for what I had.

"Enjoy your success, Jimmy," Bill said to me. "Enjoy the rewards, work hard, but remember what else is happening in the world."

Walking out of the hospital that day changed my perspective on what was really important, and it was an experience I'll never forget.

It's July in Philadelphia and Team Tennis has been living up to its billing. The place is wild, with fans screaming and cheering, throwing plastic beer cups, rooting for the home team, and I'm loving it. Then, just as I am about to serve in a close match with a lot riding on the outcome, the noise level suddenly drops long enough for me to clearly hear a guy shout,

"Hey, Connors! Why don't you just give it up and go back home to Chrissie?"

I let the ball drop and turn around.

"Who said that?"

There's a commotion in the third row, and people are pointing at a guy sitting there with a smug look on his face. I walk over and put my foot up on the advertising board. I know I can't reach the guy with my fist, but I can take a swipe at him with my racquet. I lean forward.

"Stand up, you motherfucker."

The security guards rush over and grab my arm as the guy starts to get to his feet. When he does, he just keeps going and going and going, getting bigger and bigger and bigger.

Shit.

The security guards are forcibly pulling me away and I'm not resisting, happy to go. "Fuck you. Fuck you," I shout at the guy as we're backing up. I'm so brave. But I'm no hero, and I didn't want to have to ruin my T2000.

Fast-forward to January 1975 and I'm back in Philly at the US Pro Indoors. After my match, there's a knock on the locker-room door. Bill Norris, the trainer and a good friend, answers the door.

"Jimmy, there's a guy here who wants to see you."

Probably looking for an autograph, I think. I go to the door. Shit. I know him right away. It's not easy to forget someone that size.

"You remember me?" the guy asks.

"Hey, sure. How's it going?" I say sheepishly, my voice rising two octaves.

"I'm in the bar with my girlfriend. I enjoyed the match tonight. Come and have a drink with us," the guy tells me.

Like I'm going to say no?

"Yeah, love to. I'll be there in two minutes."

In the bar he has a question: "Last year, were you really going to hit me with your racquet?"

"Well, I was certainly thinking about it, but it wouldn't have hurt you anyway."

I'm nothing if not sensible.

In August, I beat Björn Borg on clay in the Indianapolis finals, and I'm often asked whether I see that match as being the equivalent of the French Open earlier in the year, which Borg had won and I was barred from.

"You beat Borg on clay in 1974, Jimmy. His surface. Doesn't that basically give you a calendar Grand Slam?"

I don't think so, not at all. I only claim what I actually achieved. Although in the US the Indianapolis clay probably came closest to resembling Roland Garros, it wasn't the same: It was faster, and the balls were also different, lighter. The French Open in the 1970s was like playing in mud, and they used Tretorn balls, which slowed the game down even more.

Would I have liked to have that shot at beating Borg in the French Open? Hell, yeah. But would I then have gone on to win Wimbledon? Who knows? It was the politics of the different associations and the ignorance of the people involved that pissed me off the most, nothing more. They were trying to stop me from making a living just so they could vie for power and stake their claims to the money machine that guys like me were creating for them.

No wonder I had a bad attitude.

Honestly, in some ways I actually liked the fact that 1974 ended up like it did, with an asterisk by my name in the record books. After 40 years, people are still wondering if I would have won the Grand Slam. I was always told to keep a little mystery about myself, but that's the kind of mystery I could have done without.

"Hey, Connors, get us in. Come on, man, we want to see the tennis."

I'm walking through the doors of the West Side Tennis Club, in Forest Hills, to begin my quest to capture my third Slam of the year when I hear the shouts. I look over my shoulder to see two big guys waving at me from the sidewalk. I've never seen either of them before, but I like their nerve. And what was I going to say, anyway: "Gee, no, I can't. They have rules"?

What did I care about the rules?

"Yeah, OK. Let's go."

My two new friends waited for me while I got changed, then walked with me to my match. It quickly got around that these two guys were my bodyguards. Why argue with the myth?

For the next 18 years, whenever I was in New York, Doug Henderson, who became my friend, followed me wherever I went. Doug even had T-shirts made up with THE JAMES GANG printed on them. And that's what it was all about, as far as I was concerned: entertaining people and being a little bit different.

At the US Open, just like at Wimbledon, the crowds were against me, but at least they were there. I had tricky matches all through the tournament—Jeff Borowiak in the first round, four sets; John Alexander in the third round, four sets; Kodes in the fourth round, four sets; and Alex Metreveli in the quarters, four sets—but I never felt threatened. In the final, for the second time, I was going up against the people's favorite, Ken Rosewall, and once again, I reached perfection, only quicker. To reach such a peak once in your life is lucky, but to experience the sensation twice within two months is truly amazing, and it never happened again in the rest of my career. It took me just under 70 minutes to win, 6-1, 6-0, 6-1, and complete the Connors Slam.

And, boy, did that piss everybody off.

Unfortunately, Chrissie lost in the semis in Forest Hills to Evonne Goolagong. Instead of celebrating and having her knocking on my bedroom door the night before my final, like at Wimbledon, I was put in the position of trying to console her. Her reaction was totally understandable, but it made partying pretty hard work. There it was again. You can't have two number ones in a relationship. It's just not going to work.

Because of our schedules, Chrissie and I had been away from each other for long stretches over that summer. Neither of us liked it, but we had jobs to do. I spent more time with Nasty than I did with Chrissie, and even if we talked on the phone a lot, it was clear to me that things weren't all that good between us. Or at least things weren't all that I wanted them to be.

Our wedding date was November 8, just a few weeks away, but I felt left out of the big life-changing decisions that were being made by Chrissie. Our telephone conversations now seemed one-sided. This is what's happening. This is the way it's going to be. I started to wonder: If things were like this now, what was life going to be like when we were married?

Listen, an issue had arisen as a result of youthful passion and a decision had to be made as a couple.

I was staying in an apartment and Nasty was there when Chrissie called to say she was coming out to LA to take care of that "issue." I was perfectly happy to let nature take its course and accept responsibility for what was to come. Chrissie, however, had already made up her mind that the timing was bad and too much was riding on her future. She asked me to handle the details.

I said something like: "Well, thanks for letting me know. Since I don't have any say in the matter, then I guess I'm just here to help."

I put the phone down and Nasty looked at me.

"Jimbo, you're not staying in tonight, are you?"

"Well, I guess not."

That all happened during one of only two pro tournaments I didn't win in 1974. After my conversation with Chrissie, and a night out with Nasty, I was tired.

In mid-September, I won my second Pacific Southwest tournament, beating Harold Solomon in the finals, and then went to my next event in San Francisco, where my buddy Bobby Kreiss was also playing, so I knew there was some fun in store. After I lost my quarterfinal, Bob and I had dinner and ended up in the sky-lounge bar, in the Mark Hopkins Hotel.

Looking out over the city, the question I didn't want to ask and didn't want to answer once again bubbled to the surface. Why was I getting married now? My true feelings on the subject had been building for a while, and I knew what I had to do.

I went back to my room and called Chrissie. It was a horrible feeling, but I knew it was over. Getting married wasn't going to be good for either of us.

"I've been thinking. We're pretty young; maybe we should take a step back and think about giving this a little more time," I said.

She was on the East Coast and it was late, but she did not hesitate.

"OK, if that's what you think. I've got a match tomorrow. Not a problem."

"Right. Bye."

That was it.

Chrissie remembers it as a six-hour discussion, but I can only assume she's thinking about all the other conversations that led up to it. As I remember it, we had reached a major decision in a matter of seconds, with the understanding that it was probably better for the both of us.

I was sad. I loved her and we had both put a lot of effort into our relationship, but it kept going back to the same old question: Can two number ones exist in the same family? It wouldn't have worked for us and it was better that we figured it out early on.

In public, we announced that we had just postponed our wedding, but I knew that it was over. Going backward was not for me. It's easy to see now that our relationship was never going to work out. One of us was going to have to give in; I knew it wouldn't be me, and I doubt it would have been her.

9

BATTLE OF THE BALLS

t's mid–December 1974 and I've just moved into my new house up in the Hollywood Hills, above Sunset Boulevard. My buddies Dino Martin and Desi Arnaz Jr. have their own places right next door, and they're coming around for a drink before I pack my bags and head to the airport to catch a plane to Australia to defend my Open title.

I go out onto my balcony and look at the view across to the mountains. To my right, the sun reflects off the water of my swimming pool. How good can it get? I have space to grow here, to put down some roots. It's the kind of place that suits me. My new pad is what the greatest year of my life has bought for me. This house is everything I've ever wanted . . . isn't it?

I've even got a new girlfriend. Well, kind of. We met at a party on Thanksgiving, a few weeks after Chrissie and I called off our engagement. We've had some fun times but I'm not looking for anything serious, and neither is she. That's what makes it so nice. No pressure.

I'll be spending Christmas at the Australian Open again, in order to defend my title, hopefully ringing in the New Year in the finals. Yeah, I'm looking forward to it.

New Year's Day 1975 and I'm back in the finals at the Kooyong Stadium. It's me, the number one seed, versus the local hero, former world number one, Wimbledon and US Open champion John Newcombe, and we're set to fight it out in the Melbourne heat. The tournament has been pretty straightforward so far—I've dropped just one set—but none of that matters now. Here we are with 16,000 Newcombe fans and about a million goddamn flies buzzing around my head and crawling all over my back. I swear, when one of those suckers lands on me it leaves a bruise. They even give us fly repellant, which seems to attract even more of them. As if worrying about Newcombe isn't enough.

It's a set apiece and I'm down 2-3 on serve. Newcombe hits a crosscourt forehand return, just inside the line. Love-15. I have to get my next first serve in, wide to his backhand . . . Shit, it's out— but wait, it's called good. I'll take it, thank you very much. The crowd doesn't like it, but then again, he's their guy.

OK, a solid serve, a short return, get down low like Pancho says, half volley deep, and Newcombe hits it long. He gives me a shocked look. That was out by a mile, matey. 30-15. Now I have to mix it up, serve down the line this time, straight and strong, and here we go, Newk's not happy again and his fans are screaming, "Fault! Fault!"

It's getting pretty hot out here and it's not just the sun.

Screw it. You can have it, Newk, I don't need it. I'm going to serve a double fault to even things up. There, back to 40-30.

Now let's play tennis.

I've been asked over the years whether I dumped that final, whether, when I gave Newcombe that point by deliberately double-faulting, it was so I could line up a big-money revenge Challenge Match in Vegas.

Are you kidding? I have never tanked a match in my life. Take a look at the fourth set in Melbourne, for Christ's sake. I fought like crazy to save match point at 3-5, and in the tiebreaker I came back from being down to earn set points of my own. I was unable to convert them and Newcombe took it in four sets. Well, that's what they put the net up for, to go out and play and see who wins. He was better than I was that day and it's as simple as that. No worries, as they say Down Under, but it certainly made me think twice about ever giving a point away again.

"Jimmy Connors probably thinks he's the next-best thing to 7 Up."

I got really annoyed at those words from the great Australian tennis player Rod Laver, who won two Grand Slams and owns the record for the most singles titles (200) in the history of tennis. He was ranked number one in the world for seven consecutive years. And here he's slagging me off. Normally I'd just shrug and move on, but coming from Laver—not only an exceptional player but one of the true gentlemen in the game—I've got to be honest: It got under my skin.

Hell, I'm thinking, maybe I am the next-best thing to 7 Up. I mean, I just demolished Ken Rosewall in the US Open and have beaten virtually everyone I've met this year. What's left?

Bill Riordan is waiting for me in the locker room at Forest Hills. I'm not even tired; I've barely broken a sweat out there against Rosewall, and my mind is racing. I hand Bill my racquet and he shakes my hand.

"Hey, champ, you did good today. What are you doing tomorrow?"

"Get me Laver," I say.

That's how it happened. It wasn't rehearsed. I wasn't told to say it by Bill. It was a throwaway line, but, boy, did it start a firestorm.

Bill's promotional blood started pumping, and he contacted Laver's people. They talked about how long Laver would need to get into shape—six months, Rod said. Bill then spoke to the guys he knew in Vegas—he wasn't exactly a stranger there—and told them,

"I'll get the money, I'll bring the talent, you build the court," and they went for it.

Winner takes all. $100,000. In the desert.

I returned from Australia in January 1975 via the Bahamas, where I won on the outdoor courts, then through Birmingham, Alabama, to pick up my 34th career tournament victory, and headed to La Costa and Pancho. He knew Laver's game inside-out, and together we devised our strategy.

"Play to his forehand, deep," Pancho said, "because the return will be short. And move forward every chance you get. He hits with so much topspin that you have to jump all over it."

What he was telling me was to hit hard and deep to the middle and cut off his angles. Got it.

My next stop was Vegas, where Riordan had engineered the first of his fake controversies to crank up the hype for the Challenge Match. Instead of checking in at Caesars Palace, Mom, Pancho, Bill, and I went to the nearby Tropicana Hotel, where Ash Resnick welcomed us with open arms. (You know Ash, right? He was the guy credited with bringing all the high rollers to Vegas by organizing the first big-money junkets. Rumor had it that he also knew people in organized crime. Allegedly. We were good friends, but I had to be careful, because I heard that the worst job in town was starting his car . . .) Bill told the press that our preparations had been compromised by the "unacceptable" rooms that we'd been offered at Caesars Palace. Nonsense. We had been given more than enough space by Caesars; Bill just wanted to give the papers something to write about.

He then hit the Laver camp with another broadside, turning the heat up even more. Laver had been practicing with the heavier Wilson balls, so Bill made another commotion and said we wanted Dunlop balls for the match. We lost that battle. Laver's people then said they wanted the cans of balls opened two days before the match "to let them breathe," which was code for "to slow them down." That's bullshit, we responded; no one in the history of the game has ever done that. We flipped a coin and the cans were opened. Lost another one. I told you I was a crap gambler, even if it is in my blood.

When the details of the match had been finalized, in November, both camps had settled on Bob Howe as the referee and Gus Lanna as the umpire. Bob, an Australian, had won four mixed-doubles Grand Slam titles, including Wimbledon in 1958, and Gus was a highly experienced umpire and an old friend of mine. Then Caesars Palace officials decided to appoint their tennis director, none other than Pancho Gonzales, as referee. Riordan jumped on it and threatened to call the whole thing off unless Gonzales stepped down.

I couldn't give a damn about any of that, but Bill loved to stir the pot, and so I let him do it while I concentrated on my tennis. That's what I was good at. It was all resolved, of course, with Pancho as referee and Bob as assistant referee.

Not that I was beyond a little fire stoking myself when the opportunity presented itself. The day before the first practice session, which was open to the public as well as the press, I handed Bill a slip of paper.

He smiled when he read it.

"Sure, Jimmy. Consider it done."

When I walked on court the next day, the fans who had gathered early, including a pack of workmen desperately trying to finish building the seats in time, did a double take. There across the back of my warm-up jacket, printed in giant letters, were the words for all the world to see: BETTER THAN 7 UP.

Winner-takes-all was Bill's genius marketing spin. All you have to do is look at the viewing figures. CBS broadcast the Laver Challenge Match, putting up $60,000 for the privilege, pitching it directly against ABC's well-established *Wide World of Sports* in the schedule. They spanked them in the ratings, with more than a 33 share to *Wide World*'s 28.

Those are football or baseball numbers. But tennis? Unheard of. Bobby Riggs and Billie Jean King had laid the groundwork in September 1973, with their Battle of the Sexes, but Riordan raised the bar. It was the money, of course, that drew the big ratings; people who didn't know a drop shot from a tee shot were tuning in because they were curious to watch two champions from different eras slug it out for a gigantic pot of cash. The winner's prize money, $100,000, was beyond anything that tennis had seen, more than what I walked away with by winning the 1974 US Open.

We were setting a new standard, making the sports world sit up and take notice. Suddenly tennis was big business, and Bill was in the catbird seat, pulling in TV money, sponsor fees, and a bundle from Caesars Palace to make up the purse. I say "purse" because that's what prizefighters called it. Bill had created the World Heavyweight Championship of Tennis, and Caesars was only too happy to construct a 4,000-seat stadium that resembled a tennis court disguised as a boxing ring. I'd never seen anything like it before. The fans were right up against the court, close enough for us to sweat on them. It was an intense, combative atmosphere. And the noise! Man, it made the air thick. Bill even introduced our courtside cornermen: Roy Emerson for Laver and Pancho Segura for me.

Laver delays his entrance, a touch of showmanship on his part, which gives me a few minutes to take in the scene. What the hell? The fans are booing me. Really? I'm in Las Vegas. I'm from the USA! Rod's Australian, and I know he has a lot of fans, but come on! All it does is get me more pumped up.

The place is in an uproar for Laver. It's Christians-and-lions time. OK, so he's a tennis legend, and, yeah, he's come out of retirement to play, but even so, this is just bizarre. I'm sensitive. Don't you know that by now? You back me into a corner and I'm going to come out swinging . . .

I'm jumping up and down trying to get my Tiger Juices flowing. Let's get it on. Where is Laver? I scan the ringside seats and see Clint Eastwood, Charlton Heston, Johnny Carson—all American icons, and it looks like they're cheering for Laver. It's too much.

"Fuck you! Fuck you! Fuck you!" I yell.

Now I'm dancing around the court and flipping the bird at everyone. They're all just faces in a hostile crowd, even the stars of stage and screen at courtside.

Afterward I heard that Carson took my antics personally. Years later, I went on his *Tonight Show*, and he was still nervous, tiptoeing around anything remotely controversial. Johnny, wherever you are, my friend, I wasn't offended by your support for Laver. I know you loved tennis, and your presence at the match just gave it more credibility. You know my motto: You can be for me or against me, I don't care, just as long as you are there.

It's the sounds of the match that have stayed with me over the years. Every shot echoed around that tight stadium like a bullet ricocheting off the walls. The crowd quickly got sucked into the action, and we fed off their energy and emotion.

It was an historic occasion. People were witnessing the changing of the guard in tennis. Laver: the elder statesman, low-key, experienced, a finesse player able to fight off the onslaught of groundstrokes that this young, cocky kid threw at him. I raised my game; he matched me. He raised his, and I shut him down. We played some sick tennis out there. The first two sets went my way, but in the third, when Rod should have been tiring, he began to punch killer volley after killer volley into the corners and drilled passing shots down the line, leaving me to shake my head in awe.

We're in the fourth set and Rod has somehow managed to save five match points. The great old comedienne Totie Fields is in the front row, where she's been heckling me throughout the match. Now she's leaping out of her seat and yelling for Laver every time he staves off defeat. As I waste another opportunity to put him away, Totie lets out an ear-piercing shriek of delight. I whirl around and give her the finger.

"Shut. Up."

Yeah, I know, not very classy, but Totie was a tough cookie, and she could take it as well as she could dish it out.

Holding serve drained Rod. He had battled hard to stay in the match, but the heat and the intensity finally got to him, and I took the final two games easily to win the set 7-5. It was a victory that not only served to confirm my top-dog status in the sport but also put a whopping 100 grand in my pocket. I don't think Rod was complaining, either; he walked away with a check for $60,000. Not bad for the loser of a winner-takes-all match.

The problem with a misspent youth is that you misspend it. In Beverly Hills, I find I have a taste for the good life, but I keep it under control, refusing to let it interfere with my tennis. I stick by that into my early twenties, rigidly disciplined when I have to be, but now I feel invincible. OK, Newcombe has proved that isn't strictly true, but that was on the other side of the world. Here in my backyard, I rule, and nothing and no one can touch me. Now, if you'll excuse me, I've got some partying to catch up on.

That's how I felt through most of 1975. After all the success of the previous year, people warned me to be careful of the slump that would follow, but I ignored them. What slump? That isn't going to happen to me. I'm too smart and too damn good.

At the start of the year, I won in Salisbury and Boca Raton, to increase my total wins to four by mid-February, not including the Laver match. I had nothing to worry about and I deserved to have a good time. I had earned it. My tennis wasn't suffering, so I thought it could go on forever. The thing is, when you're number one, the heavyweight tennis champion of the world, you start to believe your own hype. There's only one direction you can travel, and it's not up.

I had broken up with my girlfriend, and I wasn't in the mood to settle down yet. Nasty and I hit the restaurants and clubs hard whenever we could—before, during, and after tournaments. If there were girls around, we'd chase them. If not, no problem—we had fun just hanging out with our buddies. Besides, there were plenty of times when Nasty would show up at my door in the wee hours with twins on his arm. There's nothing better for your game than a lively session of mixed doubles at 2 a.m.

Right through the 1970s and into the '80s, it was wild. We were treated like rock stars, A-list celebrities, but I kept my private life a mystery as much as I could. But still, with all the stuff that was being written about me, after 1974 in particular, the attention I was getting went off the charts. Wherever I went, people would turn and stare. And look at the places the tour would take us: Maui, San Diego, Palm Springs, New York. They had everything a red-blooded American man could ever want. Everything. And then there was Paris, London, Tokyo, Rio de Janeiro, Monte Carlo. It's almost like a dream to me now.

Did I make the most of it? In 1975 I did, no question about it. Along with Nasty, there was "Broadway Vitas" Gerulaitis. His personality and charisma were infectious, and he would hold court when we went out for dinner at the Playboy Club, for drinks at the Daisy, or to discos like Studio 54, in New York, and Annabel's, in London. I would sit with him in the VIP banquette—a drink in one hand, a model in the other—thinking, "Not bad for a working-class kid from East St. Louis."

Drugs were everywhere, especially cocaine, and there was no getting away from it. I'd walk into a bar or restaurant and people would be openly snorting lines of coke right off the table. That was never my scene. I didn't need to go looking for more vices. Girls? No problem. Alcohol? I was good at that, too, but although I came from an Irish background, I was never a big drinker during my prime (but I certainly made up for it later on). When I was out socializing, I'd have a beer or wine, very rarely hard liquor. I wanted to stay in control; that's part of my nature. I never allowed myself to become completely shit-faced in public. Falling out of a bar and not remembering how I got home wasn't my thing. At least, not then.

I was always careful to avoid guilt by association, especially when I was in the company of known druggies. Timing has always been one of my strengths, and if I saw trouble on the horizon, I made sure I was out of there before it arrived. I was living my dream and I wasn't about to blow it for some half-assed high. I don't want to sound corny, but my drug of choice had always been tennis.

I was lucky to have friends who watched my back. I remember one evening when I was offered a line of coke; before I could even respond, Vitas had the guy by the collar and was dragging him toward the door, saying, "I told you to keep that shit away from Connors!"

A few years later, my buddy Gerry Goldberg and I were at a party in Milan. It was wall to wall with Italian models. At some point, we went into the kitchen to refill our glasses, and we saw several of the girls with straws stuck up their noses. It didn't take me long to figure out that this wasn't some new fashion trend.

"Gerry, come on," I said, grabbing his sleeve, "we're out of here. If I'm caught around this stuff, I'm screwed."

We bounded down the steps three at a time to the sidewalk; I wasn't hanging around for someone to take a photograph of me with those girls in the background. Presto! Career over.

No, it was gambling that did it for me. I was an action junkie. In Vegas or London I would play craps, blackjack, whatever. At Wimbledon I would bet on myself in each round. Every year. The local bookmakers knew me well. In the US, if I wanted to put my money on sports, I had no trouble finding someone to take my bet. On tour the players gambled with each other on backgammon or cards, normally gin. I needed that buzz and thought I could handle it.

The problem in 1975 was that I forgot all of the lessons I had been taught. Mom used to say, "Jimmy, remember, what you don't get accomplished by midnight probably won't get accomplished at all." And just to make sure I got the point, she'd add, "There comes a time when you have to back off. The fun starts to go down and the trouble starts to go up."

Pancho would say something similar to Spencer and me when we headed out to the Daisy Club: "Good luck, boys, just don't fuck up!"

Up until 1975, I always heeded those warnings. There was nothing I wouldn't do to get the jump on my opponents. Because there was usually only one court available in the places we were playing on tour, I would rise at five in the morning to get an hour of practice in. I'd call up one of my buddies—Spencer, Schneider, or, later, John Lloyd—and ask them to come meet me before anyone else was even awake. From nine o'clock on you would be lucky to get 15 minutes on your own before someone else was trying to muscle their way onto the court. At 6 a.m. we would have the court to ourselves. By the time my opponents were eating breakfast, I knew I already had an advantage over them. But after the Laver challenge, none of that was happening. Tennis stopped being my priority, and, boy, did I pay the price for it.

I began to come home from a night out at five in the morning. I was sleeping all day, feeling groggy, and drinking more than I should. My diet didn't help, either. Even at the best of times, breakfast was usually a Pepsi and a Snickers bar. Eating healthy just wasn't my style. If you're not working all that sugar off in practice, it doesn't take long for it to catch up with you, and I was losing the battle of the bulge.

Following the success of the Laver challenge, Bill kept the money train rolling with an encore against Newcombe. It was the perfect match: the two best players in the world, slugging it out for supremacy in Vegas, not to mention revenge for my loss in Australia. No matter how you billed it, this was going to be way bigger than Connors–Laver. Don't screw up, Jimmy, I told myself. Make sure you're ready. So how come a couple of weeks before the match I wound up in the hospital suffering from fatigue?

I first began to feel tired after Boca Raton. At first I laughed off the symptoms—the headaches, the breathlessness, the lethargy—blaming Nasty and Vitas for being such bad influences. But I continued to feel like I'd been rode hard and put away wet, and before long I found myself struggling to get out of bed, let alone play tennis.

I talked to Bill and we decided what I really needed was a break. I had been on the go constantly for over a year and I was just plain worn out.

"I'm going to skip the next tournament," I told him. "I just don't feel like I'm ready."

"Do what you gotta do, Jimmy. I'll take care of it."

So I missed a couple of tournaments. Everyone did from time to time. Playing so many matches back to back is exhausting, whether you feel good or not. It's when you're tired or weak that you're most likely to do yourself real harm, and I wasn't prepared to risk long-term injury. I knew how I needed to feel to play right, and if I couldn't meet those standards, it was better for me to take a break.

It wasn't like I was the only guy in the world playing tennis; it just felt like it sometimes.

Of course the press had a field day with my taking time off. You know how they are. If I burped, it made good copy, so missing an occasional tournament was headline news. I was never happy about having to pull out—I don't like letting people down—but sometimes you have to put your well-being first.

At the start of March, I began to worry that it wasn't just fatigue that was dragging me down, and when I felt pains in my chest one morning right before leaving for an event in Washington, I got spooked. I've always had a little bit of an irregular heartbeat, and normally when that happened, I took it as a sign that I needed to get some rest and regain my energy. This time, though, I thought it might be something serious.

"Bill, I'm canceling the trip to DC and I'm going to the hospital. I think I'm having a heart attack."

I called Dr. Earl Woods, whom I'd known for years, and he checked me in to the hospital for a series of tests. When the tests came back, he told me I wasn't gonna die. But he and the others doctors insisted on keeping me in the hospital for five or six days, just to make sure everything was OK.

I was diagnosed with mononucleosis, otherwise known as glandular fever, and I was told that the only cure was to stay in bed and rest. I was already doing that, and, boy, was it boring. After a few days of lying around, drinking Pepsi, and watching TV, I thought my head would explode. Luckily, there was a tennis court close to the hospital, and I persuaded the nurses to let me sneak out for an hour a day to jump some rope and hit a few balls. If they had refused, I think I would have leaped out the window. I'm not good at doing nothing.

The press found out and followed me down to the court. By

then I was feeling a lot better. My heart rate was back to normal, but that didn't stop me from milking the situation. As I was warming up and a small crowd started to gather, I suddenly clutched my chest.

"Help, someone! I can't breathe!"

No one moved.

"Help, someone! I'm having a heart attack!"

No one moved.

So much for my acting chops. Don't give up the day job, Jimmy.

I was discharged from the hospital after 10 days. By then, I was almost sane and feeling 100 percent better, but I was way behind where I wanted to be in terms of preparation for Newcombe. I needed to get some match practice—and quick. Bill provided the solution and, as ever, found an angle to go with it.

"Jimmy, there's a tournament in Denver next week. I can get you in."

"Bill, that's WCT. I'm not exactly their favorite guy. They'll love telling me to go screw myself, and I don't want to give them that opportunity."

"Are you kidding? Newcombe's scheduled to play. I know the guys there, Ray Benton and his buddies, and they'll make some noise to save face, but they'll let you in. You and Newk in a warm-up match to the main event? Come on!"

As Bill predicted, Benton rattled his saber, saying he was concerned it was all a publicity stunt and that I was going to leave him stranded at the last minute with some fake injury, so he made me post a $10,000 security bond. Then Newk got upset when the announcement was made of my late entry. He had to win in Denver to overtake Ashe in the WCT rankings, and he didn't like the idea of me coming along and ruining his party.

Then, to top it all off, Newcombe pulled out of the tournament, claiming I had no class, trying to force my way in. What? Winning my qualifying matches had gotten me into the tournament. Can you imagine the number one player in the world having to qualify? Bobby Kreiss and I even entered the doubles—the practice was what I was looking for—and in the singles I beat Brian Gottfried in the finals. I left Denver ready and eager for the Newcombe match. I couldn't wait to get to Las Vegas.

As usual, Bill had been right. The ruckus in Colorado was just the thing to light the fuse ahead of the Caesars Palace match. Connors–Newcombe had become an even hotter ticket. Newcombe might have skipped town in Denver, but he couldn't hide forever.

Everyone expected the sparks to fly when I arrived on the Strip, but I like to keep people guessing about what's coming next. So I stayed polite and quiet all week, keeping a low profile, even showering and changing in my hotel so I could stay clear of any locker-room tension. I was saving my usual controversial self for the match.

But first we had to deal with Bill's obligatory circus. His opening gambit was to attempt to buy all the ringside tickets, saying that the "hometown" support Laver got back in February had been unfair. Our request was refused, probably because the organizers thought I was about 490 friends short of filling those 500 seats.

Next we argued over the surface. They wanted the older, faster Supreme Court carpet, which we used for the Laver match, while we preferred the more recent, slower version, which would blunt the pace of Newcombe's big serve. Newk didn't like that at all.

"I will make no more concessions for Jimmy Connors," he said. "As far as I'm concerned, this is my Alamo."

Okey-dokey. Which side were you on at the Alamo, Newk?

We lost the coin toss on the surface, but I didn't care, because Pop was coming to Vegas to watch me play for the first time in years. With him in my corner, I honestly felt unbeatable. There was no way in hell I was going to let my grandfather see me whine about the playing conditions.

While all of this was going on, Pancho and I stayed focused on developing a strategy to defeat Newcombe. The first issue was his serve, which had inflicted considerable damage in Australia. Would it have the same force on the Vegas surface? To help answer that question we added a new member to the James Gang, a young up-and-coming British pro named John Feaver, who had one of the biggest serves on the tour. It was high noon in Vegas. I told you I liked westerns.

As Feaver fired his missiles at me on the practice court, I quickly got a sense of what I was going to face against Newk. I realized it would come down to Newk's serve and volley against my return of serve—strength versus strength.

Pancho also identified a critical weakness in Newcombe's game.

"He doesn't move too well, Jimmy. He's a big guy, and he looks good until it comes to rallies and dealing with anything around his ankles. Keep the ball low and use your backhand slice and that will keep him off balance."

And that's what I did. I broke his serve in the first set and took it 6-3. I could have used a little air in the pavilion; man, it was hot and stuffy. A couple of fans even passed out—Newcombe fans, I'm guessing, who couldn't take it after I broke him twice in the third and then once again in the fourth to close out the match.

In terms of prize money, the Newcombe challenge dwarfed the

Mom and Dad enjoyed a busy social life in the early days of their marriage.

My trifecta of coaches: Mom, Two-Mom, and Pancho Segura at a tournament in the 1940s. When they were younger, Pancho tried to romance Mom but faced competition from Jimmy Evert, Chrissie's father. They both failed.

Mom striking a pose in her early teens when she was a rising star on the women's professional circuit. Later, she coached Hollywood celebrities like Mickey Rooney and Errol Flynn.

Hitting with Mom on our homemade court in Belleville. Playing tennis left-handed was natural for me.

My older brother, Johnny, and me running moonshine in our go-cart.

Me and Johnny in our basement practicing the technique taught to us by our grandfather, Pop, a former prizefighter who once sparred with Joe Louis. "I can take a punch," Johnny used to say proudly, neglecting to add he knew how to throw one, too.

Me and Pop. He was responsible for developing my footwork by making me jump rope every day. I can still hear him saying, "Pick up your feet, Jimmy. Just another 20 minutes."

Johnny, Mom, and me after a tournament. Johnny loved tennis but it wasn't his life, which allowed Mom to devote herself to my game.
(Courtesy of Art Seitz)

Mom may have made some mistakes along the way, but I knew she always had my best interests at heart.
(Courtesy of Art Seitz)

Even while cruising the Venice canals, my buddy Nasty was always on the lookout for beautiful women. Fortunately, I had one of my own at home, so I could just relax.

Nasty, my friend Gerry Goldberg, and me on the loose in Florida. This is just trouble! *(Courtesy of Art Seitz)*

Nasty and me performing with the Monte Carlo philharmonic. I think I'll keep my day job.

Horsing around in the locker room at Roland Garros. Wait, is that a newspaper? What? We can't *read*. *(Courtesy of Art Seitz)*

Nasty and me having a serious tactical discussion during a tournament about what clubs we'd be hitting that night.

My friend Vitas Gerulaitis had rock-star sex appeal but was also a great champion. Here we are at Wimbledon in 1978 before our semifinal match. *(Courtesy of Art Seitz)*

With Patrick McEnroe and Vitas in Scotland. I found it much easier to relax with Patrick than with his older brother, WhatsHisName. *(Courtesy of Hamish Campbell for THE SCOTSMAN)*

I dated Miss World Marjie Wallace for a year. We broke up after she appeared on the cover of *People* magazine, with the headline MARJIE AND HER MEN. My "bodyguard" Doug Henderson kept the stalkers at bay. *(Courtesy of Art Seitz)*

Walking on water at Caesars Palace before one of my big-money winner-takes-all challenge matches. *(Courtesy of Art Seitz)*

With my manager, Bill Riordan. You can guess how this conversation was going: "We can sue this guy and this guy . . ." "What? Huh?" *(Courtesy of Art Seitz)*

With Chrissie in 1974. Nice haircut, Jimmy. Where'd you leave the bowl?.

Nasty, Chrissie, me, and my buddy Spencer Segura. Who is that on the pedestal? Oh, yeah—all of us! We thought.

Chrissie and me with our Wimbledon silverware. The Love Double cleans up!

(All photographs courtesy of Art Seitz)

Laver match. With CBS throwing $600,000 into the pot for TV rights, Caesars Palace adding $250,000, and foreign TV adding an additional $150,000, I rolled out of town this time with half a million in my pocket, leaving Newk to console himself with a mere $300,000.

The television ratings were once again through the roof, and the high rollers who had come to watch the tennis happily stopped off at the casino tables before and after the match. Planning for Connors–Newcombe III started pretty much right away. But for me, the big thrill was seeing my name in lights, on the giant neon Caesars sign that loomed over the Strip. It was proof that there was more to playing tennis than just the game itself. It was now as much about entertainment as it was hitting the ball down the line.

The battle for the French Open once again played out on the red clay of Roland Garros without the presence of one James Scott Connors. It wasn't because of another ban this time; I was just pissed at how I'd been treated the year before, so I decided against entering. Instead, I flew to England early to give myself plenty of time to acclimate to the weather and grass courts. I had a title to defend.

There was no Queen's Club tournament that year (I don't know why; it disappeared from the schedule for three years, beginning in 1974), which meant I entered the field in Nottingham, where I made it through two hard-fought matches against Bobby Kreiss and Brian Gottfried before losing out to my old college rival Roscoe Tanner in the quarterfinals.

It had been a decent run, and even though I was still a little too interested in the London nightlife for my own good, I was confident going into Wimbledon. The only question—and it was a big one—was could I do it without Pancho? His relationship with Mom had been strained since the Newcombe Challenge Match, for which Pancho had been given a huge amount of credit across the sports pages, and rightfully so. The press had been saying that it was his savvy coaching that had turned my game around after the defeat by Newcombe in Australia. Suddenly, Pancho was being portrayed as my savior, and it made Mom uncomfortable.

There was also a deeper tension between them, on the management side of my career. Requests were still coming in from IMG and other agencies, begging me to sign with them. These were being channeled through Pancho, whose ideas on the subject were now changing, maybe because he felt I was missing out on some lucrative opportunities.

"McCormack wants to meet with Jimmy, Gloria. Maybe now is the time to think about some sponsorship deals?"

"Donald Dell is organizing an exhibition and he wants Jimmy. Hell, Gloria, it's worth considering."

Mom thought she was being backed into a corner, and you know what happens when a Connors feels threatened. It ain't pretty. Mom started to make snap decisions; one day she would agree to sign a deal and the next day she would say we couldn't trust anyone. Pancho found himself pulled in two different directions. A deal was on, then it was off, and then it was on again. It must've been frustrating for both of them.

I could sense the growing tension, but I ignored it. I didn't want to be forced to take sides. If it looked like the conversation was going to turn ugly, I would excuse myself to go outside and work on my serve. Chickenshit move? Absolutely. That's why I don't really know the full details of what went down, other than the fact that Pancho wanted to formalize our association now that there was big money to be made from the Challenge Matches. Pancho felt that he deserved recognition and compensation above the loose arrangements that we had always had, and I couldn't fault him for that.

Mom, however, had her doubts about the direction Pancho was taking my tennis. He wanted to work more on my short game, but Mom was convinced my serve and overheads were what needed improving. Whether this was just a smoke screen, I can't say for sure, but when the issue of a formal contract with Pancho came up, Mom told him she thought that it was time for a break and that maybe we could revisit his arrangement again after the summer.

Pancho says he didn't take Mom's decision personally, that he was more disappointed than hurt. He compared it to a tennis match with points won and points lost. I hope that's true. After everything Pancho and I had been through, it must have been hard for him not to see it as a slap in the face. I should've stood up to Mom on that one, but that was easier said than done. I wish I had made it clear that they were equally responsible for whatever success came my way, that they were both geniuses in their own right.

Instead, I withdrew and let Mom decide how things were going to be, because that's pretty much how it always went. For a guy who excelled at confrontation on the court, I ran from it elsewhere. Mom was dynamic, she had a fierce will, and, most important, she had my best interests at heart. I had no doubt about her intentions, but it didn't mean she always made the right decisions.

If Two-Mom had still been around, the situation might have turned out differently. My grandmother was a stabilizing influence on Mom and would have helped her see both sides more clearly. I think it's fair to say that Mom made mistakes from time to time.

So Pancho and I drifted apart for a while. There was no one dramatic moment where he picked up his racquets and stormed out;

he simply stopped traveling with me. I wanted to think that things were going so well in my career that maybe his absence wouldn't be a big deal. Deep down, though, I knew it mattered.

I was getting tired. I'd been on a relentless schedule for 18 months and I had reached a plateau. I was finding it difficult to raise my game, to maintain the tempo, and the bright lights of fame were becoming increasingly seductive. With Pancho gone, I gave into those temptations a little too much.

10

NO ONE'S CUP OF TEA

Two days before the start of Wimbledon in 1975, I picked up a newspaper and turned straight to the sports section. The headline read: CONNORS SUES ASHE.

What sonuvabitch has gone and done that? As if I didn't know. I'm in the middle of a multimillion-dollar lawsuit against Jack Kramer, Donald Dell, and the ATP, and here I am launching a new one.

Nice move, Bill.

I discovered that Riordan had filed two lawsuits in Indianapolis, claiming damages of $5 million in total for libelous comments that had apparently been directed at us. The first concerned a letter written by Arthur Ashe, as ATP president, in which he referred to me as "unpatriotic." The second complaint ran along the same lines, originating in an article written by Bob Briner, the ATP's secretary. He supposedly called Riordan a "nihilist." Is that even an insult? Let me get my dictionary.

Once again, I was completely in the dark. It was all about Bill seeking revenge for a $3 million slander suit brought by Kramer against us—for what, I never did find out. How many more legal battles was I going to be sucked into? I was losing track. Something had to give, but not before I dealt with a little tournament at the All-England Club.

Whether my opponent was friend or foe, my attitude going into tennis matches never changed. I was out to beat whoever was across the net from me, no matter what my personal feelings were about them. Now, I liked John Lloyd a lot and we were buddies, but he understood as well as I did that once you walked onto the court, business was business.

Chasing a drop shot early in my first-round match on the damp grass of Centre Court, I slipped and hyperextended my knee. I didn't think much about it at the time; I carried on playing and won 6-2, 6-3, 6-1. But once the adrenaline rush of my first Wimbledon title defense was over, all that changed. I felt a degree of pain that I had never experienced before.

I thought I would be OK after some rest, but when I woke up the next morning, the pain had intensified; my knee was completely swollen and unable to support my weight. I needed to get it checked out. I got in touch with Bill and he found me the top physiotherapist at Chelsea Football Club, one of England's leading soccer teams, which had the facilities to treat this kind of injury. After they examined me, it turned out I had a couple of hairline factures in my shin—painful but treatable. Thanks, Lloydy, I'm blaming this on you.

The physiotherapist's advice was simple: rest. The timing could not have been worse. There were only two tournaments that I would have even considered playing while badly injured: Wimbledon and the US Open. As Pancho always told me, once you walk out there, be prepared to play, or don't walk out there. Well, I thought I was ready. The physiotherapist wrapped up my leg and off I went to practice. I knew that once I was on the court, I would forget about the medical warnings.

After every match I won in those two weeks, I would immediately go for an intensive treatment of ultrasound, ice, and massage—and I wasn't above taking a fistful of painkillers, either. I kept the injury as secret as I could, refusing to wear even an Ace bandage; I wasn't going to give anyone an edge.

I advanced to the final without losing a set, but 24 hours before my showdown with Ashe, the physio warned me once again to take it easy; he was afraid the fractures were getting worse.

So why did I continue to play? Because I'm an idiot. I did decide to take the day off before the final, though.

As we left the physiotherapist's office, Bill turned to me and said, "Don't worry, kid, you're strong enough, you're young enough, and you're good enough. You'll be fine. I'm not worried."

He dropped me off at the hotel and told me he had a few errands to run.

"Rest, Jimmy. I'll see you later."

"Not a problem," I said.

By match time the next day, I'm ready to go. I start off steadily, but I can't find my rhythm; I'm sluggish and Ashe is playing perfect tennis. I lose the first two sets easily, 6-1, 6-1, and now I'm getting desperate. Funny how things happen when you're on the brink; a shot here, a lucky break there, and I win the third set, 7-5. I go up a service break early in the fourth set and I'm starting to feel like I have the momentum, but that doesn't last long. My shots lack pace; they catch the tape and fall backward. The recovery I think I've engineered turns out to be a figment of my imagination. Ashe comes back strong to win the set, the match, and the Wimbledon title.

After his victory, Ashe turned to the crowd and raised his fist in triumph. He was a popular winner—and he was playing for black America, as well as representing all the members of the ATP. He deserved to revel in his moment.

Arthur's game was flawless that day; he had figured out the way to play me. By reducing the speed and length of his shots, he constantly brought me into the net before passing or lobbing me.

The book on me at the time was that I was a one-dimensional player, a grinder and fighter, someone who never gave up, but that basically all I had were my groundstrokes. Excuse me, but look at any match you want back then and, if you know anything about tennis, you'll see me mixing it up throughout. If things weren't going my way, I knew how to adapt, how to try something new. Sometimes they were just small alterations in my play, as I figured out a strategy for countering my opponent. I could end up playing five or six different ways in one match, but whichever style I used, my game was all about precision and aggression. I was always about taking chances, going for it, playing with no fear, and being willing to accept the consequences if it didn't come off. That's the way I was taught, and being as stubborn as I was, I wasn't going to change that basic philosophy for anybody.

Oh, yeah, there's one thing I forgot to tell you. After Bill had dropped me off at the hotel the previous day, one of his "errands" was to go to Ladbrokes, the local betting shop, and put a bundle on Ashe to beat me in the final. I was the heavy favorite, and I understand Bill made out quite well. Can you believe it? And he didn't even share his winnings, the cheapskate. No wonder I didn't trust a soul. What's that saying? Keep your friends close and your enemies closer? I built my emotional wall another few feet higher.

Ashe didn't like me. He resented all the money I was making from my Challenge Matches, on the grounds that they would diminish the prestige of the Grand Slams. And he didn't appreciate my attitude toward the Davis Cup. As for how he felt about Riordan's multiple lawsuits, well, we never talked about that. Arthur didn't have the balls to confront me; instead, he left a note in my locker at Wimbledon outlining his position.

Well, that speaks volumes, doesn't it? All he had to do was come up and talk to me face to face, man to man, but he chose not to. It annoyed me, but not so much as when he walked out on to Centre

Court wearing his Davis Cup jacket, with USA emblazoned across his chest.

In 1974, probably 90 percent of the fans at Wimbledon had been rooting for Ken Rosewall. In 1975, you guessed it, 90 percent of the fans were rooting for Arthur Ashe. What's a guy gotta do to win friends around here? It took me a few more years to find out the answer to that question.

I did have a small cheering section. Sitting in the box alongside Mom and Bill was the British actress Susan George. Susan and I had met earlier in the summer, and there was a lot of tabloid speculation that we were dating. We weren't. We were just good friends. Susan was still with the singer Jack Jones, but he wasn't in town, and since she enjoyed tennis, I invited her to be my guest.

During the second week of the tournament, the All-England Club authorities called me in, supposedly to explain a negative comment I had made to the press about the state of the grass. As far as I was concerned, that wasn't the real reason they decided to interrogate me right in the middle of the tournament. I was in no mood to stand there and be lectured. I had better things to think about, like trying to win their goddamn championship and not being 100 percent fit. I've never been a whiner and I wasn't about to start now. So I just emptied both barrels.

"This is bullshit and we all know what's going on here," I told them. "Instead of worrying about the tennis, all you care about is what the press is saying about your precious grass. How about paying less attention to what I do off the court and more to what I do on it. Give me a break. And while you're at it, why don't you bring that bowler hat back to East St. Louis and see how you get treated?"

I knew I wasn't their favorite person, but I was who I was, and as far as I was concerned, to put it in terms they can understand, they could sod off, the wankers.

I think part of the reason the All-England Club was annoyed at my attitude was that they had gotten a lot of mileage out of Chrissie and me the year before and didn't appreciate that a big fuss had been made out of my showing up with Susan George. It's not always about the tennis, is it?

In the spring of 1975, the US papers had reported seeing Chrissie and me out shopping together in LA, holding hands. In the photos they published I was still wearing a necklace she had given me with the inscription SUPER on it. Then there was an interview I'd done in which I said I missed her. That was true: I did miss her. We'd been together for a long time (at least, that was how it felt back then), and you can't just switch that off. Since we had publicly said we hadn't broken up and that our wedding was just postponed, I could see how people would be talking.

I still cared about Chrissie, but that didn't mean we were getting back together. We were always going to bump into each other after we split up, at tournaments or exhibitions, and we had friends in common. When we did see each other over that period, we were happy to spend time together. As for the necklace, why wouldn't I wear it? I liked it and I've still got it today.

All the whispering and gossiping came to a head during Chrissie's semifinal against Billie Jean King at Wimbledon, when Susan and I walked into the players' box to watch the conclusion of the final set. At the time Chrissie led 3-0, but she went on to lose the next six games in a row. According to the press, this was apparently my fault, because I was sitting with Susan. To be fair, Chrissie never once blamed the loss on me, saying she didn't even know I was there.

We knew we had to do something to stop all the rumors. It was starting to be a distraction, which neither of us needed. The day after her loss to Billie Jean, we issued a joint statement confirming that our wedding plans were now permanently off. As I said at the time, "She's going out with other guys and I'm going out with other girls. But the most important thing for me is that Chrissie and I are still good friends."

What I said was true. If Chrissie had been upset with me for taking Susan to Wimbledon, do you think a few months later we would have been found sitting very publicly with each other making a date? OK, so it was not exactly a romantic date; this was on a staged TV show, where Chrissie asked me to play mixed doubles with her against Billie Jean and Marty Riessen for a CBS special called *Love Doubles*. I even gave Chrissie a kiss on the cheek when I said yes. Granted, it was pretty cheesy, but it showed that we were still friends and we had moved on.

After my Wimbledon defeat (which I took pretty hard, by the way), I had a week off before I was thrown back into the circuit of summer tournaments leading up to the US Open. I was putting on a pound a day just thinking about it, but in the meantime I had to take time out to cut a hit record.

Didn't see that coming, did you?

Flash back to the summer of 1974. Bill and I are sitting in a restaurant in Las Vegas, talking about—what else?—money. Specifically, we were discussing how to make more of it. The prize money in those days had a lot fewer zeros on the checks than they do today.

"It's show business, Jimmy," Bill says. "Movies, TV, records, concerts. That's where the real money is nowadays and that's where you want to be."

"Well, what's stopping us? I can sing a little."

"Show me."

I go through a few bars of "White Christmas." All right, so under that kind of pressure I folded. They were the only lyrics I could remember.

"You're not half bad, kid. If you're serious, I'll see what I can do." Really?

"I'm willing to take a shot," I say. "Go ahead." I mean, how long could I play tennis? I've gotta think about my future. Anybody got a food stamp?

Nine months later, following the Newcombe Challenge Match in Vegas, Bill and I are sitting next to Paul Anka's cousin at dinner. The subject of me recording a song comes up and the cousin promises to introduce me to Anka. He was as good as his word and I met with Paul a week later. I didn't even have to audition.

"Yeah, sure, Jimmy, come on in. We'll make a record."

Paul promised to write a couple of numbers, and when I was in New York for the US Open, I went into the studio and laid down the tracks: "Girl, You Turn Me On," which, it seemed to me, Paul had written in 30 seconds, and "Guitar Man." I was convinced I would be number one on *Billboard* in no time. I could even see myself on *American Top 40* with Casey Kasem.

Oh, yeah. Fat, drunk, and stupid. I can do anything.

My singing debut would be broadcast nationwide from New York's Ed Sullivan Theater on a new TV show, *Saturday Night Live with Howard Cosell*, two weeks after the US Open.

"Always take care of your business, Jimmy." Sure, Two-Mom, that's what I'm doing.

In 1975, Forest Hills decided to tear up their grass courts and replace them with the slower Har-Tru clay. What the hell were they thinking? The US Open was our national championship, and they decided to install a surface that was more familiar and beneficial to European and South American players. Didn't they want homegrown winners?

Doom and gloom dominated the lead-up to the tournament, with commentators predicting that no US player would even reach the quarterfinals on the new surface. They weren't far from the truth—only Eddie Dibbs and I made it that far—and when Borg defeated Eddie, I was the only American in the men's semis, facing Borg. He was coming off the second of his six French Open titles and about to play on his best surface, so he was widely considered the favorite. I felt otherwise. Earlier in the week, I had the good fortune of meeting up with Pancho when he came to New York, even though he was no longer officially my coach, and we sat down to discuss tactics. Pancho suggested patience against Borg.

"Jimmy, I've been watching you on TV. You're hitting the ball well off the ground, so stick with that. Borg with his topspin—the ball will bounce a little high, so move in and take the ball early, hitting hard and deep to the middle. Wait for the short reply and get to the net. Be patient and wait for your chance."

That's exactly how it worked out. I kept my concentration and broke him once in each set to win 7-5, 7-5, 7-5. I had beaten the clay-court champ, defying the odds, and I took all the positives from that into the final against Manuel Orantes, of Spain.

Pancho told me to concentrate on two things with Orantes: the weakness of his forehand, and to rush the net whenever he was preparing to make a shot.

"He puts so much slice on it that it comes over high. Pounce on it, take it out of the air before he has time to react."

I didn't listen. Going up against Orantes in the US Open final was, to be honest, a day I would like to forget.

With Orantes having come back from an almost impossible position, down two sets to love against Guillermo Vilas in the semis, I thought he would be worn out. His match had finished so late that night that I don't think he even went back to the hotel, and I was convinced that would work to my advantage. The opposite was true. Orantes may have been exhausted, but he'd just played the match of his life, was full of confidence and adrenaline, and he ran me ragged. And in a lot of ways the match highlighted a major problem that had plagued me all year. Carrying those extra 20 pounds of weight was starting to take its toll on me. If I could reach the ball, I could hit it pretty good, but getting to it was a hell of a struggle.

Orantes beat me in straight sets, 6-4, 6-3, 6-3, and the whole time all I could hear from the stands was *"Olé! Olé! Olé!"* I should have been used to that by now, the home crowd cheering for the foreign player, and it was the third time in a year that the crowd was rooting for my opponent in the final of a Slam. But I'd be lying if I said it didn't bother me at the Open in 1975. It made me mad and even more determined to win the fans over the next chance I got. At the same time, I told myself that I didn't care what the fans thought. Why? Because I knew I was about to be Sinatra's opening act. Yeah, baby, the Chairman of the Board and me.

The big night arrived, September 20, with Howard Cosell introducing his famous musical guests: Sinatra, Shirley Bassey, John Denver, the cast from the Broadway hit *The Wiz*, plus a new Scottish pop group called the Bay City Rollers, who were making their first appearance on US television. ABC had pulled out all the stops to make sure that Howard's pilot was a ratings bonanza. Oh, wait, I forgot, I was there, too.

Nervous? Let's put it this way: I'd played tennis in front of thousands of people live and millions on TV and hardly broke a sweat, but a few seconds before I was about to stroll out in front of the cameras, microphone in hand, and strike a casual pose against the piano, I had already changed my shirt three times just from the anticipation of doing something outside my comfort zone. Well, what could you do? I went out there wearing jeans, clogs, and pit stains the size of tennis balls. You know, Mr. Cool.

To make matters worse, a few minutes before my big entrance, Paul Anka had presented me with a contract, which I assumed was to cover my "show-business career." I was happy to sign up with him, to sing his songs, and appreciative of all the help he had given me. It just so happened that my buddy Spencer was there in the studio.

"Spence, take a look at this," I said, handing him the contract. "I'm sure it's fine, but since you're here, let me know what you think."

Spencer had just been accepted to law school, and it took him all of 15 seconds to give me his opinion.

"You can't sign this. It has a clause that includes income from some of your tennis-related activities."

Oops.

"So," I asked him, "is that a bad thing?"

"Ya think?" Spencer grinned.

To be fair, I can't say for sure if Mr. Anka was trying to pull a fast one—maybe he thought he was offering me a good deal—but I wasn't impressed. If Spencer read it right and there was a clause like that, there was no way I could sign the contract. I guess I don't have to tell you that we haven't stayed in touch since.

As for my high-profile debut in the company of all those showbiz giants, well, Howard Cosell's new show lasted barely three months before it was cancelled, which was two and three quarter months longer than my singing career. "Girl, You Turn Me On" was never released, and my new singing career was over when I hit the last note. I took that show down in a hurry. But remember Riordan's words: "Any publicity . . ."

Right after Wimbledon I had managed to persuade Bill to quietly withdraw the Arthur Ashe libel suit. Then a week before the US

Open, after hours locked away in discussions with the ATP, Jack Kramer, Donald Dell, and Bill settled our dispute with them.

"We've come out of a long, dark night," he told the press. "We smashed the monopoly in tennis. Now it's open tennis for everyone."

Was it worth it? Hope you got everything you wanted out of it, Bill. I, on the other hand, would have that hanging over me for life. See, we're still talking about it. Here, let me simplify this for you: I was young. I didn't understand it then, don't understand it now.

Bill said that we had won, but the reality was different. The whole episode had been an incredible waste of time, energy, and money; neither side came out on top. As I recall, we ended up getting nowhere near the level of damages claimed in the press (obviously, I didn't see a penny of it from Bill), but it wasn't the outcome that really mattered. It had all been an unwelcome sideshow. All I wanted to do was play tennis.

With all the legal bullshit behind us, I was asked if I wanted to join the Davis Cup team for their upcoming match against Venezuela. Even though I found it hard to shake the association between the Davis Cup and Two-Mom's passing—I had been practicing with the team in Jamaica when she died—I tentatively said yes; I didn't want to make a full-time commitment. I've always been a little superstitious, and in my mind the Davis Cup represented bad luck. The main reason I never embraced the competition the way people thought I should have had nothing to do with money or giving up my time, and it wasn't about deserting the US cause; it was just a very negative feeling deep inside that was hard for me to shake. In reality, my participation could have backfired for the team if my heart wasn't in it. And that's just what happened.

In 1975, Tony Trabert had replaced Dennis Ralston as captain, and his approach suited me; he wasn't always telling us what to do or how to behave. Our preparations were relaxed and I was happy to be sharing a room with my buddy Vitas. In addition, my friend Bill Norris, the ATP trainer, came along. So why not go play some tennis and hang out with a few of my buddies. How bad could it be?

We defeated Venezuela comfortably, which set us on our way to a North American Zone elimination playoff against Mexico in December. But first I had to go back to London for the Dewar's Cup, which was played at the famous Royal Albert Hall. I'd been offered a guarantee for my participation, a set amount of money I would take home, win or lose, which was not common practice in those days and had to be on the QT (although everybody did it). Just before the finals against Eddie Dibbs, one of the organizers came up to me in the locker room and handed me an envelope containing my guarantee. When I looked at the check, I blew my stack.

"What the fuck is this?! We agreed the amount was going to be in pounds, and this is dollars?"

The exchange rate at the time was about $2 to £1. I thought someone was trying to rip me off and I was really pissed. Even though I wanted to walk away, I couldn't: The hall was full, and we were about to go onto the court. Despite all that, I started out strong, winning the first set with ease, but Dibbs, being the battler that he is, hung tough. The more difficult Eddie made it for me, the more I thought about being shortchanged. We played for three hours, and in the end I couldn't keep my emotions together and lost in three sets.

When the match ended, I stormed out of the stadium and back to my hotel to shower and change. Then the phone rang. It was Nasty.

"Get back here. We're in the doubles final."

I told him I wasn't in the mood.

"Come on, Connors boy, get back here. We'll have some fun."

Because I always do what I'm told, I got in a cab and headed back to Albert Hall. When I walked into the locker room, I could see Nasty had taken care of everything.

Nasty and I walked onto the court ready to play. We took off our jackets, and when the crowd saw that we were wearing tuxedo shirts and bow ties under them, the booing started. And it didn't stop there.

After the first game, Nasty goes and pulls out a magnum of champagne from an ice bucket he had placed by the side of the court. He shakes up the bottle, uncorks it, and sprays the crowd. You can imagine how happy they were to have their tuxedoes drenched in champagne, even if it was an expensive vintage. Then Nasty pours us each a glass; we toast, knock back our drinks, and return to the court.

At the next changeover, we had another glass of bubbly. Now, remember, I've already played singles for three hours, I haven't eaten, I'm tired, it's hot inside the hall, and I'm drinking champagne. Tipsy time. Nasty and I were laughing so hard that neither of us could even see the ball. But we were the only two people laughing, and the crowd hadn't stopped booing. Fuck it. We could take it, and, anyway, the match only lasted 35 minutes.

To give our opponents—Karl Meiler, from West Germany, and Wojciech Fibak, from Poland—credit, they ignored us, kept their concentration, and won the match against the two clowns.

By anyone else's standards, my year would have been considered a success. Three Grand Slam finals plus a win in that WCT tournament in Denver that I entered at the last minute and three more victories in Bermuda, Hawaii, and North Conway, New Hampshire. But compared with 1974, it was disastrous. I had fallen into the trap of thinking I could do what I wanted off the court and still perform the way I needed to on it. Things were rapidly spinning out of control.

My year was coming to an end and the only thing left was the

Davis Cup tie in Mexico. I knew I needed to change some things personally and professionally.

My relationship with Bill Riordan was heading in the wrong direction. He had already scheduled two winner-takes-all matches for the spring of 1976, but that was the extent of my obligations to him. We decided to go our separate ways.

Unfortunately, there were a few financial discrepancies to resolve first, when the accountants discovered that some money I was owed from the Newcombe Challenge Match was missing. I thought it was probably just an oversight on the part of Caesars Palace; I knew the guys there and was certain they could help me straighten it out, so I told Mom I'd take care of it. But when I called Caesars Palace to ask about the check, they told me they'd sent it out months ago. After some investigating, we found out that the money had been mailed to Bill, but he had returned it straight to Caesars to settle his gambling debts.

I was furious, but Bill claimed that the payment was rightfully his, and in May of 1976 he filed yet another lawsuit, this one aimed squarely at me. He said that he was owed 15 percent of all of my earnings since March 1972 for services as my exclusive personal manager. I've got to give him credit for being consistent.

With Bill out of the picture, Mom took full control of the business. Every contract, sponsorship deal, and request to play in a tournament now went directly through her. At first I was glad; she'd always fought my battles off the court. A good thing, since if anyone approached me with a request, I'd usually agree, even settling on a fee myself, just because I don't like to say no. Then I'd tell them they had to talk to Mom about the details. They would call Mom and she'd cut them off if she didn't like their terms.

As a result, most agents and promoters hated dealing with her.

They would try to drive a wedge between us, but that was impossible. This wasn't just business; this was family. So they retaliated by ridiculing her achievements whenever they could, which only toughened her up and confirmed her belief: It's us against them, Jimmy.

Sure, in tournaments that mentality gave me an edge, fueling my killer instinct when playing a faceless opponent. That's how I won my matches, but off the court there was a downside. I became wary of people, and, truthfully, I still am.

Could I have made more money when I was at the top of my game if someone other than my mother had been looking after my business interests? The answer is yes. Mom had trust issues, and her management cost me financially because I didn't establish enduring relationships within the tennis world. Now ask me if I give a damn? You can bet your life that I don't. Every decision my mother made was with her heart in the right place, and that's all that matters to me. Loyalty.

Eventually I signed with IMG for a year, and during that year I won Wimbledon and the US Open and they made me nothing. Then I signed with Donald Dell's ProServ agency and they made me a boatload of money, and I made them just as much. The difference was that during the time that Mom looked after my deals, when I had a week off, I really had a week off. With the management firms, it seemed that my time wasn't really my own, and that was what Mom tried to protect me from.

Acapulco in December should be paradise, right?

After an unfortunate performance in Mexico City, I needed to get away. I had lost the deciding rubber match of the Davis Cup tie to Raúl Ramírez, in an atmosphere of total chaos. The Mexican supporters screamed for their hero and then swarmed onto the court to lift him onto their shoulders. It was a disaster, and the USA's third exit in a row at that stage of the competition.

So I'm on the Pacific coast, in Mexico's most famous resort. I've earned almost $1 million this year, won nine tournaments, made it to three Grand Slam finals, played in the most-watched tennis matches ever televised, represented my country in the Davis Cup, and was even on the cover of *Time* magazine.

I'm number one in the world, according to the ATP. So why do I feel like shit?

Spencer came with me to the Davis Cup, and we decided afterward to grab a few days of sun and relaxation in Acapulco. But once we started hanging out at Carlos and Charlie's, a bar and restaurant that was the center of nightlife for the rich and beautiful, we quickly gave up on the idea of getting any rest. Our routine consisted of waking up bleary-eyed and heading out to the beach, where we continued to do nothing but damage to ourselves.

One day, on the way out of our hotel, I pass a mirror. I know I've been out of control, but I really don't like what I see. My gut is hanging over my shorts, my face is puffy, my eyes are bloodshot slits—oh, and by the way, I'm 185 fat-ass pounds. Oh, my God. Number one in the world? Who am I kidding? I've broken all the rules I've stood by over the course of my career. There's only one thing to do. Get back to the basics.

I picked up the phone and dialed the only person I knew I would listen to. Mom.

11

THE POINT'S NOT OVER 'TIL IT'S OVER

had come to the end of a hellish year, a year of too many off-court distractions, which had a detrimental effect on my game. When I placed that call to Mom from Acapulco, I knew I had to get my priorities straight so that I could once again focus on tennis.

The first thing I did was move from my house in the Hollywood Hills. Despite my initial excitement about the place—it was a pretty cool pad—it had never really felt like home. I needed to find a quieter spot, one that required a lot less upkeep, where I didn't have to worry about the gardener, the pool guy, and the trash man.

I found it nearby. Except for the bedrooms, it was a huge open space that even had room in my bar area for a pool table and pinball machine. My favorite spot was next to the fireplace, where I could sit in my leather chair and look out over the lights of LA. A bottle of Suave Bola and I'm set.

Mom came out to stay for a month; I enjoyed some good home cooking and she helped me work on my game and get back in shape for the start of the 1976 season. By the time I hit the courts in Birmingham, Alabama, at the end of January, I'd lost almost 20 pounds. I beat Billy Martin in straight sets in the singles final, and Erik Van Dillen and I took the doubles title. I was back on track.

I also had a new girlfriend, who just happened to live in the same apartment building as Chrissie, right down the street from my place. That was . . . interesting. I still wanted to keep my private life private, so there was a lot of sneaking around. I really didn't want to bump into Chrissie; it would have been awkward for both of us.

I'd met my new girlfriend back in November at a birthday party at one of my favorite restaurants in LA, Mr. Chow's. Dino Martin had persuaded me to go by telling me that there might be someone there I'd be interested in.

He wasn't wrong.

Spencer, Dino, Desi, and I had a big table with plenty of beautiful women sitting around, but there was only one who caught my eye. Fortunately, there was an empty seat next to her.

"Good luck, son," Spencer said, grinning at me.

Her name was Marjie Wallace, and she had been Miss World 1973 before she lost her crown due to some ridiculous rule about not dating celebrities. Hmmm . . . Marjie moved with a fast crowd and had dated the soccer star George Best, the Grand Prix driver Peter Revson, and even the singer Tom Jones. She was easy to talk to and fun to be around. And, by the way, did I mention she was hot?

After that night at Mr. Chow's we started spending a lot of time together, traveling to tournaments, going out for dinner, or just hanging around my apartment. Pretty soon she was a semi-permanent fixture at my place (and we even got a dog, Sneakers, a schnauzer), but she never officially moved in. That wasn't her style, and it wasn't mine.

Marjie had just been through a tough couple of years. Revson had died in a racing accident in March 1974, only weeks after she'd been stripped of her Miss World title. A few months later, she had been taken to the hospital after an accidental overdose of sleeping pills. I didn't know any of this when I first met her, and by the time we started going out, she seemed to have recovered, and drugs were never a part of our life when we were together.

I was preparing for my third Challenge Match in Las Vegas, this time against Manuel Orantes, whom I'd lost to at the 1975 Open. I had defeated Borg at the US Pro Indoors in Philadelphia at the end of January, but I still thought there was something missing in my game. Even though I was in much better shape than I'd been for a long time, that killer instinct of 1974 hadn't fully returned, and I couldn't shake the dull, tired feeling that had nagged me over the previous 12 months. I gave an interview at the time in which I described myself as having been a "pussy" on the court. That just about summed up how I felt about my game, and I promised myself that I would fix that at Caesars Palace.

Even though Bill and I had parted company, he was still promoting the Challenge Match. And, in the way that only Bill could, he started to stir the pot again, claiming that because I had been struggling with my fitness throughout most of 1975, I had deliberately dodged opponents. I knew that this was just Bill being Bill, but it struck a nerve.

He was right about the condition I'd been in, and I wanted to show him that even without his help I could look after myself. At the weigh-in (yeah, the weigh-in, another one of Bill's inventions), I registered a healthy 170 pounds, compared with the 185 pounds I'd been carrying around New York in September. But I still wasn't satisfied with my fitness, and I had a few more pounds to lose to get to where I wanted to be.

Orantes's straight-sets victory over me in the US Open meant that once again the Challenge Match would draw a whole lot of attention. CBS was airing it as another World Heavyweight Championship of Tennis, and Caesars Palace rolled out the red carpet across the casino floor so that we could walk to the court through a crowd of fans.

Unfortunately, the match didn't live up to the billing. Unlike at Forest Hills, this time I decided to follow Pancho's advice, rushing net to cut off my opponent's backhand slice and being more aggressive on his second serve, even though Mom was unsure about the tactic.

"OK, Pancho, I'll attack whenever I can."

"Good, Jimmy, good. And if that doesn't work, drop it. It's fine. Do what you need to do to win."

Pancho understood both my game and my personality better than anyone. And, yes, he was back in my corner and effectively my full-time coach again. The strain between Mom and Pancho had eased, if not healed. Pancho had made it clear to me that if I ever wanted his help or advice, all I had to do was ask. Which I did before playing Borg at the previous Open and again at my tournament win in Alabama at the beginning of the year. After the Orantes Challenge Match, Pancho would be beside me almost without exception for the rest of the year.

Orantes was not at the top of his game, and it was one of those days when everything went right for me. I think nerves played a big part in his performance, and I was able to take advantage of that from early on. The match was over in little more than an hour, and happily for Caesars Palace, the fans were able to take out their frustrations in the casino. If I'd been smarter when it became obvious after the first set that Manuel was struggling on the faster indoor court, as opposed to the slower clay of Forest Hills, I'd have taken my time and won anyway in the end. Then maybe Caesars would have signed us up for another Challenge Match. But Orantes was too good a player for me to give him any opening to get back into the match. Winning was the only thing that mattered, and I had to do it any way I could.

I was still pissed at the French tennis authorities for banning me in 1974, and once again I ignored Roland Garros in 1976, making Wimbledon my first Grand Slam of the year. I arrived in England after six tournament victories, as well as playing my part in the USA's 6–1 World Cup victory over Australia in March. My confidence was high.

I had a fairly easy passage to the quarterfinals, feeling that I was getting better after every match, until I ran into Roscoe Tanner. The weather had turned very hot, the grass on Centre Court at the All-England Club was bone-dry, and because of the heat, the ball traveled through the air like a bullet. Tanner's big serve proved to be a devastating weapon. Although I did everything I could to meet the challenge, he was too good on the day and sent me on a quick trip back home.

I hated losing any match, but I usually found it pretty easy to put losses behind me and move on. Having to leave early this time was not OK with me, though. Mom had set up some endorsements and advertising deals that included big bonuses if I won Wimbledon. As I said to a reporter at the time when he asked how much the defeat hurt, "I'm down two million bucks, buddy."

I could've been exaggerating, but not by much.

After winning three tournaments (in Washington, North Conway, and Indianapolis), I went into the West Side Tennis Club for the US Open in my best shape in almost two years. With Pancho riding shotgun, I felt confident that I could climb out of my Grand Slam slump.

That was the thing about Pancho—I knew that when I looked

up into the stands, I would see someone who wanted the victory as much as I did, and I was determined to please him.

I played some of my best tennis ever at that Open. By the quarterfinals I hadn't dropped a set, but I knew that if I was going to win the championship, I would have to raise my level of performance even further. To get to the finals I had to beat top clay-court specialists, Jan Kodes and Guillermo Vilas, back-to-back, and those two victories were exactly what I needed for my confidence. Laying in wait in the finals was the French Open champion and the best player in the world on clay, Björn Borg.

Now, for all the advice Pancho had given me throughout my career, he always kept in mind what Mom had said to him when she first brought me to Beverly Hills: "Do what you want with him, Pancho; make him better, but don't change his game." And that's exactly how we approached everything, working on new dimensions to supplement my natural game, not to replace it. In the 1975 semis, Pancho had advised me to slug it out from the baseline, but the night before this final, we decided to mix things up. We both knew that my game had developed over the past year and I was eager to see how the other strategies I had incorporated into it would work. No better time than the finals of a Grand Slam to try something new, right?

"Play to your strengths, Jimmy. Forget about him. Think only of what you are doing best. You are moving well and you're hitting the ball flatter than ever. Tomorrow, use that. Attack him; that's where your winning game is. Finish the points early."

With his speed, Borg could chase down every ball and make impossible shots. My new approach was to hit sharper angles, moving the Swede forward so that he couldn't stay in his baseline comfort zone. When I had the chance, I would hit deep to the corners and come to the net; that would shorten the points and disrupt his rhythm. But against Borg especially, I remembered Two-Mom and Mom's rule of thumb: "Always expect the ball to come back, Jimmy."

Never, ever think the point is over until it actually is. If I hit a perfect shot, way out wide, I always stayed ready for it to come back. The question was whether my game was at a level where I could match him, groundstroke for groundstroke, like I had the previous year.

New York fans have never been a quiet, unemotional bunch. That's what made the US Open so great; it was volatile, exciting, and aggressively loud for every match. And in 1976 the volume was turned up to a new level of craziness, thanks to my buddy Nasty.

I always tried to watch Nasty's matches whenever I could. His ability to make shots that were beyond everyone else was amazing. And then there was his attitude, which, in the second round, against the German Hans-Jürgen Pohmann, reached new heights—or should I say new lows? Yes, it was brutal—but what a show. The match turned into one of the most controversial of all time, and the fans and players poured in to see it as word spread around Forest Hills.

There was tension on the court from the very first point. I don't know why exactly, but Nasty told me later that he didn't like Pohmann's face, which would've been enough for Nasty. And the crowd could sense trouble brewing, which only added to the enjoyment. Nasty had been questioning calls during the first set, but when a fan called one of Nasty's shots out in the first-set tie-breaker, Nasty went berserk. He forced the point to be replayed, and after that he never calmed down.

As he challenged more calls in the second set, the crowd started booing him and throwing coins and drinks onto the court. Nasty responded by screaming even louder, spitting, and flipping them off. I thought, Nasty was going to spontaneously combust. One minute the fans hurled abuse at him, and then the next cheered him when he made another incredible shot. Believe me, Nasty ate it up.

Toward the end of the match, after Pohmann fell to the ground for the third time with cramps, the gloves came off. Nasty was sick of Pohmann's theatrics, and the two of them traded almost as many insults as shots. Nasty won the match but refused to shake either the umpire's or his opponent's hand. Instead, as they headed off the court, Nasty launched his parting shot at Pohmann, calling him a Nazi. All the players raced to the locker room to see what was going to happen next, and we weren't disappointed. Pohmann went after Nasty. Fortunately, one of the players intervened. I've gotta think that Pohmann would have had the best of it, but I'm glad it didn't come to that. It would have been a black eye for tennis—and probably one for Nasty as well. Oh, man, the pressures of the US Open. God, was tennis fun back then.

After all of that, the fans needed something even more momentous to finish off those 12 days of mayhem—and they got it in the final. Some of the shots that Borg and I played that day—he with his little wooden racquet and me with my T2000—were just flat-out crazy. The crowd responded with the kind of passion that showed their appreciation for fierce competitors and great tennis.

The first set went according to plan. I came into net when I could, following up my punishing groundstrokes by taking the ball out of the air whenever possible, not letting Borg settle into a rhythm. In the second set, I was hitting the ball so flat to the corners that I missed a few shots, both out wide and into the net, giving Borg a way back into the match, but I refused to let it put me off my game. I was playing to win, continuing to go for my shots.

Sitting back and letting Borg dictate the play—playing it safe like a lot of guys and hoping for the best—wasn't an option for me. Those missed shots just made me press even harder. Keep playing your game, Jimmy. That's what you do best. If you lose, OK, you lose, but it happens on your terms.

Going into the third set, I stuck to my game. I kept hitting flat, deep balls to the baseline, not letting Borg build on the momentum of winning the second set. It worked. The match had sapped our energy, and winning the tiebreaker in the third set proved to be the turning point. Fighting to the end is what tennis is all about for me, and with Borg you could take nothing for granted. But I got on top early in the fourth, won the title on my third match point, and added another Grand Slam to my collection.

In December 1975, I was supposedly finished—just a chubby, washed-up, fading superstar with no manager, no coach, and no fiancée.

By September 1976, I had my fourth Grand Slam, Mom looking after my business, Pancho in the stands, and Miss World to wake up to.

Washed-up ain't so bad.

"Jimmy, I've got to go home. Today. There's a flight this afternoon. I'm going to pack and call a cab to take me to the airport. I know it's short notice, sorry, but something has come up in LA."

It was November, and Marjie and I were having breakfast in our hotel suite in London. I was supposed to play the Wembley final that evening.

"What do you mean?" I asked her. "What's up? Is everything OK?"

"It's just work, Jimmy, nothing to worry about. You'll be OK here without me. Lornie will keep you company. Everything's fine."

She was right about one thing: My buddy from Illinois, Lornie Kuhle, was with me on tour. Mom wasn't traveling with me anymore, but she could still figure out if I was struggling by just watching my matches on television, then she'd call me to offer a solution. That's why I call her a genius, but maybe it was just because she really cared. She had an amazing ability to assess and analyze the smallest details of my game that needed work.

For his part, Lornie was a great organizer of my daily schedule, and he was able to take the pressure off me. We played a lot of backgammon, and there was always a chance that guys would be looking for a money game. We were happy to oblige.

One time, Lornie and I were at a tournament in Frankfurt and ran into some buddies who just happened to have a backgammon board. We stayed up four nights straight playing in their hotel room, Lornie and me against the two of them. The only time I left the room was to go play my matches. I'm making $250,000 for the event and I'm more excited about having a chance to win a couple thousand bucks on the backgammon board. It's crucial to have your priorities straight.

The other good thing about having Lornie along was that he understood tennis. As he says himself, he was a frustrated player who never made it, but he was close to Bobby Riggs and had picked up a lot of tips from him, which he was more than happy to pass on when we practiced. I didn't always listen, of course, but if Mom had talked to Lornie and given him a piece of advice on a part of my game, he would pass on exactly what she'd said. He became her mouthpiece.

"Tell Jimmy's he's tossing the ball too far out front on the second serve."

"He's not getting down low enough on the short balls. He's got to bend his knees more. Take the ball even earlier."

Lornie was good for my confidence, and he could also tell me when I was out of control. We had known each other for so long that I didn't mind, and he was usually right, anyway.

I couldn't get a straight answer out of Marjie all morning about why she had to leave. She kept saying that something had come up, it was important for her career, and she had to be back in LA to deal with it.

"Sure, but what is it?"

"It doesn't matter, Jimmy. It's not important. I've got to go, bye-bye, see you in LA in a few days. Good luck with your match."

And she was gone. That left me to take some revenge on Roscoe Tanner for my Wimbledon defeat by winning my 12th tournament of the year and securing my third-consecutive number one spot in the world rankings.

When I arrived back at LAX, I saw Marjie's face smiling at me from the cover of *People* magazine, with the headline MARJIE AND HER MEN. She hadn't even told me she had done the interview. OK, I get it. She's got to live her own life; that's fine by me. She wanted to be back in LA when the magazine came out. I know I wasn't headed to the altar, and I'm pretty sure she wasn't, either.

I called her when I got back to my apartment and told her I thought the piece was good and asked if she wanted to meet me for dinner. I knew how much the cover story meant to her, since she was trying to rebuild her career. But the fact that Marjie hadn't said a word to me about it, even though my face was there alongside George Best and Pete Revson, told me that we'd started the down-hill slide a little sooner than I expected.

We weren't over quite yet. I was hoping to enjoy some time off with Marjie in LA before the next tournament. But then my brother, Johnny, called from Belleville.

"You'd better come on home. Daddy's got cancer and it's not good."

Marjie and I hopped on the first plane out.

My dad, who hadn't been sick a day in his life, had been complaining of aches and pains in his back for a while and had been going to a chiropractor, but it wasn't helping. He decided to get some tests done, and when the doctors saw a spot on his lung, Dad went into the hospital for a biopsy. Once they opened him up, they realized that he had cancer that had started in his lungs and spread into his chest wall, his spine, bones, and just about everywhere in his body. The surgeon told Johnny and Mom that it was hopeless and that Dad wouldn't be going home.

It was strange, but a few weeks before Johnny had made that call to me, I had a weird feeling that I should be back home in Belleville. I can't even explain it; it was just an uncomfortable feeling that something was up. I even had a dream in which Dad was standing on a cliff, calling for me. Like he was saying, "Come back, I've got a problem, come back."

I ended up staying in Belleville for the nine weeks that my father was in the hospital. I wasn't looking for absolution; I was there because I wanted to be.

We made sure that someone was with Dad 24 hours a day. Mom wanted to be constantly by his side, but even when we'd send her home for a rest, she made my dad dinner so that he didn't have to eat the hospital food. My dad's sisters and their husbands and kids also took their turns, but it was usually Mom, Johnny, and me. My dad always thought he was coming home, but he was so fragile that he broke his back while he was lying in bed.

It was during those terrible nine weeks that my dad and I got the closest we had been in our lives. I'd spend hours at his bedside, and when he'd wake up, we'd talk, really talk, about things that previously would have been off limits, out of bounds. It was as though everything that had ever existed in our lives was contained in those hours together.

I remember that when Johnny and I were kids, Dad would hate it when we farted at the table. I mean he really hated it. In the hospital, with cancer invading his stomach, there were times when he would pass gas and the smell practically filled the whole hospital. I'm sitting there one night, and as I'm gagging on his fumes he grins.

"See, not so pleasant, right?"

Tennis had never been Dad's thing—it was his social life that was important to him—but it had, without a doubt, taken Mom and me away from him. But in the hospital, he told me he had seen what tennis had given me, and he understood that it wasn't just something Mom wanted to do. He realized that it had been a means to an end. My dad told me that he was always proud of me no matter what.

Sometimes you wait a lifetime for those kinds of words from your dad, and when they come, they mean everything.

I hadn't touched a racquet while I'd been in Belleville, and I was due to play the US Pro Indoor tournament in Philadelphia. I had decided not to go, but Dad said, "Jimmy, I'd like to see you play. Go win that tournament for me."

Marjie and I went to Philadelphia on January 23, and a week later I lost to Dick Stockton in five sets in the final. After the match, I called Mom from the hotel.

"Daddy's probably not going to last another day," she told me. "You need to get right back here."

Johnny picked Marjie and me up at the airport. I was tired and really hungry and we were driving down Main Street, so Johnny says, "Let's stop at Steak 'n Shake and get you something to eat." Steak 'n Shake had always been a favorite.

"No, I have a bad feeling I'd better get up to Dad's room."

"It'll only take five minutes," says Johnny. "You want a hamburger or not?"

"Johnny, just take me to Dad."

At the hospital, Johnny and I stood on either side of the bed, holding Dad's hands. Although he was slipping in and out of consciousness, he knew we were there and squeezed our hands as a sign of recognition.

Mom went out for a moment to get a cup of coffee. Dad took three big breaths, and on the last one he didn't exhale. I looked up at the clock and it was 10:22 p.m. The sports were on the local news, showing me losing the tournament in Philadelphia.

Not much more to say about that.

We spent the week after Dad's death helping Mom with all the arrangements. Dad was to be laid out at Brickler Funeral Home. The casket was open, and the wake lasted for two whole days. Dad knew everyone in the surrounding area, not just Belleville and East St. Louis but all of St. Louis and beyond. People just kept on coming: Johnny's friends, my friends, the mayors of several nearby cities, and all of my dad's buddies, including the great baseball players Stan Musial and Red Schoendienst, coach and manager of the St. Louis Cardinals at the time. They all came to pay their respects.

The funeral service was held in the Blessed Sacrament Church, and from there we went to the gravesite to lay Dad to rest. When we returned to our house, the party kicked off and didn't stop for 24 hours. The next day Dad's friends were still there drinking. It was a full-blown Irish funeral, a testament to the affection people felt for him. He was only 56 years old when he died but he had lived a full life.

After Dad's death, Mom was in a state of disbelief. Two-Mom had died five years before, and that had hit Mom hard, and now she was burying her husband. I was going back on the road, Johnny was living his own life, and she was alone. So in one way it was good that she had tennis to dive back into. After we buried Dad, Mom did what she had been taught to do: get on with it. And I did exactly the same thing, although looking back now I realize it probably wasn't the smartest thing I could have done.

A week after Dad's funeral I went to Toronto for a WCT tournament. I didn't really want to go, but I had an obligation and I thought it was better for me to keep busy. I was playing my good friend Eddie Dibbs in the semifinal when I had a total meltdown. After a few questionable line calls went against me, I lost my shit and jumped up onto the umpire's stand, grabbed him by the shirt, and was about to jerk him out of his chair when the thought occurred to me: Maybe this isn't such a good idea.

Dibbs, pal that he is, said to the umpire, "You can't let him do that! You have to default him."

It makes me laugh now.

"Yeah," I said quietly, "thanks for the help, you asshole."

12

MEETING MY MATCH

Marjie and I split for good not long after my father's death. We'd been together for more than a year, and although it was unspoken, I knew both of us felt that the relationship had run its course. I think Marjie realized around the time of the *People* article that the lifestyle I was leading wasn't really what she was looking for. Even though she'd dated other sports stars and was accustomed to the on- and off-season routine, tennis lasted all year round. George Best might have played two soccer games a week, Pete Revson might have raced twice a month, but I was playing tournaments that went on for a week, two for the big ones, sometimes with matches on consecutive days. When I wasn't playing, I had no desire to be in the public eye. I didn't want to have my photograph in the papers, and I hardly needed the added publicity. The less people knew about my private life, the happier I was. But that wasn't how Marjie rolled in those days.

I drove over to where she was staying with a friend, and we talked in my car.

"I don't know," I said, "but I think we're not going anyplace with this. I think our relationship is . . ." I searched for the right words, which Marjie already had.

"I think you're right," she said. "It's been fun . . ."

Even though on the surface it sounded casual, it was an emotional conversation. We both knew our relationship was over, but it didn't immediately erase the feelings we had for each other. At least for me. Looking back at it now, I wonder why all the women I broke up with took the news so easily.

March 1977. After the all-too-quick Orantes Challenge Match, Caesars Palace announced that they didn't want to host a fourth round of the winner-takes-all contests. Well, here I go again. First the breakups in my love life; now I'm being dumped by my beloved Vegas hotel.

But Caesars' attitude wasn't going to stop Bill. It didn't take him long to find a resort that was more than happy to host the next event. He moved the whole package to the Cerromar Beach Hotel, in Puerto Rico, where Nasty and I would go head to head for a winner-takes-all purse of $250,000, with CBS televising the match in prime time.

This was a big deal with a lot of money at stake, but as usual, Bill wanted more. I don't blame him; that's what he was good at, creating controversy and interest. This time, Bill's malarkey was that Nasty and I had gone from best of friends to bitter enemies.

Whenever Nasty and I played each other, we put our relationship to one side, and it was all about who was better on the day. It was no secret that this was tough for me; he knew my game inside out, and he was also good at taking advantage of our friendship. In any case, it was time for me to start asserting myself and earning back his respect. We both had tempers and were never shy about insulting each other across the net. We more than earned the nickname the press hung on us: "The Bad Boys of Tennis."

Once Bill got started marketing the match and manufacturing controversy to sell tickets, the tennis press, which will print any story that is fed to them (OK, there were some exceptions, like Mike Lupica, Neil Amdur, and Bud Collins—I'm sure I've left out a few more, but not many), was more than happy to report that Nasty and I had had a major falling-out.

In a pre-match press conference in Puerto Rico, Bill said that the rift occurred in a tournament Nasty and I had played the previous year. "They were big buddies for a while," he told the reporters, "but the split began in Nottingham, England, before Wimbledon. They were playing for $30,000 in the final. Each had won a set, and it began raining slightly in the third. Nastase got a service break, and Connors said, 'Let's quit,' and walked off the court."

Nothing could be further from the truth. So what really happened in Nottingham? The rain started falling before we even got onto the court, but since people were already in their seats, Nasty and I agreed to play as best we could. We slipped and slid our way through two sets, taking one apiece. It was entertaining and the fans enjoyed it. But at 1-1 in the third, with a service break each and the rain still coming down, conditions were getting a little too dangerous, so we agreed to stop the match and split the prize money. We may be tennis players, but we're not stupid. No one complained. We walked off the court to applause and laughter and hit the bar for a beer.

After the press gobbled up Bill's nonsense about Nasty's and my big fight, Nasty fed them even more baloney. He said that I was trying to get out of the match because less than two weeks before I'd defaulted in my final in Toronto against Dick Stockton, faking a knee injury. Never mind that I was leading 6-5 in the first set and had just lost my dad.

"Jimmy, for sure, don't want to see me on the court. For two years, I tried to get him in a Challenge Match, but he does not challenge me."

Well, maybe if you had been world number one for as long as Laver or had beaten me in a Grand Slam final like Newcombe or Orantes, I would've given you a call before now, Nasty.

And he didn't stop there: "I like Jimmy, but I know I have the game to beat him. And Jimmy, he knows it, too. It's Jimmy's way, always something wrong with him before a big tournament."

Classic. Of course I wasn't making a big deal about my knee injury, just as I hadn't made any excuses when I fractured my leg at Wimbledon in 1975, so I kept my mouth shut. I knew if I said anything, then the whole thing would blow up in my face and the press would crucify me. I thought about one of my favorite quotes, "Revenge is a meal best served cold," and that's what I was planning on doing. They could say anything they wanted to, but they would see the results on the court.

Puerto Rico was beautiful, hot and windy. Not ideal for tennis. In the days leading up to the match, Nasty and I didn't spend much time together, which only stoked the rumors of our feud. Over the years I had often practiced with Nasty, but how dumb was it to expect us to do that before a Challenge Match? He brought his practice partner and I brought mine. If people wanted to read something into that, then let them. It was irrelevant to me, and I think Nasty probably felt the same way.

One of my old UCLA teammates, Jeff Austin (Tracy's brother), agreed to be my on-court coach for the match. We were good friends, and he was able to hit the kind of shots that I knew I'd have to deal with when I played Nastase. Of course, Nasty was a little crazy and there are some things you just can't prepare for.

It turned out that the conditions in Puerto Rico worked in my favor. My hard flat groundstrokes weren't much affected by the wind, but because of the amount of topspin Nasty employed, he had trouble controlling his shots. I won in four sets, in what turned out to be a pretty calm match, but that became a footnote compared with the controversy over what I'd allegedly said to Nasty that morning. There had been a terrible earthquake in Bucharest, and as soon as I heard the news, my first thought was for Nasty's family. Before we went out on court, I said to him, "Nasty, I hope your mom and everyone are OK."

Nasty remembers it differently. In his autobiography, I'm quoted saying something like "Nasty, you better call home. You might not have a house anymore."

I had no idea that Nasty hadn't yet heard about the earthquake. I'll admit it wasn't beyond me to try to dig out any advantage I could over my opponents by getting them riled up before a match, but this wasn't one of those times. I was genuinely concerned about his family; I'd been to Romania with Nasty and met his mother, and you know how I am about mothers!

St. Louis Arena, a week later. It's the semifinals of the WCT tournament, and Nasty has a disgusted look on his face because of what he feels is another bad call in my favor. He stands there for so long that I start to get bored and mimic his expression, to the delight of the crowd. Nasty walks to the net.

"This stinks, Connors boy. They only clap for you."

"What do you expect? This is my home. But if you want to win that bad, I'll give it to you."

"Screw you."

I go on to win 7–5, 6–4. Career tally against Nasty: 15–6. I'm reeling him in.

As for the press, I'm sure that moment at the net provided many of its members with further proof that Nasty and I were no longer on speaking terms.

After the match, we went out for dinner together. As usual.

The next month, in Vegas, April 10: Nasty and I are in each other's faces. It must be another big money match.

"You're not a little baby. So quit acting like one."

"Fuck you, Connors boy! Maybe you should go get your mommy."

"Now, you know better than that. Don't bring mothers into it."

He's just questioned a line call and I'm pissed. We're in the first set of the $100,000 winner-takes-all WCT Challenge Cup, where I'm defending a 13-match unbeaten run at Caesars Palace. There's a lot at stake—the money, my streak, and revenge for Puerto Rico—and so we're both feeling the pressure. Nothing new.

I start fast and I'm up 5-1 in the first set before I hit the wall. I'm lucky to win the set, and nothing goes right from there. Nasty's game picks up and he's anticipating my every move, giving me no time to set for my shots. He senses things starting to change in his favor and he starts taunting me. Now all the imaginary animosity from before is becoming real. Now I do hate him. I can't get my emotions under control, and my game, well, what the hell? Nasty wins the next three sets and the title.

I refuse to talk to the press after the match. I know what they're going to ask; it'll be all about how Nasty and I used to be friends and now we hate each other. In reality, all they know is what we want them to know. So keep guessing, boys. Nasty and I have been friends since I was 16 years old. So what if we blow up over a match or two? It was all part of our show. We were friends. We still are today.

In May of 1977, I was still in the legal dispute with Bill Riordan about the share of my earnings he was demanding, and as a part of my counterclaim, a letter of agreement, which spelled out the financial terms of the Orantes Challenge Match, was attached as an appendix. The *Washington Post* picked this up at the same time as the *New York Times* was digging into the details of my match with Nasty in Puerto Rico.

Both newspapers came to the same conclusion: that the winner-takes-all matches weren't really winner-takes-all. No shit. Was anybody really surprised? Did people honestly think we were going to play high-profile matches, with millions of people watching on TV, and the loser was going to walk away empty-handed? That's crazy. Caesars Palace did put up the cash for the winner in those events they hosted, and, yes, money from sponsorships, television rights, et cetera, all went into a pot. Whether we actually received everything we should have—that's irrelevant now. In my opinion, if I had lost, the appeal of the Challenge Matches would have ended. Nobody else could have carried it, and I had a good thing going. Winning was the priority, but the loser's cut was still substantial. At least that's what I've heard.

I'm grateful for the opportunity to have been able to play the four Challenge Matches, against four of the greatest players in tennis history. It was Bill Riordan's vision and the participation of Caesars Palace, CBS, and all the sponsors that really made them possible. Next to Billie Jean King and Bobbie Riggs's Battle of the Sexes, my Challenge Matches were some of the most watched tennis matches ever. Like 'em or not, they did their job by creating more interest, inspiring more participation, and increasing the popularity of the game.

I had stayed loyal to Bill Riordan's circuit for several years, resisting the temptation of signing with the WCT, even when Nasty did, in 1974. But by 1977, so much had changed in my life that I decided it was time to accept Lamar Hunt's offer. While Riordan's traveling road show was going to places like Little Rock and Salisbury, Hunt was taking his events to Mexico City, Rotterdam, Bologna, Monte Carlo, Toronto, and London. He was helping to promote tennis internationally.

I signed with the WCT for a year. What a mistake that was. I should have agreed to a 10-year deal. And I won't pretend the money they offered didn't play a part in my decision.

The WCT series ran from January through May, with points on offer from each event, as well as big prize money. The top eight players would then come together in Dallas to see who would be the WCT champion of the year. On top of that, players signing a WCT contract were given a financial guarantee—in my case, $750,000 to play five events, plus prize money. That would grab anyone's attention, but the appeal of the WCT was way more than that. Tennis was changing, and I wanted to be at the heart of it. But the main reason I ultimately signed with the WCT was for the chance to work with Lamar Hunt.

A well-known Texas oilman, Mr. Hunt was just as passionate about sports as he was about his many business interests. He was one of the original investors in the Chicago Bulls; earlier, he had founded the American Football League, in 1960, and three years later moved his Dallas Texans to Kansas City, where they became the Kansas City Chiefs. He was instrumental in persuading the AFL and NFL to merge in 1966, which led to the creation of the Super Bowl. So you can thank Lamar Hunt for every Super Bowl party you've ever been to, and all the guacamole you've eaten there.

Hunt was a gentleman: fair, honest, down-to-earth, a class act. And, boy, did he look after his players, treating them better than he treated himself. I was on a number of flights when he would make sure I flew first-class while he rode coach with the people who worked for the WCT.

Lamar Hunt was good for tennis. He generated money, interest, and excitement, and the Dallas finals started to rival the Slams. Of course, it's precisely because of his success that the tennis establishment tried to get rid of him. They didn't like the competition and they were always looking for ways to destroy what he was creating. They pretty much succeeded the year after I signed up. They negotiated the merger of Jack Kramer's Grand Prix circuit with the WCT. Even though the Dallas finals continued into the late 1980s, the magic had gone out of it. But, in my opinion, if that merger hadn't happened and Hunt had ended up owning tennis, the game would have been better off.

In my first and only full WCT season, I made it through to the finals in Dallas, a classy event where all the seats were sold out. I played Dick Stockton and was lucky to escape with a four-set victory. I later played in two more WCT finals, both against a young, curly-haired, bandana-wearing left-hander from New York with a bad attitude, winning in 1980 and losing in 1984. We'll come to him in a minute.

But I'll always have great memories of that first final in 1977. It was a standout year for me, a year when the WCT and Lamar Hunt were, for a brief, happy moment, the future of tennis.

Just when you're not expecting it, your life changes dramatically. In May 1977, I met the only true competition for my love of tennis.

Spencer and I had been invited to Hugh Hefner's Playboy Mansion for the filming of an ABC special to celebrate the Playmate of the Year. When he asked me if I was planning to attend, I said, "Are you crazy? Of course I'm going."

I'd been to previous events at the mansion—the Midsummer Night's Dream Party, a Halloween Party, various boxing matches—each one more elaborate than the last. Other times I stopped by just to enjoy the scenery, you know, strolling through his private zoo . . . checking out his video-game room . . . Who am I kidding? I went there because he had the biggest collection of beautiful women in the world.

And this time, Hef pulled out all the stops. There were cocktail waiters in tuxedos, gorgeous women, champagne flowing, gorgeous women . . .

After an hour or so of hanging out, seeing old friends and making new ones, I gathered with all the guests at the foot of the stairs for the presentation of the Playmate of the Year. With the cameras rolling, Hef, dressed, as always, in his silk bathrobe and pajamas, and holding his trusty pipe, announced, "Ladies and gentlemen, please welcome your Playmate of the Year 1977, Miss Patti McGuire."

And there she was. The *life*-changer. The last thing I was looking for and the end of my life as I knew it.

She walked down the stairs and was given a huge bouquet of roses from . . . is that Alice Cooper? I hardly recognized him without his makeup.

Patti was the most beautiful girl I'd ever seen. All I could do was stare at her. "Hi, Mom and Dad," she said. "I want to thank Hef, because if he hadn't invented the Playmate, none of us would be here. I'd like to thank Pompeo Posar, my photographer, because I love him. Thank you, everyone."

And that was it. She walked into the crowd and I followed her. I knew I had some fierce competition, but that's never stopped me before. I approached her and tried to stay as cool as possible.

"Congratulations," I said, "and I think it was really nice of you to remember your parents."

"Thank you," she said before she turned and walked away. Not exactly the reaction I was hoping for.

I looked at Spencer.

"I guess we can go now," I said.

Later, Patti would tell me that her girlfriend Deborah Svensk had a crush on me, and she didn't want to complicate their friendship.

I wouldn't see Patti McGuire again for a year.

It's Wimbledon 1977, my first Grand Slam of the year, and London is buzzing on and off the court. At the same time that Queen Elizabeth is celebrating her Silver Jubilee, the All-England Club is marking its centenary, with a parade before the opening match featuring 42 of the 52 surviving past singles champions.

There are British flags flying almost everywhere you look, and a strong whiff of patriotism is in the air. This is not a good time to piss off the locals.

On the Saturday before the start of the tournament, I'm hitting with John Newcombe and Lornie Kuhle on a private grass court at the home where Newcombe is staying. It's wet, and I wouldn't normally risk playing under these conditions but I'm short on grass-court practice.

Newk serves to my backhand, and as I set myself for the return, the ball skids off the damp grass, forcing me to readjust my grip at the last minute. As I'm about to hit the shot, my right hand slips and my thumb catches in the prongs of my open-throated T2000. When I make contact with the ball, my thumb is jerked back hard.

"Shit! I think I've broken my fucking thumb!"

I try hitting for a minute or two, but it's no use. My thumb is turning black.

"You need a doctor, Jimmy," Lornie says.

We go to St. George's Hospital, on Hyde Park Corner, where they X-ray my hand. When the technician comes out with the results he is both smiling and shaking his head.

"Well Mr. Connors, I'm glad I didn't have a fiver on you to win the title. Your thumb is broken. There's going to be no Wimbledon for you this year, I'm afraid."

"Thanks," I say, "but don't fucking bet on it."

I returned to the hotel to stick my hand in ice, and early the next morning I was back at St George's to try and figure out a solution.

By now my thumb was swollen and throbbing. It hurt like hell and I was having trouble holding on to the racquet, let alone gripping it tight enough to deal with the speed and the unreliable bounce of Wimbledon's grass courts.

The doc put a splint on my thumb so that it was sticking out at an angle away from the racquet. Lornie and I then went off to the practice courts to hit some balls. The splint was uncomfortable, but what bothered me most was the clicking of the metal bandage against my metal T2000. Looking back, I should have left it alone; the noise could have driven my opponents crazy.

After half an hour of practice, it was clear that the splint wasn't working.

"Shit, Lornie, we're going to have to go back. I know it's never going to be a hundred percent, but if he can change the splint even a little, it might help."

Back at the hospital, the doc put a cotton sleeve over the metal splint, and an hour later Lornie and I were back on the court.

"How's it feel now, Jimmy?"

"Better, but still not right. At least the clicking sound is gone."

This went on all day, back and forth between the court and hospital until it was too dark to play.

"Jimmy," the doctor said to me on our last visit of the day (by now we were on a first-name basis), "I think I can see a way to tweak the splint some more. I'll work on it tonight. Come back first thing in the morning to pick it up."

"Thanks but I'm playing tomorrow, so if we don't fix it by lunchtime, I'm screwed."

I'm almost the first one on the practice courts at Wimbledon the next day, trying out the latest version of my splint. It's an improvement, but it's still not right. I can't control my shots like I know I'll have to.

I call the doc from the pay phone by the locker room and tell him what I think the problem is.

"Can you bring a new one over here? I'm really sorry. I don't think I can make it to your office and back again before I'm due on court. The centenary parade is at one o'clock. I've got to be there."

Two hours later, I see Lornie running toward me. He's been over at the gates waiting to meet the doctor so he can bring him to the practice courts. He's alone.

"You're not going to believe this, Jimmy. They won't let him in! He doesn't have a ticket!"

I look at my watch. 12:30. Shit.

"I tried to explain to the security guys, but they won't listen."

I run over to the fence, where the doctor hands me the new splint.

"Jimmy, go hit a few balls. Quickly. See how it feels."

Now I'm really beginning to sweat. On my way back I run into Nasty. He's heading in the opposite direction, to Centre Court, where the big parade of past champions starts in 20 minutes.

"Nasty, I need your help."

"But Jimmy, we . . ."

"Give me a minute, son. I need you to hit with me."

He agrees and pushes me pretty hard. My thumb feels OK. Not perfect, but good enough.

12:55. I race back to the doc, who's waiting by the fence.

"Thanks. It'll get me through my match. Tomorrow we can work on it some more."

I arrive at the entrance to Centre Court too late. I've missed my place in the parade by a few minutes. Only 41 surviving champions receive a medal from the Duke of Kent. But I'm pretty sure I'm not going to be missed, even though I'm the top seed this year. And an official at the door confirms it for me.

"It's no big deal, Jimmy," he says.

Man, was he ever wrong.

The booing starts the second I walk out onto Centre Court. I'm the third match that afternoon, and word has obviously traveled fast around the grounds. Even people who weren't at the parade have heard about me standing up the Duke of Kent, and they all seem to agree. Connors not only thinks he's better than 7 Up; he thinks he's better than royalty.

I've pissed off the locals. Good work, Jimmy.

To make matters worse, I'm playing a Brit, Richard Lewis, in the first round. Being the villain doesn't worry me; I like it, as you've probably gathered by now, but even by my own low standards it's clear this match is going to be brutal. Better just get it over with.

Lewis serves the first point of the match. I get ready to return it. Backhand. This is the first real test of my thumb, and the grass is still damp. Can't worry about any of that now.

BOOF! Lewis's serve shoots off the wet grass at a weird angle and flies right into my crotch, and the pain in my thumb is now nothing compared with the pain in my nuts. Down I go. I'm on my knees and 15,000 people jump to their feet to cheer and clap. Jeez! You would have thought that a Brit had just won Wimbledon instead of just nearly neutering me.

I win the match with nuts the size of grapefruits, 6-3, 6-2, 6-4. *Take that*, I think as I go and sit in a bucket of ice.

The next day I went back to St. George's for a tweak on the splint and that was the end of it. I never mentioned it again and no one seemed to notice.

That was the good news. The bad news was that the press went into a full tabloid frenzy when I didn't make the parade, and the prissy Wimbledon authorities called me into the principal's office, once again, to tell me how much they didn't appreciate my bad manners. Come on, guys, it's not like I looked up the Queen's skirt. I was just doing everything I could to fulfill my obligation to you people as a professional tennis player. So back off!

I'm still seething as I'm being driven back to my hotel. We're waiting at a traffic light when a guy in a truck honks his horn at us.

"Connors, hey! Jimmy Connors!" he shouts.

Here we go. This is all I need, some asshole about to give me a hard time. I roll down the window, ready to launch a few verbal missiles. And he says in his Cockney accent, "Nice one, Connors. Fuck the Duke!" and sticks out his middle finger.

My kind of guy.

Seriously, I know the All-England Club is a stickler for rules, but let's put the blame where it should be: All the Club had to do was to allow the doctor to enter its hallowed grounds for five minutes. I would have had my emergency splint, I would have made the centenary parade, the truck driver wouldn't have flipped off the Duke, and none of this would have been an issue. But then again, where's the fun in that? It would have left the All-England Club with nothing to complain about.

There was a kid from New York making some noise at Wimbledon that year. He'd come through qualifying and upset some top players: Sandy Mayer in the fourth round, Phil Dent in the quarters. I never met him, never even saw him play, I didn't know anything about his game, but during those two weeks in London I was starting to hear his name.

John Patrick McEnroe. My semifinal opponent.

The first time I ever laid eyes on McEnroe was in the men's locker room at Wimbledon, minutes before we walked out onto

Centre Court. He looked like the Pillsbury Doughboy with a head-band. I had to ask myself, how the hell did he even qualify? I'd been in his shoes five years ago at the Pacific Southwest tournament, about to play the great Aussie champion Roy Emerson. I had nothing to lose that day, and Roy had everything. Now the roles were reversed and I wasn't going to give this up-and-comer an inch. If I could rattle him, I would.

He came up to me and introduced himself. I grabbed my bag and racquets and walked past him—no smile, no hello, no handshake, no acknowledgement of his existence. I'm nothing if not gracious.

It didn't take me long to figure out this skinny kid was probably going to be around for a while. But that was OK; I knew how to deal with guys like McEnroe; I'd played Nastase long enough. It didn't matter if it was his tennis or his attitude, I had to be ready. But he was still a handful. His game and his shot-making ability were impressive, and I had to do everything I could that day to win the match in four sets. It was clear to me right then that this young talent would be a force to be reckoned with in years to come. He wanted what I already had, and I understood that, but I also knew he was going to have to fight me for it.

After I got rid of McEnroe, only Björn Borg stood in the way of my second Wimbledon title.

I had a good record against Borg going into that final, and although he was the defending champion, I was confident I had the game to beat him on grass, a surface that we had never competed on. Borg was a very good grass player—don't get me wrong. His run of five consecutive Wimbledon titles, including one against McEnroe when Mac was the best in the world on the surface, proves that. He was superfast and never missed a ball. But he wasn't invincible. None of us were.

Borg should have lost to Mark Edmondson in the second round

in 1977, when he was two sets down. A year later, in a first-round match, Victor Amaya was leading him two sets to one, and again in 1979 Vijay Amritraj had match points against Borg but failed to convert them. What was going on? Was Borg bored playing all those early-round matches and had lost interest? Maybe, but then something would happen; he'd get a lucky break, or his opponent would relax and let him back into it by playing a careless shot, and you could imagine Borg thinking, "Screw it, I may as well give it a go." He had a reputation of being ice-cold, but I never bought that. Everybody feels something on the inside, whether they show it or not.

Borg had one big advantage on grass—his underrated volley. It was soft, and he didn't bury you when he was at the net. Normally that would be a weakness, but not in the second week of Wimbledon, because by then all the serve-and-volley guys—and there were a lot of them—would have bruised (that's tennis talk for tearing up the grass) the section of court between the service line and the net. Exactly where Borg's short volleys would land and die instantly. That was tough to play against.

Looking at Wimbledon today, it's almost like a different tournament. They lay a more durable grass now, which allows the ball to bounce up, almost like on a hard court. Even by the finals, the grass looks like it hasn't even been played on. With players staying back more, it's now just along the baseline that any damage to the court is noticeable. Actually, it's more like six feet behind the baseline, where the guys seem to play today.

In my day, the bounces were inconsistent and very low, so taking the ball out of the air was more of a priority. Wimbledon was not accustomed to baseline tennis back then; most past champions were serve-and-volley specialists. Borg–Connors was a different kind of battle.

The other key element behind Borg's success is that Wimbledon suited his personality. Like Roger Federer in recent years, Borg's polite demeanor embodied the values the All-England Club considered sacred: tradition and keeping your mouth shut. Apparently, they thought I had a weakness in those areas. I always felt some tension whenever I walked through the gates, knowing I had to temper my behavior. Borg was comfortable there, and it showed in his tennis.

The 1977 final went all the way to the fifth, both of us playing at the top of our games, but not simultaneously. I won the opening set with ease; I couldn't do a thing wrong. But you could never relax against Borg, especially in the finals. Once he found his stride, I lost my concentration, and Borg won the next two sets easily.

Pancho was watching from the players' box, and I knew what he was thinking. There's no point sitting back now. Attack and go for the jugular. I break serve at 6-5 to take the match to the final set.

Then I blink and find myself 0-4 down. How did that happen?

Dig deep. You're not out of this yet.

I pull it back to 4-4, 15-0 on my serve. The momentum is all with me, and Borg looks shattered. I'm not used to seeing that.

Keep the pressure on, Jimmy.

I'm getting ready to serve, bouncing the ball, when I hear a shout from the crowd, a wiseass comment I can't quite make out. It's followed by some laughter.

Just ignore it, Jimmy, keep concentrating. You are two games away from your second title.

I can't help it. I look up to where the loudmouth in the stands is sitting and the spell is broken. I double-fault and don't win another point in the match.

Really? I'm that thin-skinned that I let some idiot get in my head?

I guess so.

I got back to LA after being gone a month, and written in dust across the hoods of my Porsche and my 1968 Ferrari was a welcome-home message:

u fucking loser!

Another fan I didn't know I had.

Some guy's calling me a loser and I've got a Porsche and Ferrari in my parking space and I've just played the Wimbledon final. I had to laugh.

It's been a month since the final with Borg and I've hardly played at all. I had to pull out against Cliff Richey in San Antonio when I couldn't hold my racquet the way I needed to.

And now I'm sitting in an office in Belleville, talking to a doctor buddy of mine who is looking at my thumb. I knew there was a problem when I took the splint off and my thumb was frozen in place. I guess it didn't set right.

"Jimmy, hang on a minute, I have to do something. Put your hand on the table and let my nurse take a good look at it," the doc says.

I lay my right hand down flat, spreading the fingers. The nurse asks me a question but I miss it. I ask her to repeat what she said.

Crack!

I spin around to see my doctor just as he smacks my thumb with a rubber mallet! What the . . . ? I clench my left fist to pop him one, just as the room begins to spin.

I'm only out for a few seconds. When I come around, he's sitting next to me and my hand is throbbing like crazy.

"Should I be mad at you?" I ask.

"Sorry, Jimmy, but it was the only way. Your thumb needed to be reset, which means it had to be rebroken. I could have put you under first, but I figured if I told you that, you'd never go for it."

He was probably right. I don't think I would ever have risked an operation on my hand. I would have just given myself the rest of the year to see if I could work out a way to play with my thumb as it was. So thank God for that rubber mallet; within three weeks I was pretty much back to normal. Just in time for the US Open.

It's a good thing I've never worried about winning any popularity contests, because the New York fans at Forest Hills that year were ruthless. They made the Wimbledon crowd look like a bunch of . . . well, like a bunch of well-behaved Brits.

New Yorkers were in no mood to fool around during that ridiculously hot summer. They were still pissed off about the July 13 blackout, which caused looting in the streets and fires across the city. They were in the middle of electing a new Mayor, Ed Koch or Mario Cuomo, and the choice had polarized the voters. The only good news was that they had finally arrested Son of Sam, the serial killer who had terrorized the city for far too long, and that the Yankees were poised to return to the World Series following their defeat the previous year by the Cincinnati Reds.

So emotions were running high, and even today, 35 years later, it's considered the wildest US Open ever.

Well, to start with, a large crowd of fans staged a sit-in when the officials tried to switch an afternoon match to the evening. They then had to move one of the evening matches forward in order to avoid a riot. Then there was an anti-apartheid protest (against the participation of South African players), and a bomb threat, and someone in the crowd was even shot during the third-round McEnroe–Dibbs match, apparently the result of a stray bullet fired in Queens.

The atmosphere was tense and volatile, but it took me until the semifinals to really blow things up. My back had been giving me trouble, so I'd been pretty quiet, trying to close out my matches as quickly as I could, and I hadn't dropped a set by the time I met the unseeded Italian Corrado Barazzutti in the semis.

We were 3-3 in the first set. Barazzutti had questioned about nine line calls already, and I was getting ready to lose it.

At break point against me, I passed him with a backhand, right on the line, and it was called in. Barazzutti just stood there and stared down at some imaginary mark in the clay.

"Come on! Not again! The ball was good!" I yelled.

He still didn't move. So I did. I ran round the net to where he was standing and used my shoe to rub out whatever he was looking at. For a second no one could believe what had just happened. Neither could I. Oops. Even I knew I'd gone too far.

The fans went bat-shit crazy, booing and screaming as though I'd caused another citywide blackout. The umpire tried to maintain some order, but it was useless. The noise level was deafening. Eventually he made himself heard.

"Mr. Connors, I know you did that in fun, right?"

"Oh, yeah. How'd you know?"

"OK, the ball was good. Play on."

I didn't think it was possible for the fans to get even louder, but they did, and they called me everything they could think of, and New Yorkers have rich imaginations. Now I was pissed. I'd won the point fairly, I'd done nothing (much) wrong, and I was the only American still standing in our national tournament.

I finally turned to the stands and confronted the hecklers.

"I'm all you've got left in this tournament! You should be pulling for me, not him!"

Come on, guys! I'm the defending US Open champion. Work with me here. Cut me some frickin' slack!

They weren't listening, and the biggest cheers of the night came whenever I missed a shot. OK, if this is the way it's going to be, fine. I still like the energy here in New York.

By the end of the match, I still hadn't dropped a set.

That semi was nothing compared with the final, which was just plain ugly. I took the first set 6-2 against Argentina's Guillermo Vilas, and it was all downhill from there. I lost the second set 6-3, the third in a tiebreaker. In the fourth, at match point, I hit a forehand down the line, Vilas chipped a return, and I buried the easy volley. It was good, I know it was, but Vilas was glaring at the linesman. *Screw him. I've won the point. It's deuce.*

I turn around and walk to my service line. What the hell is going on? Why are the fans pouring onto the court and lifting Vilas onto their shoulders? Then John Corman, the umpire, raises his hand and points.

"Mr. Vilas wins . . ."

More and more people are swarming around, bumping me, pushing me, swearing at me. It's nuts out here, not to mention dangerous. I pick up my bag and my friend Doug Henderson acts like a blocking back for me on our way off the court. It's pandemonium, and Vilas is the US Open champion.

How's my mood? Cranky at best. I was swinging at the onrushing fans just like my brother Johnny taught me. Of course, I would get criticized for not shaking Vilas's hand, because in case you haven't heard, tennis is a gentlemen's game. Are you kidding me?

Within minutes, Pancho, Mom, Doug, and I are in our Ford Pinto and long gone. That was the last time the US Open was played on clay and held at Forest Hills. Well, nothing like going out with a bang.

I might have been down but I wasn't out. Four months later I was back in New York, playing Vilas in the Masters at Madison Square

Garden. It was late at night and fans were hanging from the rafters and cheering the tennis we were playing.

Somehow, something had changed since Forest Hills, and I still don't know why. The atmosphere in the Garden that night was new to me. I lost the match 7–5 in the third, after making a big comeback, and through it all I could feel that the fans were on my side. It was like they finally got me. I was a fighter, I gave them everything, and now they were taking me in as one of their own.

In my interview on the court at the end of the match, I gave the crowd a message: "Don't count me out." They responded with a huge roar, which carried me through the rest of the tournament, including victory in the finals over Borg. From the ovation I received, it was clear that this was the result the New Yorkers had come to see.

13

BJÖRN AGAIN

'll chase that sonuvabitch Borg to the ends of the earth.

Borg has just beaten me 6-2, 6-2, 6-3 in the 1978 Wimbledon final and I'm hot. Losing three finals in four years on those grass courts does that to you, and when asked how I feel about losing, I respond that I'm not about to roll over and accept the result without a fight. It's intended as a compliment to Borg, but of course the press sees it as being disrespectful to the reigning champion.

Borg had announced he would consider playing the Australian Open at the end of the year if he still had a chance at the Grand Slam. He'd already won the French and now Wimbledon, and he was the only one who *could* win it. I couldn't let that happen. I wanted to hunt him down and even the score as soon as I could. If that meant flying halfway around the world to Australia, then that's what I was going to do. Fortunately, I didn't have to travel that far, because first he had to win the US Open.

I am in the backgammon room at Pips International, in Beverly Hills—one of my favorite places, a restaurant, bar, and disco run by my buddy Joe DeCarlo. I called Joe earlier in the evening to ask if Lornie and I could come over and hang with him, since I just got back from Wimbledon. I walk in and see Joe sitting at the table with Patti McGuire.

I came here for two reasons: to relax and blow off some steam, but that all changes the moment I see Patti.

I hadn't been looking for love that night at Hef's mansion, but I found her and then I lost her, and this time I wasn't going to let her get away.

I'd had a busy year, and at the same time I was trying to find a way to hook up with Patti again. I found out we had a mutual friend in James Caan's sister Barbara, and whenever I'd see her, I'd ask about Patti. I also tried through Barbara's other brother, Ronnie. I'd bump into him at parties in LA and ask the same questions. But none of it got me anywhere. And now, here she is, sitting next to me, playing backgammon with Joe. After a little while Joe has to go off and attend to some of his other customers, leaving Patti and me on our own. She asks if I want to play backgammon with her. We play two games and she kicks my ass.

"Jeez," I say, "this just isn't my week."

"What do you mean?"

"I just lost in the finals of a really big tournament."

Patti doesn't really know anything about tennis and she doesn't follow it. She smiles.

"Well, if I would have known that, I would have tanked and let you win to make you feel better."

We decide to go into the disco, and we're having a great time dancing and I'm thinking, "Man, this is too good to be true. Something has to go wrong." Then Patti decides to call it a night. I don't want her to leave, and I try and stall a little.

"Patti, can I ask you four questions before you leave?"

"Sure."

"Do you play tennis?"

"No."

"Have you ever been to a tournament?"

"No."

"Watched one on TV?"

"No."

"Do you know who I am?"

"Yes, because you were on the cover of *Time* magazine."

I want to ask her one more question, but think I've pushed it far enough for one evening, and getting a no if I ask her out would be devastating.

The next day I call Joe.

"Hey, Joe, I was just wondering, do you know anything about Patti's social status? I'd like to give her a call."

"Jimmy, it's not really my place to say, but I can check to see if it's OK for you to call her if you want."

He telephones me an hour later. "I've spoken to Patti. Here's her number. Good luck."

That was the start. As Joe said to Patti afterward, "Jesus Christ, I give him your number and I don't hear anything from either of you for a week!" I'm patting myself on the back right now.

Our first date is at Carlos and Charlie's, the club on Sunset Boulevard. I find out she grew up less than 40 minutes from where I was born, but on the St. Louis side of the river.

Late that night, we go back to my apartment, and I know for sure I'm never going to let her leave. Not in a chain-her-in-the-basement kind of way (although it does cross my mind); I just don't want to be where she isn't. Early the next morning, Mom pounds on my door. She's been staying in my second bedroom, and I guess I forgot to tell Patti about that.

"Jimbo, it's nine o'clock," Mom calls out.

Patti bolts up in bed.

"Who the hell is that?"

"Oh, that's just my mom," I say.

"Your mom? Are you kidding me?!"

"Jimbo, you up?" calls Mom.

"*Jimbo?*" Patti whispers, looking at me. "I didn't know anyone was called Jimbo anymore except on *The Waltons*."

"That's Jim Bob, you twit," I say, laughing. "It's OK, she's cool."

"Oh, crap. This really isn't going to look good."

Patti jumps out of bed and rushes to get her clothes on. She's going to try and sneak out before Mom sees her.

"No, come and meet her," I say.

I introduce Patti to Mom, and Mom looks pleased to meet her, I'm sure figuring she'll never see her again. Just another one of Jimbo's girls.

Patti and I only have a few days together before I'm back on the road again, heading for the clay courts of the Washington Star International. I know I'm going to miss her; the past few days have been everything I could ever have hoped for. More, in fact.

While I'm in DC, Patti and Joe call me from a table at Pips, where they're having dinner.

"Hey, guess what?" says Patti. "We're just sitting a couple of tables down from one of your old friends, Marjie Wallace, and her new husband, Michael Kline. Would you like to say hi?"

"No," I say, laughing. I really wouldn't. Patti and I chat for a moment, and then I make one of the best decisions of my life.

"I want you to come to Washington," I say. "How does that sound?"

"OK, I'll get a flight tomorrow."

Simple as that.

Washington, DC, was a miserable 100 degrees with humidity in the nineties. Playing in that kind of weather is hard work and sucks the life out of you, with the added bonus of making everyone short-tempered. I guess it was a good thing that Patti was getting to see me in that cranky state before she found herself in too deep with me.

In the quarters I faced Hans Gildemeister, of Chile, in a match where he stopped play for almost 10 minutes, arguing a call, and then went on to question every shot that came within three inches of any line. Finally, I'd had enough. The next time he disputed a call, I told him to stop his whining.

"Play the game!" I said. "God darn it. It's hot out here." God *darn* it? Yeah, I know it doesn't sound like me, but Patti was in the stands and I was trying to impress her with my maturity.

When Gildemeister answered me, he didn't bother toning it down at all. I glanced up at Patti, hoping she'd think I was the gentleman on the court. I don't think she was fooled for a second.

On the day of the finals, the temperature hit 108 suffocating degrees, and I came up against my buddy, Eddie Dibbs, in the best shape of his life and willing to stay out there all day. He'd already won over $500,000 in prize money that year, more than anyone else on the US circuit. Unfortunately for him, there was no way I was going to lose that match with Patti watching. I had to show her that I could at least earn a living.

It was brutal. Halfway through the match I had to change shoes; the ones I was wearing were soaked with sweat. Nowadays they have what's called a "comfort break" for the players and the opportunity to leave the court anytime they want. But back then we couldn't leave the court at all. So what's a guy to do when he's gotta, you know, go? I was pouring sweat and soaking wet, and the clay court was already damp, so I took a leak right there. (It wasn't one of those Secretariat kind of things, but I did hit the service line.) I kept a smile on my face the entire time, and nobody noticed, not even the eagle-eyed members of the press.

The intensity of the heat drained Eddie and me of energy but not determination. It was a war of attrition, and the winner would be the last man standing, but hopefully not in my puddle. Eventually, relying on guts and relentless stubbornness, I was able to outlast Dibbs. Unlike Patti, it wasn't pretty.

After DC, Patti agreed to come with me to Indianapolis for the national Clay Courts, her second-ever tennis tournament. But before that, we had to fly back to LA so I could pick up some fresh clothes. There wasn't a dry-cleaner in the world who wanted to touch what I'd been wearing to win that tournament.

In Indianapolis, I wanted Patti to stay, but she had to fly back to LA after my first match for a modeling assignment. Fortunately, Patti returned in time to see me play some of the best clay-court tennis of my career, beating Mac in the quarters, Orantes in the semis, and Spain's José Higueras in the finals. I realize that it wasn't simply that I wanted to impress her but that something more important was happening: I was happy.

Patti, an independent woman in every sense, insisted on paying for all her plane tickets. "I'm here because I want to be with you," she said. "Nothing else." Even though she didn't know much about tennis, she enjoyed cheering me on; after the matches were over, she wasn't interested in them. Which was fine with me. I've never wanted to live and breathe tennis after I walked off the court. Tennis was important, it was my business, and it had offered me an escape from East St. Louis, but when it was done, it was done.

I could relax with Patti after my matches. We didn't need to be seen out and about in public. Pretty quickly I knew she was the person I'd been looking for all my life. I wasn't planning on going anywhere else, and I hoped she wasn't either.

My winning streak continued through mid-August at the first-ever Grand Prix tournament staged at the Topnotch Resort, in Stowe, Vermont, where I beat Tim Gullikson in straight sets, my 69th tournament win. By then, the press had noticed Patti but didn't know who she was. She became the "mystery woman" for the gossip columns, and Patti and I let them keep guessing. We wanted to hold on to our privacy for as long as possible.

Our cover was blown at the US Open in September, the first Open at Flushing Meadows, when photos of us together appeared in various magazines. However, we still managed to keep Patti's identity secret in the early stages of the tournament. She was watching me practice on the first day she arrived, and during the session I noticed Chrissie approach Lornie. Later, I asked him what they talked about.

"Oh, nothing much. She just asked who the girl was."

"What did you say?"

"I just said, uh, a new fan."

"Good."

The next day at practice, I was hitting with Chico Hagey, a tennis player from San Diego. We were the only ones out there; it was raining and the courts were wet. I was taking it easy, feeling relaxed and not running down every ball. At one point, Chico hit a winner down the line that I, standing like a statue at the net, made no attempt to reach. As I walked back to the baseline, I pulled my sweat pants down and mooned him for just a second to let him know how I felt about his shot. I assure you that, had I noticed the group of spectators who had gathered to watch the session, I would have been more discreet, but the days of keeping a little mystery about myself were apparently over.

It's two sets all and I'm down 2–5 in the fifth against Adriano Panatta when I climb out of my hole and go up 6–5. Panatta is serving at deuce and I'm about to hit one of the most memorable shots of my career.

Panatta puts his serve wide to my left. I manage to get my racquet on it crosscourt, but shorter than I wanted. The ball lands in Pancho's "winning zone," inside the service line. Shit. *Move, Jimmy.*

He's going down the line, but his half-volley isn't deep enough. I return down the line, but he hasn't moved, so he's got the whole court wide open for a crosscourt winner. I'm on a full run, hoping to get there just in time.

The ball is dying. I'm not going to make . . .

Feels like I'm going to hit the wall of spectators courtside.

I swing.

And I watch as the ball *goes around the net-cord judge's head and* . . .

I can't see what's happening.

The line judge is keeping his hands down.

Fucking-A! It's IN?

I've seen the footage since that match. The ball flashing over the highest part of the net, past Panatta, who doesn't move a muscle, the shot clipping the line, me leaping in the air, arms raised in triumph. I knew then that the match was mine. It can destroy you to have a sure winner snatched away like that. Sure enough, Panatta double-faulted the next point, a lucky escape for me, and I moved on to the quarters.

The shot of my life? Panatta said it best after the match.

"In Italy we say he never dies."

Yeah, that about sums me up.

I liked Borg. Still do. We were acquaintances when we were fighting each other to be the best during the 1970s. Later on, in the 1990s, when the Senior Tour came along, we became closer. But back then he was very quiet and kept himself apart from most of the guys, except his coach, Lennart Bergelin, and Vitas. When he wasn't on the court he was up in his room reading. Was it comic books or Shakespeare? I don't know. But he sure wasn't going to tell anyone.

The press dubbed him "Ice Borg." He was cool and kept his emotions to himself. I used to throw my best material at him on the court and he never cracked a smile. Jeez, what a waste. The fans saw, and still see, Borg in a different way from, say, Mac, Nasty, Vitas, or me. We were transparent. Fans could relate to us, maybe imagine going out with us for a beer, talking about sports, or girls, but no one knew what to expect from Borg.

However, as he got older it was like he'd been let out of a cage. The trouble is, I didn't have the stamina to keep up with him, but to be honest with you he was a lot of fun. But more on that later.

When Borg and I played, the tennis felt almost secondary to our battle of wills. His topspin style, speed around the court, and patience went against everything I stood for. I wanted to hit the ball flat, take chances, and be aggressive. Against him, that was a tough task. When Mac and I played we brought the best out in each other, because I played to his strengths and he played to mine. With Borg it was as though we were playing our own game regardless of what the other guy was doing, until one of us came out on top. Seems funny to me that I never beat him at Wimbledon, where I thought I had the advantage, and in turn he never beat me at the US Open, where maybe he had the edge. Go figure.

Against Borg I knew I had to be at the top of my game, especially because there was so much attention and drama created around every match we played. That's why I said I'd follow him to the ends of the earth; I didn't want him to feel too comfortable if he beat me. I didn't want him to settle in and gain more confidence. There were only two other guys I felt that way about, Mac and Lendl. The three of them were my toughest challenges. They raised their games when they faced me, no doubt about it; they all wanted to kick my ass. I took it as a compliment.

I beat Borg at Flushing Meadows that year as bad as he beat me at Wimbledon, and because of that I became the only player ever to win the Open on three different surfaces. It was my fifth career Grand Slam title and my third US Open title.

The turnaround in my relationship with the New York fans that had started with my victory at the Garden in January felt complete that day at the Open. After the match, I thanked all 20,000 of them.

"I play my best tennis when I come to New York. Whether you like me or not, I like you."

At the end of September, Patti and I went to Vegas for a couple of days of R&R. Then we were off to Argentina, where I was playing a four-man exhibition against José Luis Clerc, Nasty, and Borg—which I ended up winning. Then I was winging my way to Australia to play the Sydney indoor tournament.

Patti had her own apartment on Maple Drive, in Beverly Hills, but since I was going to be out of the country, I wanted her to stay in my place with Mom because, as I told her, I thought she'd be safer there.

"You just want to keep an eye on me," Patti said. "You're not fooling anyone." I was also hoping she and Mom would get closer, and I think they did. Patti told me they cooked together, went shopping, and enjoyed each other's company.

From Australia I was off to Japan for the Tokyo indoor tournament. I didn't like being away from Patti and I had a conversation with a guy who worked in Mom's office, Joe Roundtree, in which I confided I was thinking about asking Patti to marry me. I asked Patti to fly to Japan and had Joe accompany her. Of course, he spilled the beans on the plane. Later, Patti told me that her first thought was "Whoa, we haven't been together that long," then she thought it was sweet and it made her feel good to know that I was serious about her.

Patti and I were slow-dancing in a Japanese nightclub and I was worried that, if I waited too long, she might get to know me better and lose interest!

"Let's go back to the hotel and make a baby," I said. The words just came out of my mouth. Being a good Irish Catholic, it was my way of asking her to marry me.

"OK," she said, and that was her way of saying yes. We're from the Midwest. That's how we roll.

She told me afterward that it was the moment she knew for certain that I really loved her. She hadn't thought about starting a family before then. As she said later, "I grew up during women's lib. It wasn't my be-all-and-end-all to be a mother. But when you said those words, I melted."

We were married a few weeks later, in a small Shinto ceremony in Japan, just the two of us and a friend. Quiet, and exactly what we wanted. The next March we had a simple family blessing in Belleville. Mom and Johnny were there, plus Patti's parents, her aunt Nita, and her sister. The whole thing lasted about 90 seconds. I wore a flannel shirt, jeans, and cowboy boots. Patti looked pretty in a rose and lace-silk dress.

We could have made a big thing of it with Patti's connections. I'm sure *Playboy* would have enjoyed laying on a lavish event for publicity, but that wasn't what we were about at the time. We've talked about the possibility of renewing our vows, but we've had a lot of friends who have done that, and the marriage took a nosedive afterward. I'm too superstitious to go down that road.

I think it's fair to say that when Patti and I announced that we'd gotten married, we weren't exactly everybody's best bet to succeed as a couple, and mainly for one reason: Most people thought I was probably too tough to live with.

But the truth is, even our friends had their doubts.

Many years later, when we were at a seniors' event in Dallas, drinking a few margaritas with Eddie Dibbs and Dick Stockton, the conversation turned to our wedding.

"You know, when you guys got married," Dick said to us, "out of all the tennis players and wives on the tour, we thought you'd never last. In fact, we thought you'd be the first to go."

Well, 33 years later we are still going strong, although I am not saying we haven't had some rough patches, mostly as a result of my stupidity. But we've come through it all.

Mom didn't always make it easy, either. When we first got together, she was happy Patti was around, a nice Midwestern girl, but as we grew more serious, Mom found it hard to accept that Patti was another woman in my life who I was turning to for advice. I can understand that, I guess; she thought she was protecting me, worried as she was that Patti might be out to take advantage of me, which is sad, because nothing could be further from the truth. Patti had a successful career when we met. She didn't need anything from me.

Mom kept Patti at arm's length for a lot of years, which was difficult for Patti to deal with, because she's such a strong family person. "Gloria, all I want is to be a family," Patti said to Mom once. "I understand what you are protecting. I know that you have poured your life's blood into Jimmy and his career. Let me be a part of that." Still, Mom found it hard to see that Patti saw something in me other than fame and fortune.

Six weeks after Patti gave birth to our son, we moved from LA to Florida. Mom never came to see us there, nor did she visit when we moved back to California a few years later. Mom loved being in Belleville. I got that. She had friends there and her coaching, but that wasn't the reason for her staying away from us. She was making a statement.

Yet she always loved spending time with our kids, having them sleep over at her house as often as possible. In fact, she would do too much, organizing events and outings when all the kids wanted to do was hang around the friends they'd made in Belleville. I think Mom had to feel she was needed, and then she overcompensated, when in reality she had nothing to prove. All Patti and I ever wanted, all the kids ever wanted, was for Grandma to share our lives both at home and in Belleville.

Is there a secret to a long marriage? I don't know; all I can talk about is what works for us, and that comes down to one thing. We love each other. Patti said it at our wedding in Belleville when Mom asked her how she knew I was the man for her.

"Jimmy made me laugh," Patti answered, "and the others made me cry." That's a huge part of it. We still crack each other up today, just as we did on that first night together at Pips.

We also understand each other's need for independence. Without that we wouldn't have made it this long. For the first two decades of our marriage, I was probably away, on average, 38 weeks of the year, on the main tour and then later with the seniors. You have to know how to survive on your own in those circumstances. That still applies today, and fortunately we have our own passions. With me it's golf and playing tennis, while Patti competes in high-level ballroom dancing, takes care of our home, and has a lot of good friends.

Patti recognized early on that I was two people: the one on court who pumped my fists and swore at umpires and the one who came home to her and the kids.

Patti didn't find it easy to cope with the different sides of my personality. When I played tennis, I'd leave any personal distractions behind. If Patti and I had a fight (and we've had a few) that wasn't resolved before a match, I'd come off the court afterward and go find her. Knowing I had another match to play, she had the wisdom to say, "OK, Jimmy, we'll talk about it later."

That need of mine to avoid confrontation off the court could be frustrating in another way, because I would let things fester. If something upsets me, I won't bring it up until much later, when something completely unrelated sets me off. Whenever that happened, Patti would look at me and smile, as if to say, "What's wrong with you? That's six weeks ago, that's over." And I would calm down.

All of this took a while for us both to learn since our relationship worked backward. We were lovers first, soon husband and wife, followed quickly by mother and father, and then we were friends. Best friends. I guess I just can't do things like everyone else.

We were living in LA and waiting for the birth of our first child, who was already two weeks past his due date of July 20. I had just come back from Wimbledon and arranged to take some time off so that I could be around for Brett to make his grand entrance. I had committed to a series of exhibitions in Europe, and I could only be released from my obligations by an "Act of God," or they would sue me. Patti and I agreed that having a baby qualified as an AOG, but the tournament organizers didn't see it that way. I stayed with her in LA as long as I could, driving her nuts as we waited for the baby to arrive. I couldn't leave the house without asking Patti, "Are you sure it's OK for me to play golf?"

"Please go," Patti would say. She wanted me out of her hair so she could take a nap and get a break from my anxiety.

Finally, I was off to Europe but made it back on American soil for a tournament in North Conway, New Hampshire. It was Tuesday morning, July 31, and I called Patti before I got ready to go out and play my match. We're talking. Then . . .

"Ow! Ow. What was that?" Patti says.

"What? What's wrong?" I asked.

"I think I'm having my first labor pains."

Holy shit!

She had a standing appointment with her doctor, our good friend Lloyd Greig, and she calmly drove herself to his office. When she got there, she and Lloyd called to confirm she was in labor.

"How long do I have, doc?" I asked.

"About eight hours," he said.

OK. No pressure. I'm only 3,000 miles away.

I went out and beat Eliot Teltscher in under an hour in straight sets. Now we had to find a way to get me out of New Hampshire and back to LA. There was a small airfield nearby, where Mom and I rented a Learjet and headed west. On the plane I was a nervous wreck. The worst and best thing about it was there was a phone on the plane. I tried to reach Patti every 15 or 20 minutes but never got to talk to her. As if I weren't worried enough, one of the engines lost power over Kansas City. We went into a free fall until the engine got some air and fired back up again. And if you've ever been in one of those situations, you know you soil your shorts in a hurry. We stopped in Kansas City to refuel, then continued on to California.

There was no phone in the labor room, so every time I called Patti, I was put through to the nurse's station. They had Patti's friend, Judy, come to the phone.

"I don't want to talk to you. I need to talk to Patti!" I shouted. Grace under pressure—it's one of my strengths.

"She's fine, Jimmy, she's fine," Judy said calmly, "but she hasn't had the baby yet."

We finally got into LAX, where my good friend Dr. Earl Woods met us. He had stopped at the hospital to check on Patti before picking us up. "Whatever you do, don't let Jimmy drive," Patti had cautioned Dr. Woods. But I jumped behind the wheel and got us to the hospital, half an hour away, in about five minutes.

When I walked in her room, Patti had already been in labor for 13 hours. "You look like shit," I said

"So do you," she said, laughing.

After another six hours of labor, the doctors decided to give Patti a C-section. The baby's head was turned the wrong way, and his heartbeat had gone down too far. In the operating room, I stayed next to Patti's head, holding her hand as our son, Brett, was born at 3:02 in the morning. And just in time—his umbilical cord was wrapped three times around his neck.

The doctors were running around, calling for a whole bunch of tests, because they were concerned about Brett's rapid heartbeat and that he had swallowed some of the meconium, which is high in bacteria. They said they wanted to do a spinal tap on him. Patti was crying and hanging onto my hand.

"Jimmy, they can't do that on a newborn," she said. "Don't let them do that to our baby."

"OK," I said. I took charge and told Dr. Greig, "You do what you think should be done for Brett. You're the doctor."

Oh, yeah. I took over, all right.

After Dr. Greig put Brett in the neonatal section, there was no way I was going to let him out of my sight. By seven o'clock the next morning, little Brett was stable, but he had to have an IV on his head with a Dixie cup over it so he wouldn't pull it out. His heels were purple from all the blood tests, and his thigh was bruised from the antibiotic shots they gave him twice a day. Patti was sleeping and I finally went home to try to do the same. The minute my head hit the pillow, the phone rang. It was Nasty. We had a $500 bet: I said I was having a boy, he said I was having a girl. I told you I'd bet on anything.

"Connors, you sonuvabitch, you little weak thing, how can you have a boy?"

Nasty had a girl at that time and he had that Eastern European thing about having sons. Not that we're competitive or anything.

Patti and Brett ended up staying in the hospital for 10 days, during which time I had to go to Indianapolis for a tournament and then fly right back to bring Patti and the baby home. And let me tell you this, I was a hands-on father and I enjoyed every minute of it.

I could change a diaper with the best of them. (Whoa! How did all *that* come out of something so little?!) I was completely in love with my new family.

Patti and I agreed that we didn't get married and have a family so that I could be apart from her and Brett for more than half the year. We made the decision that we would travel as a family for as long as we could.

Brett went to his first tennis tournament, the US Open, at the age of one month and two days old. I hoped having him and Patti along would act as a good-luck charm to turn around my Grand Slam fortunes. Two disappointing semifinal exits, to Victor Pecci in Paris and Borg at Wimbledon (my fourth-consecutive straight-sets loss to him), had threatened my hopes of retaining the world-number one ranking for a sixth-consecutive year.

Traveling with my new family worked out just fine. Patti would carry Brett in a baby sling, I'd grab our suitcases, and that was that. Baby Brett didn't seem to mind flying at all.

During the day, when I was playing, Patti arranged for babysitters (the tournament directors were a huge help in that respect) so that she could come and watch. Nighttime was harder, since we weren't able to take turns every time the baby woke up. The reality was I needed a good night's sleep in order to play. I hadn't been able to perform at Wimbledon when I was 22, after being up most of the night partying, and I didn't stand a chance at 27, so Patti assumed all the responsibility for getting up with Brett in the middle of the night while we were on the road.

I loved traveling with Patti and Brett. In Hong Kong in November, I watched my son roll from his stomach onto his back for the first time; in Palm Springs in February, he cut his first tooth; and in Paris in May, he took his first steps.

For the first nine months of his life, he thrived on the different locations, the various people who babysat him, but then, suddenly, separation anxiety set in, and he didn't want to be away from Patti and me. That's when we decided to hire a nanny, someone whom Brett could learn to be comfortable around while we kept traveling as a family. We hired Adela, from Guatemala, to be Brett's nanny when we were on the road, then she became our housekeeper when we were home because Patti and I enjoyed our roles as parents.

When Brett was still just a couple of months old, we moved from my bachelor apartment in the Hollywood Hills to a penthouse suite at the Turnberry Isle Resort, in Florida, overlooking the tennis courts. For the next three years it proved to be one hell of a great place to live, and you never knew who you'd see coming through the lobby: Elton John, Lauren Bacall, Eddie Van Halen, just to name a few. Then there was the action on the courts.

I don't know how many thousands of dollars I won and lost down there, but that wasn't really the point. Guys were lining up to take me on. I would play right-handed so I could work on my footwork and conditioning, and that just made the matches even more interesting. Those days and nights down on those Turnberry courts were a lot like the fun times at the Beverly Hills Tennis Club. The pressure of losing a few bucks might not have been the same, but the thrill of picking up your winnings never got old.

Friends would pass through Turnberry all the time. In between tournaments Nasty might come stay, and if we had the time, we'd rent a yacht, take the family, and go exploring in the ocean right off our doorstep. If Patti liked the idea of taking a trip to the Caribbean, then off we'd go. I knew I could arrange another exhibition with Nasty to pay for it. The money was coming in fast, and going out at the same speed.

If my buddies and I ever started to believe we were big shots, something would usually happen to bring us back down to earth. During the first year I lived in Florida, Nasty and I decided to charter the boat *Monkey Business* (long before Gary Hart's ill-fated cruise) for a trip to the Bahamas, and we brought along my friend Gerry Goldberg.

Gerry had been the tournament director at the Montreal Challenge Cup in December 1979, where I suffered my sixth-consecutive defeat to Borg in the same year. I wasn't in the best of moods, but I liked Gerry. I invited him to go drinking with Nasty and me that night, and we've been friends since then. He's sat next to me on many bar stools and at even more casino tables. He and his wife were frequent visitors to Turnberry while Patti and I lived there. He became the bookmaker for the on-court action. When Nasty, Gerry, and I got down to the Bahamas, we decided to go look for a place to hit some balls, and we found an empty court with no one around. We'd been playing for about 15 minutes when this guy appears out of nowhere and just kind of stands there, staring at us. Not in a friendly way.

"Hi, how are you doing?" I called over, suddenly feeling pretty uncomfortable. The guy's glare didn't soften.

"Get out of here," he barked.

Gerry decided to intervene. "Hey, buddy, this is Jimmy Connors and Ilie Nastase. Sorry if it's your court, but we couldn't find anyone to ask."

"I don't give a fuck who you are. Get off this court. Now."

OK. This doesn't happen very often.

Nasty walked over to me, looking nervous. He's not someone who's often intimidated, but there was something going on that neither of us wanted any part of.

"This guy's serious. We're out of here, right, Connors boy?"

Right.

Back on board the *Monkey Business*, we told one of the crew what happened.

"Oh, my God, guys, you're lucky to get out of there in one piece. I know that court. It belongs to Bebe Rebozo, Nixon's moneyman. You don't mess around with him."

Sometimes you just have to say "What the fuck" and move on. But sometimes you say it quietly.

It's official after my Montreal Challenge Cup defeat by Borg: According to the press, the Borg–Connors era is over. It's not a rivalry anymore but an embarrassment. Jimmy's finished. Welcome to the new Borg–McEnroe decade.

Well, screw that. Yes, it's true, I didn't win a Slam in 1979, didn't even make a final, but it was a busy year and I had a new wife and a new baby, and that takes some getting used to.

I was happy with my life, and I knew I could figure out how to improve my game. Over my vacation, I thought, I'll hit the courts, practice hard, and next year I'll make another comeback. That's what I do.

After Mac beat me in New York in September, I said three words to the press:

"I'll be back."

Who was I? The Terminator? Believe it or not, I said it first.

What I didn't know as I was making my grand plans for the beginning of the eighties was that it would take me two years before I'd be proved right. A little longer than I expected. What the hell.

14

BACK FROM THE DEAD

The Masters in January 1980 was a disappointment, but a week later I secured my sixth-straight Birmingham International Indoor title, winning in straight sets over Eliot Teltscher. Seven days later, I captured my fourth US Pro Indoor championship in Philadelphia, beating McEnroe in a five-set final.

"Unfortunately, I guess he's starting to play a little better again," Mac told the press after I kicked his ass.

Then it was on to the WCT Tennis Invitational, a round-robin tournament in mid-February in Salisbury, Maryland.

Vijay Amritraj waits patiently at the net, like the gentleman that he is, as I jog toward him to shake his hand. Not surprisingly, he has a huge grin on his face. A 6–3, 6–3 victory will do that for you.

"Well played, Vijay. You deserved it today."

I don't want to say anything else because I'm too pissed at myself for the way I played. The Salisbury crowd, fans I've grown to know well over the years, are applauding, but not for me. Time to get out of here, Jimmy.

I grab my bag and sling it over my left shoulder. Don't know why I did that. I always carry it on my right. Now where is Patti? There she is, coming down to meet me as I walk off the court. I want to head straight back to the hotel. No point in hanging around the locker room . . .

Then . . . WHAT?! I see a guy climb out of the stands and run at Patti. Now he's got his arm around her neck and she's struggling to get away.

I'm sprinting toward my wife. I'm in no mood for this shit.

I'm at a fighting weight of 160 pounds, I'm in the best shape I've been in for years, and I reach them in seconds.

There's a lot of pushing and shouting around Patti, but no one is doing anything.

I shove someone out of my way and grab the guy's hair with my right hand as I spin my bag off my shoulder. As I pull him forward my left comes free just in time.

Boom! I land a haymaker. He goes down with a thud. Thanks for the lessons when I was growing up, Pop!

I try and jump on the guy, but security pulls me back. There it is again, that flash of memory, Mom getting pummeled in Jones Park, but this time I'm not powerless.

I grab Patti. She's shaken, but safe now.

"I thought you were going to kill him," says Patti.

"I tried," I say, and I still want to.

I'm supposed to play Nasty the next day, and as I walk out of there an hour after the attack on Patti, I have an ice pack on my left hand and my wrist is throbbing.

The next morning the swelling is still there, but the pain has eased up enough for me to play. Patti isn't hurt too badly other than her neck being a little stiff, and once we discover who the punk is, we decide not to involve the police. Turns out he wanted a kiss from Patti. No excuses. I still wanted to kill him.

With no serious damage done to Patti (my punch was described in the press as a "textbook left," which is always good for your reputation), the organizers decided to treat the incident lightly. As Nasty and I walked onto the court, the loudspeakers up on the roof exploded with the theme from *Rocky*.

I beat Nasty 6-4, 6-4 in an uneventful match, setting up a show-down with Borg, which I had to win to make it through to the finals. Instead, I walked away with my eighth-consecutive loss to the new world number one. Just for the record, the seventh in that sequence came during the Grand Prix Masters at Madison Square Garden a month before, another round-robin event, where at least I came within two points of ending the run before losing out in a third-set tiebreaker.

After my loss to Borg, Vitas Gerulaitis beat me 7-5, 6-2, playing incredible tennis. It was my first loss to him since 1972, bringing our career record to 16-2 in my favor. But no one cared about that, because Vitas, as always, managed to steal the show. At the post-match press conference, Vitas gave the world his memorable line:

"Let that be a lesson to you all. Nobody beats Vitas Gerulaitis 17 times in a row."

Classic.

From Maryland I went to Memphis to defend my US National In-door title, losing to McEnroe in a close final 7-6, 7-6, which put him on top of the ATP rankings for the first time, where he lasted for three weeks.

The rollercoaster ride continued into April. In a four-man invitational in Brussels, I lost to Mac 6-1, 7-5, which I then followed up with a win over him in the International Tennis Competition, in Tokyo, picking up a $110,000 check in the process.

By the end of April the tally for the year stood at Borg 2, Connors 0; McEnroe 2, Connors 2.

Borg or McEnroe, McEnroe or Borg.

The beginning of the Borg–McEnroe decade? Really? We'll see about that.

May through September are the business months in tennis, and I'm not going into them fighting for second place. I'm out to regain my number one spot. And it all starts here in Dallas at the WCT finals. OK, Borg isn't playing, but Mac is, and we're meeting in the final.

During a pre-match press conference, Mac makes the statement that it would have been nice to have been able to play me when I was at my best.

Do you really want to know what I was like when I was at my best? You're about to find out, son. I win the match in four sets and give him a taste of what it would have been like to play me in the early 1970s.

The year's tally after Dallas? McEnroe 2, Connors 3.

Time to chase down Borg in Paris.

I don't like the fact that today all four Grand Slams have 32 seeded players. It gives the top guys too much protection. They changed it from 16 in 2001 at Wimbledon and the US Open, followed a year later by the French and Australian Opens. In my opinion that didn't benefit tennis.

Sure, the big names have to be looked after in the early rounds, because those are the guys who sell the tickets, but to keep as many as 32 players protected—I think that's just nuts. When I was playing, we had eight seeded players, which seems about right to me. When the draw was made you could be facing a top-20 or -30 opponent, which meant a fan wouldn't know which match to watch, because there were so many good ones, and that made the tournaments exciting from the very first ball served.

It was certainly the case in Paris in 1980, thanks to Patti.

Patti had the honor of making the draw for the French Open and she didn't do me any favors. My first round opponent, Adriano Panatta, the 1976 champion and winner in Florence the previous week, was ranked 28th in the world at the beginning of the year.

Although I'd missed the French Open for five years (it took four years for me to get rid of my anger and frustration after being banned in 1974), I always knew Roland Garros suited me. Not the surface or the balls they used, which slowed everything down too much for my game, but the atmosphere. It was hot, dirty, close, and noisy . . . and I loved it. You had to be ready to grind it out. I'd buy a ticket for that any day.

Panatta takes me to four sets. In round two I meet the Frenchman Jean-François Caujolle, and the scoreboard says it all: 3-6, 2-6, 2-5, 30-40. Match point to the hometown favorite. The 18,000 fans are howling their approval and I'm a point away from defeat. They don't know me well here, but they've decided they don't like me. Not today, anyway. OK. Keep grinding and win this game. Connors 3-5.

I take the set 7-5, after which there can be only one winner and the crowd knows it. Their booing lacked the conviction it had had before. I win the next two sets, 6-1, 6-1, and go on to round three.

With Borg in the other half of the draw, I was convinced there could only be one final, and one winner, and I could feel my career Slam getting closer.

Until Gerulaitis came along again and spoiled it. I'd thought my Madison Square Garden loss was a fluke. My targets were McEnroe (who lost to Paul McNamee in the third round) and Borg, but in the semifinal Vitas matched me stroke for stroke in a seesaw match that went to five sets, which I didn't think I would lose until he aced me on his fifth match point. By that stage the crowd was on its feet for both of us. As disappointed as I was with the result, I knew my romance with Paris had begun.

I loved everything about that city—the restaurants, the cafés, the boutiques, the Louvre, taking Brett for a walk in the parks. Of course the photographers wanted a piece of us, especially in the first couple of years of our marriage but that was OK, because we never did anything very exciting, and soon they got bored with us.

The only time we had any trouble in Paris was a day or two after the Caujolle match in 1980. Patti, I, and our nanny, Adela, were walking down the Champs-Élysées, enjoying a day off, with Brett riding on my shoulders. The sidewalk was crowded and I was just enjoying bouncing Brett up and down, listening to him laugh, when suddenly Adela was tugging at my sleeve in a panic.

"Mr. Connors! Mrs. Connors!"

Looking over, I spotted a couple of guys moving Patti toward a side alley, maneuvering her off the street without actually grabbing her. I gave Brett to Adela and charged through the crowd of shoppers and tourists.

Patti could see me coming and started shouting. I couldn't hear what she was saying, but I thought she was calling for help. I lunged toward the guys and heard Patti yell, "Don't get into a fight! Don't get into a fight! You'll hurt your hand. You're playing tomorrow!"

I was about to ignore Patti's warning when Patti broke loose. I grabbed her hand and we got out of there. I don't even want to think about what those guys wanted with my wife.

Paris was always an adventure. I remember when Brett was almost three years old and we were staying at the Hilton, and he'd been running up and down the hallway outside our room, burning off some energy before bedtime. Patti and I were watching him from our doorway when, to our horror, he walked into an open elevator car, the doors closed, and he was gone. We jumped into the next elevator, but by the time we reached the lobby Brett was nowhere to be seen. In a panic we looked under sofas, in the bar (well, he *is* my kid), and asked everyone in the place if they'd spotted him. Suddenly, Claude, the concierge, came in through the front entrance with our son in his arms.

"Monsieur Connors. Do not worry. I have little Brett. I saw him run out and chased after him. When I caught him he asked me to take him to the park. He wants ice cream, I think."

I never knew that having a family would be so hard on the nerves.

Then, a few years later (and not because of the Brett incident), we decided to try a different hotel and moved to the Plaza Athénée, on Avenue Montaigne, the hotel where I'd been invited by Sinatra to join him for a cocktail.

Nasty picks Patti and me up at Charles de Gaulle Airport, drives us to the hotel, and comes up to our room for a drink. As we're waiting for our bags, I open the curtains to look at the view of the city skyline. About five minutes later there's a knock on the door. Nasty answers and talks to the bellhop for a few seconds.

"Connors boy, there's a note here for you," he says. "It's from Marlene."

Who?

I open the letter. "To Jimmy. I have just seen you arrive. Good luck in your matches. Marlene Dietrich." Noooooo. How did she even know we were here? A minute later the telephone rings and Nasty starts speaking in French and then hands me the phone.

The voice is husky and unmistakable. "Jimmy, this is Marlene."

It turned out she lived in an apartment right across from the hotel and she had seen me at the window. We talked for a minute and she said she hoped I would enjoy my stay in Paris and wished me luck in the tournament. Nasty, Patti, and I couldn't believe it, and a few minutes later there was another knock at the door. This time the bellhop delivered a package: a framed photograph of Dietrich from the 1930s. Written across it were six words that still make me smile: WE JUST TALKED. FUCK THEM ALL. Attitude plus style. My kind of woman.

I'd have loved to have her come out to the stadium to watch one of my matches, but she was in her eighties by then and it just wasn't possible. Instead, we spoke regularly over the next two weeks. Talking to Marlene Dietrich made East St. Louis seem a long ways off. If I ever needed to be reminded of the life tennis had given me, all I had to do was remember Paris. And Marlene.

Some of my favorite encounters in Paris were with René Lacoste, a distinguished French player and the inventor of the racquet I used for almost 30 years, the T2000. Mr. Lacoste had been one of the French tennis stars dominating the game in the 1920s and early 1930s, and the world's number one player in 1926 and 1927. He won seven Grand Slam singles titles in the French, American, and British championships. Oh, and he also founded the Lacoste clothing firm, featuring the famous crocodile logo.

I first met Mr. Lacoste in the early 1970s when Nasty invited me to join the two of them for lunch. I was nervous as hell, but I relaxed soon after Mr. Lacoste told me how much he enjoyed following my matches. I'm not kidding, this man was amazing, what he had achieved, how he had broken new ground in almost everything he tried, and there he was telling me he liked my game. I have to tell you, that felt good.

Whenever I was in Paris I'd call Mr. Lacoste to say hello. He wasn't short on opinions, another thing I liked about him.

"Oh Jeemy, I saw you play today. You drive me crazy. You hit the ball too close to the line, too close to the net. Geeve yourself more margin of error, please."

Topspin ruled in Paris. Hitting the ball flat was almost unheard of. Almost losing in straight sets to Caujolle in 1980 wasn't the only scare

I had that afternoon. Deep into the third set, with the tournament slipping rapidly away, there was a sudden commotion in the area of Mr. Lacoste's seat, and I could see he was being helped out of his box.

All I could do was go on with the match and hope everything was OK. As soon as we walked off the court, I called Mr. Lacoste's wife to find out what had happened.

"René was not feeling so well. He had to leave."

"Madame, I am so sorry. Please tell him I'll call him later to see how he is."

A couple of hours later Mr. Lacoste called me at the hotel and I asked him if he was OK.

"Yes, Jeemy, I am fine now, thank you. But I cannot watch you anymore. Your game, the way you play, it geeves me a heart attack!"

Saturday, July 5, 1980.

Centre Court, Connors versus McEnroe, Wimbledon semifinal.

First set 4-2, 40-15, McEnroe.

For once I'm wearing the white hat and the villain is across the net. Mac serves, down the line, and it hits the T, a puff of chalk. I take a step toward my chair.

"Fault!"

I stop. So does Mac. He stares across the net, then at the umpire. I stand and wait.

The umpire makes the call. "Play a let."

Mac walks toward him. "Play a let? But I aced him."

"No, no, the call came before the ball was played."

Not sure about that.

"He never even called it. He never said anything."

"He called a fault."

"He never called a fault. He just went like that." Mac sticks his arm out, mimicking a line judge.

"He called a fault. Play a let, please."

"Could I have the referee, please?" Slow handclaps beginning around the stadium.

"No, play on."

"I'd like the referee. I'm not playing on until you get the referee. I feel I have a right to get the referee. Are you going to call the referee?"

I stand quietly, casually twirling my racquet, happy to let him wind himself up. The crowd doesn't like it, but I do. This can only work to my advantage.

"You can only call the referee on a point of law."

"But this is the point of law. I want the referee out here right now."

"You can't have it."

"But I aced him. Wait, in your opinion he could have gotten that ball?"

"Yes. He could have gone for it. Play on."

"I'd like the referee."

Realizing that this could go on forever, I walk toward the court-side seats and put one foot up against the barrier, smiling at the fans next to me.

"Play on."

"I'm not playing until you get the referee."

The umpire, Pat Smythe, has had enough. I'm surprised it took this long.

"Mr. McEnroe, you are getting a public warning. Now, please play on."

Mac, shaking his head, walks to his service line. I settle myself and look toward the umpire's chair to ask a totally innocent question.

"Two balls or one ball?"

"Two."

"Oh, jolly good." I'm trying to sound like Prince Charles, but it comes out like Dick Van Dyke in *Mary Poppins*. And the crowd loves it.

Mac hits his serve long, has a little tantrum, and smashes my return into the net. More boos from the crowd. His next serve is good, but I return it low and he nets his volley. Cheers ring out as though I've just won the championship. On the next point, Mac serves an ace to go 5-2 up, then sarcastically asks, "How was that?"

At the changeover he's still talking to the umpire. *Man, give it a rest.*

I wag my finger at him. "I'm telling you, son, keep your mouth shut out here."

And still he goes on, "I'd like the referee out here."

First set, 5-2, 15-0, my serve.

I hit it down the line, but it's called a fault.

"Ooh, I say," in my Dick Van Dyke voice. Laughs ring out everywhere except on McEnroe's side of the court.

I return serve that day as well as I have in a long time. Under pressure, with McEnroe hovering at the net, I lob him repeatedly. On his side of the net, he serves and volleys as well as anybody I have ever played, creating angles even I didn't think possible.

Despite my best efforts to try and throw him off his rhythm, I never quite manage it.

I lose the third, and in the fourth I have opportunities to pull even, and though the momentum is with me I can't quite close the gap. Mac wins the match and keeps me from playing another Wimbledon final. In the 14 matches we'd played up until then we'd only ever gone to five sets once, in Philadelphia earlier in the year, and I'd come out on top. But that day at Wimbledon, I just came up short.

A BBC commentator had likened the match to an irresistible force meeting an immovable object. Unfortunately, the irresistible force that was John McEnroe prevailed.

If he wasn't quite there already, I knew Mac was on his way to becoming the world's best tennis player. He was now ranked number one in the US, and that's what really pissed me off. I'll say it again: That title belonged to me and I wanted it back. What you saw on the court back then was genuine dislike.

Mac came out with a good line after that semifinal, which I've got to give him credit for. When asked about the nature of our relationship, he replied, "Well, we don't go out to dinner together a lot."

Even though we get along better than we used to—I'd go for a beer with him now—there's still that edge. Whenever Mac and I meet up, do I still think, *Goddammit, he beat me in the US Open*? Sure I do, but I don't lose sleep over it anymore. At the time, though, some of those matches caused me insomnia. We didn't have a soft rivalry; it was down and dirty, old-school.

Two months after Wimbledon, Mac and I met again at the Open, our third-straight Grand Slam semifinal. I had worked hard to win over the crowds in New York in 1978 and now Mac wanted them on his side. I think he thought he was the real king of New York and I was just some guy from East St. Louis trespassing on his territory. That just wasn't the case. I'd won this thing three times already, I'd spilled my blood out here, and this was *my* stadium and *my* tournament.

The Flushing Meadows fans knew what was going on. Mac had guts, he really did, but there were times when he just wanted to have everything his own way. But who didn't? The crowd demanded great tennis and became irritated when Mac held up the match with his calls for a change of umpire halfway through my run of 11 games in a row. After having lost the first set, and finding myself down a set point in the second at 4-5, I didn't lose another game until I was 2-0 up in the fourth.

Then he decided that the electronic Hawkeye device used on the service line was broken. Come on!

"The machine's wrong. It was *this* far out," he yelled at umpire Don Wiley. "Tell me when you're going to get one right, Mr. . . . Mr. *whatever-your-name-is*. Mr. Incompetent. You're wrong eighty percent of the time. You realize that?"

The crowd started booing and hollering.

The call for the umpire change came at 0-3 down in the third, after Mac complained once again about what he saw as a bad call.

"I'd like to see the referee, please."

I'd heard it all before. This shit was getting old.

At 0-2 in the fourth, Mac pulled his game back around, and as his tennis began to heat up, so did the fans. They were getting the kind of show they expected from us, and they roared their approval.

The match went to a tiebreak at 6-6 in the fifth set, a great opportunity for me to close him out. But Mac served and volleyed his way to victory, and once again I had failed to reach a Grand Slam final.

And all on Patti's birthday. That sucks.

At the beginning of the year I'd been aiming for the number one spot but ended 1980 third in the world behind Mac and Borg, and second in the US. That sucked, too.

"He's a chicken."

It's late, very late, Friday night/early Saturday morning at Madison Square Garden, January 16–17, 1981, and I'm talking to the press after beating Ivan Lendl, 7-6, 6-1. This is the sixth time I've met the

Czechoslovakian over the past 18 months, and the only set he took
off me in those matches was the previous year in Dallas. That's OK;
he's young, he's learning, but this stinks. We're at the 1981 Masters
(which is played for the year 1980), and the way the matches have
worked out, the winner tonight will meet Borg in the semis, while
the loser will be up against Gene Mayer in the other semi. Who
would you rather play?

So what happened? Lendl tanked. Everyone in the stands knew
it—the lack of effort, the shots he was missing. It's unacceptable.
He's number six in the world: He should show respect for the sport,
for his opponent, and, most important, for the fans. So let's just say I
wasn't afraid to express my opinion.

For me there is only one way to play tennis. You put yourself on
the line and fight to win, always. No questions asked. No compromise.

Over the years I grew to like Lendl. I respected his talent, conditioning, and preparation. He represented the new breed. Yeah,
maybe a bit mechanical and lacking in flair, but still a great player.
He went on to kick my ass in a lot of matches throughout the 1980s,
but not in the two that mattered most—the US Open finals of 1982
and 1983. Those are the ones I remember.

So, yeah, Lendl was OK, but I still despised what he did that
night at the Masters.

The next day, I was back out there putting everything into my
match against Borg, but before I could find my rhythm he ran away
with the first set. I took him to a tiebreaker in the second, which I
won 7-4, but I was exhausted, and at 1-5 in the third set it looked
like the match was over. Then I broke him and held to make it 3-
5, and the pressure now was back on him. It took him four match
points to finally win the match, but not before I made him earn it.

This was my ninth-consecutive loss to Borg, but I knew there would be a lot more battles to come. It reminded me of the ice cracking under my feet as a kid while I was thinking, *I can make it. I can make it.*

"You're going to get drunk tonight, aren't you?"

The next summer, Patti and I are in the car going back to our hotel after the 1981 Wimbledon semifinal. We've already stopped off at a little store not far from the grounds, where I picked up a six-pack of beer and some salt-and-vinegar potato chips. I'm already two beers down and the seat is littered with crumbs from the three bags of chips I've demolished.

"Oh, yes, I am."

Up until that afternoon I'd had a good tournament. Sure, there had been the usual confrontations with the rigid protocols, but I was accustomed to that by now. I never got completely used to the crazy formality at Wimbledon—it was their way or no way—but the older I got, the less it bugged me. This year, actually, it had been Patti who clashed with the All-England authorities. Bettina Bunge and Dick Stockton were playing mixed doubles on an outside court, and Patti was sitting in the tea room (very British, you know), watching the match through the long lens of a friend's camera.

"Excuse me, miss, no cameras are allowed in here."

"Yes, I know that, but don't worry. I'm not taking any photographs. I'm just watching our friends play."

"No cameras allowed in here, miss."

"I understand, but as I just said I'm not using it as a camera. It's really a . . ."

"Do you want me to escort you out, miss?"

"Just fucking try it." Did I mention that Patti is half Irish and half Cherokee? You think *I've* got a temper?

Everything else had gone smoothly all week. Instead of the Inn on the Park, Patti, Brett, and I were staying in an apartment just behind Harrods where we had fun socializing with our friends the Gottfrieds, cooking meals together, and playing hearts. Patti usually won. My favorite strategy, it will come as no surprise, was shooting the moon. All or nothing for me.

One night we went to the Playboy Club to meet up with Gerry Goldberg, who was also in town. After dinner we decided to head to the disco in the basement. Gerry was leading us down when he suddenly stopped and I almost fell over him.

"Gerry, what the—"

"Connors, I don't think we should do this. Let's hit the tables upstairs instead."

"But, G-Man, Patti wants to dance. Come on, we don't have to stay long."

"No, Connors, I really don't think we should."

He was looking really flustered by now. Behind me, Patti was asking what the hell was holding us up.

"Look," Gerry whispered in my ear. "Look," he said again, insistent this time, as he gestured with his head at the wall over his shoulder. "It's Patti," he hissed.

I looked up and there was a huge naked picture of my wife from one of her *Playboy* shoots.

"Hey, Patti, take a look at that," I said, pointing to the picture. Why not? I was proud of it.

She burst out laughing. "Don't I look cute?"

Until the quarters I hadn't lost a set. Then I mounted a huge comeback against Vijay Amritraj, battling back from two sets down to win the match in five sets, setting up my semifinal with Borg. Let me say something here: When you're two sets down, you can't think about time, because you don't know how long it will take to climb

246 / JIMMY CONNORS

back into the match. You just keep grinding and looking for a break or a way to make something happen. Remember, you're fighting with someone of equal ability and determination. You have to trust your own instincts and play with abandon, because you have nothing to lose. As Two Mom used to say, greed and fear are your worst enemies in that situation.

After an hour and 24 minutes in the English sunshine against Borg, with me up 6-0, 6-4 in the semifinal, it looked like his winning streak over me was about to end and I was once again going to make a Grand Slam final. Guess what? Neither of those things happened. After going two sets up and having my way with Borg, he ends up rolling me over exactly the same way. I walked out of the stadium feeling like I'd just been hit by a runaway truck with BORG painted on the side. I had never before blown a match after being two sets up, and I was in for a gut-check. You could handle that two ways; you could crumble and never be heard from again, or use the experience to grow stronger.

Flushing Meadows. September 13, 1981. It's Borg versus McEnroe for the second-consecutive Grand Slam final. Borg's serve had cut short my effort to regain the Open title, as he fired 14 aces on his way to a straight-sets victory in the semis. Now he had a chance to avenge his defeat by Mac the previous year in New York, and for Wimbledon earlier that summer.

On the final point of the match, Borg hits his service return long and leaves Louis Armstrong Stadium almost immediately, not even waiting for Mac's trophy ceremony.

He never plays another Grand Slam.

In the fall of 1981, Borg announced he was taking a break. He said that he was exhausted from too many matches and that he would only commit to seven tournaments the next year. Under the rules of the Men's International Professional Tennis Council, the governing

My two-fisted
backhand, which the
critics said was my
only shot. But it was
a damn good one!
(Courtesy of Art Seitz)

Beating Mac in the
Wimbledon finals,
1982—the longest match
in tournament history
at the time and my
second Wimbledon title.
*(Courtesy of Russ Adams
Productions)*

PLAYING AT THE 1991 US OPEN.

The Open has always been my
stage and the crowd my people.
Like I always say, the fans won me
more matches than I won myself.

Here I am leading the James Scott
Connors Philharmonic Orchestra
after coming back from 2-5 in the
final set to beat Aaron Krickstein.
Not bad for a 39-year-old geezer.

I'm still not sure how Brett grew to be so big but I'm glad he did, because no one messed with me when he was around.

Aubree takes after her mother— beautiful, elegant, and still willing to laugh at my jokes.

It took Mom years to drop her guard with Patti, but they became close toward the end of Mom's life. *(Courtesy of Art Seitz)*

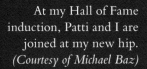

At my Hall of Fame induction, Patti and I are joined at my new hip. *(Courtesy of Michael Baz)*

With my good friend David Schneider. What? A golf cart? Really?

Mac, me, and Borg. Sorry if I turned you guys gray. *(Courtesy of Art Seitz)*

With Vitas and Patti on a night out in Paris. Wherever we went with Vitas, he was the life of the party. We miss him every day.

Mug shot, 2008. Finally, a good picture. Inmate 00001. *(Courtesy of Santa Barbara County Sheriff's Office)*

We call Sophie our "special child" even though she is now a senior citizen—just like her dad.

Me and my shrinks at the beach. Those therapy sessions were lifesaving, especially after I retired from tennis and didn't know what to do with myself. Nothing could calm me more than a long walk with the dogs.

body, seven tournaments wouldn't be enough for him to gain automatic entry into Grand Prix events, including the Slams. If he stayed away, he'd have to go through the qualifying process. He tried that in Monte Carlo and again at the Alan King Classic, in Vegas, but he failed both times. In tennis, you needed to play to keep your game up; Borg was entering too few tournaments to compete at a high level. Björn Borg officially retired at 26 years of age.

I never understood why he did it. It took everyone by surprise and disrupted the rivalry that the fans had been enjoying among the three best players—Mac, Borg, and me. What caused him at such a young age to just walk away from a sport he was so good at? He had so much success early on that maybe he didn't want to—or couldn't—keep working as hard to stay on top. If it was a case of burnout, though, that's something I will never understand. Did I miss Borg when he walked away? Hell, yeah. I wish he'd stuck around a lot longer. There was no way to replace the excitement and competitiveness of the matches we played.

I could never do what Borg did, not even after that Open, when the press wrote me off. *You know, Connors had made only eight Grand Slam semifinals out of nine over three years, and no finals. Connors used to be number one, but not anymore.*

I wasn't giving up. I still had a job to do and one that I loved more than anything in the world, except being a husband and a father.

I reinvented myself on Sunday, November 15, 1981, at Wembley, London, in the final of the Benson & Hedges Championships, broadcast live on television. Connors versus McEnroe. It wasn't just that I won, but how: from two sets down against McEnroe, the best player in the world.

I walked off that court that night, knowing one thing for sure: I was back.

15

CRACKS IN THE FOUNDATION

mmediately after beating Mac at Wembley in 1981, I flew to Tel Aviv to play a tournament. During that week, Gerry (who knew Israel well and had helped build their tennis stadium) arranged for Nasty and me to go on a private sightseeing tour on one of our days off. The Wailing Wall, an incredible place, was crowded with men in their shawls, rocking back and forth in prayer, some with their foreheads and hands touching the wall. The stones had been polished by untold numbers of people who had been there before them. Like most visitors to the wall, I'd written a few thoughts on a piece of paper and slipped it between the cracks of the stones. It was an honor to have been a guest and a part of that sacred tradition, and I left with a feeling of awe.

In January 1982, I found myself in a very different climate: minus-20-degree weather in Rosemont, Illinois, to play the Michelob Light Challenge of Champions. I knew at that point that my game was back where it should be, and Mac and I pretty much picked up where we'd left off at Wembley, carrying the fight to the tennis fans. Almost literally.

The stadium was sold out and the fans applauded, booed, heckled, and cheered for over four and a half hours for great tennis—plus the bonus of seeing the Mac & Connors Show—as the score and penalty points swung one way and then the other.

In the second set, at 0-4 down, I took a courtside seat for a few minutes after the umpire, Art Leighton (who'd been removed from his chair during one of my earlier matches in the tournament), overturned a line call when Mac's ball was clearly out. "Mr. Connors, penalty point." I graciously decided to return to the court when it was withdrawn.

At 4-4 in the set, Mac just can't stop wasting time, and I've had enough. When we played, we usually got in each other's faces—on and off the court. So I climb over the net to see if Mac needs some personal counseling. Something I think we both could have used.

The crowd boos as I point my finger at him, inches from his nose, and give him a few choice words of "advice."

Mac swats my hand away. I back off for a second to get my temper under control and then move back in as two officials step between us. I guess the officials have decided they don't want any Irish blood on their court.

Fourth set, 5-5, Mac down 30-40 and he hammers his racquet into the ground. "Mr. McEnroe, penalty point." Mac pulls on his tracksuit and stalks toward the locker room. I follow and persuade him to resume the match. I hold serve to win the fourth set 7-5. Into the fifth we go.

With a sold-out stadium of 14,000 crazed fans, we can't just leave it hanging. One of us has to walk out of here with a winner's check. A break up at 4-2, in the seventh game, Mac gets another penalty point for smashing a ball into the roof in anger when he can't reach my crosscourt winner. With the score 15-40, I would have won the game and evened up the break, but Mac walks off (again) in disgust. I like to win my matches, not to be handed them by an umpire. I refuse the penalty point, Mac's back, and I win the game and go on to finish the set and the match 6-4.

That's tennis when Mac and I are in town.

He got his revenge at the Masters later that month, when I lost to him and then to Roscoe Tanner, and again at the US Pro Indoor in Philadelphia, where I picked up a $1,000 fine and a 21-day suspension for an obscene gesture during my semifinal against Chip Hooper. You can't grab your nuts? I didn't get that memo.

All those people who wrote me off? I didn't want to make them eat their words; I wanted to ram them down their throats.

I've run into an old friend from Mexico whom I haven't seen in a while. We're at a craps table in Vegas. Not my best idea.

"Come on, buddy, give the man a marker. He's good for it," says my friend.

I shake my head.

It's Wednesday, April 21, 1982. Earlier in the day I had beaten Hank Pfister 6-3, 6-1 in the first round of the Alan King Classic, on the heels of beating Johan Kriek in Monterey after my suspension, and then, at the Los Angeles Tennis Club, taking Mel Purcell for my third Pacific Southwest title.

"No, thanks, son. I'm done. Really. I only play what's in my pocket," I said.

"Come on, take a marker, man, and let's play," my Mexican friend insists. "Another hour. You've gotta win some of that back."

I'm already down five figures. And I never, ever, take markers. But my friend has a point. I'm not playing until later tomorrow.

"All right. Five thousand bucks, that's it. One hour, maximum, then I'm out of here."

Over the next 60 minutes I'm up, then down, up again, and I can't get a break.

"Mr. Connors, another marker?"

"Sure, what the hell."

Three hours later, as I'm signing out, the cashier looks up at me, as he totals my markers. There's not a flicker of emotion. I guess they've seen it all before. Much worse.

"That's sixty thousand dollars, Mr. Connors. Do you wish to settle up now?"

"OK if I leave it to the end of the tournament?"

"Not a problem, Mr. Connors. Have a good night." Oh, yeah, thanks. And sleep well.

I just lost a lot of money. But fuck it, I like this life and it feels good being part of the action again. I love the buzz, even when it costs me 60 grand. You can't beat it. But, hell, I'm gonna have to win the tournament now to pay my debt. Smart move, Jimmy, just what you need. More pressure.

My toughest challenge in the Alan King Classic comes in the semis against Sandy Mayer, when I have to come from a set down to win, setting up a meeting with his brother Gene in the finals. When they hand me the winner's check for $60,000 on Sunday, after my opponent has been forced to retire with an injured ankle, it should have been made out to Caesars Palace, because that's where it goes. I sign it over at the casino later that evening. Problem solved. For now.

Two weeks later I receive a phone call. From Mom. All my winnings go through the business she oversees.

"Jimmy, I'm expecting that check from the Alan King tournament, but I haven't seen it yet."

Yeah, about that check. After I danced around the issue she backed off and did the math. Vegas + Connors + missing check. Hmmm.

June 1982, the Stella Artois championships at the Queen's Club. I've just beat Mac in the finals and I'm feeling a little superstitious. Last year, Mac had been the only one in the Open Era who had managed back-to-back Queen's and Wimbledon victories, and that's what I wanted to take back from him.

During the week I took it easy in practice, sometimes only going out there 15 minutes a day to check how I was feeling. I didn't want to wear myself out. I also wanted to stay eager to play, just like Mom had taught me.

I'd been putting money on myself to win Wimbledon since 1972, but as I walked into Ladbrokes this year to place my bet, there were some raised eyebrows. I can't say I blame them. I'd competed in Wimbledon for 10 years and won just once. And I hadn't won a Grand Slam since 1978, so I wasn't exactly seen as a big threat to John P. McEnroe's run of victories. Eight years between titles is a long time, and the odds on me to win were 16-1. That didn't bother me, so, gambler that I am, I opened a vein and laid down a large bet on me to win. I'm pretty sure the guys at Ladbrokes thought it was money in the bank for them. *Et tu, Ladbrokes?*

That June, Patti, Brett, and I were back at the Inn on the Park where they knew what it took to keep us happy. My mini-bar was always stocked with plenty of Snickers bars (or Marathons, as they were known in the UK) and Pepsis.

It's a first-class hotel with every luxury you can imagine, but Mom and I had originally decided to stay there because of its location, and then kept coming back because of how well we were treated. In the first couple of years, Mom used to wash my tennis clothes by hand in the bathtub after every match. Then, after I became Wimbledon champion, the hotel manager agreed to let her use the hotel washing machines and dryers. Mom didn't trust anyone else to do the job right, but Patti had a different take on the laundry situation.

"Patti, they have a service here," I said. "If you ask them, they'll wash my clothes. Every night."

"Are you nuts?! They charge four bucks a sock. I'm not paying that. If you add in Brett's clothes, it'll cost us more than the room. Anyway, they'll only end up shrinking your shirts. Someone told me there's a laundromat in Knightsbridge. I can go there every morning and I can have breakfast in a local café while I wait."

"Whatever you say." See, guys, those are the first three words you learn to say when you're married if you want to stay happy.

I wasn't about to try and change Patti's mind about the laundry. The way she saw it, I had my job to do and she had hers. She didn't tell me how to hit the ball and I didn't tell her how to run the details of our family. It worked out well for both of us.

I think of that period between the two London tournaments of 1982 as being one of the most relaxed I've enjoyed in my life.

We had no idea of the cracks that would soon appear in the foundation of our relationship, or their terrible consequences for our little family.

In the three years that Patti had been with me at Wimbledon, she had become good friends with the legendary Ted Tinling. Ted had a short career as a tennis player before becoming the personal umpire to the fabled French player Suzanne Lenglen (who won 31 championship titles between 1914 and 1926), umpiring more than a hundred of her matches. He then became a Wimbledon Player Liaison until 1949, when he designed the famous lace tennis panties that Gussie Moran wore at the All-England Club. Because of the scandal those panties created, Ted was asked to resign.

From the 1950s to the 1970s, Ted designed daring, fashionable tennis outfits for stars like Maureen Connolly, Evonne Goolagong, Billie Jean King, Chris Evert, and Martina Navratilova, just to name a few, while at the same time acting as chief of protocol for the International Tennis Federation. In 1980, Ted designed the dress for

Patti's great friend Mariana Borg, for her and Björn's wedding. He also created Chrissie's wedding gown when she married John Lloyd. I know that only because Patti told me. I wasn't invited.

So at Wimbledon in 1982, at the age of 72, Ted was the official player liaison, and one of his more challenging jobs was to make sure Mac and I stayed out of trouble, after the fireworks of the semis in 1981. We took it easy on him because we liked him.

Also, just before Wimbledon, Ted had to have surgery on his leg. Patti went to visit him while he was recovering in the hospital and returned to the hotel still laughing at a story that Ted, who was openly gay, had told her.

A couple of nights before, Ted had been asleep when he was awakened in the early hours by the sound of someone in his room. "Patti," he told her, "all my life I have wanted to wake up with a gorgeous guy standing over me, and then it finally happened. The only problem was that he was there to rob me! What sort of luck is that?"

"Don't worry, Jimmy," Patti said, "the thief ran off and Ted's OK."

That sort of summed up Ted; he always found something to laugh about, even when things weren't going his way. After he was released from the hospital, he invited Patti to the annual Women's Tennis Association pre-Wimbledon party at the Kensington Roof Garden. As Patti tells it, she was the only non–tennis player there, and Ted loved showing her off. After Patti's date with Ted, he would call us every morning just to see if we (and by that I mean Patti) needed anything, and if we did, it was done. He was a great guy, and I wondered why it took the All-England Club only 30 years to realize what a contribution Ted had made to tennis—not just his innovative designs, but also his encyclopedic knowledge of the game.

It was a very sad day for us when Ted died, in 1990. He'd become a good friend and we still miss him. Oh, and by the way, we found out after his death that he had been a British Intelligence spy during WWII in Algiers and Germany.

Because of rain, I didn't end up playing my third round until the second week of Wimbledon. I beat South African Mike Myburg and Australian John Alexander, then faced Californian Drew Gitlin, ranked 185th in world. That turned out to be a pretty interesting match, because he played out of his skin. In the fourth set, with the match going on three hours and the fans calling for a postponement because it was too dark for them to see the ball, I finished him off in the tiebreaker with a lucky return. Man, was I happy to be back in my hotel room that night, without worrying about resuming the match the next day.

The telephone by my bed rings early the next morning. Still half asleep, I answer.

"Hello?"

"Hey, Jimmy, what are you doing?" It's my brother's voice.

"I'm still in bed, I'm not playing today. What's going on? Where are you?"

"I'm in the lobby."

"What?"

It turns out that Mom, who was in Belleville, had called Johnny over the weekend and told him to fly to London to help me out, without even asking me if I needed him. Although I didn't know it at the time, he was there for a reason.

I think Mom was still trying to look out for my best interests, and she probably wasn't aware that sending Johnny to Wimbledon would just put more pressure on me. With Patti, I was already well taken care of. She kept me grounded, helped me relax and escape from tennis—which was exactly what I needed if I was going to succeed

in proving my critics wrong. Johnny's arrival was a minor inconve-
nience, but I was happy to see him. So Ted arranged for two cars.

However, all too quickly I got into a pattern of riding with the
guys in one car—me, Johnny, and Lornie, who had come with us to
London—while Patti, Brett, and Adela rode in the other. Patti was
being pushed aside, and I didn't even notice. That proved to be the
first crack in my relationship with Patti.

After I defeated Paul McNamee on my way to a quarterfinal
match with Gene Mayer, I had a conversation with Mac. It had
been raining hard throughout the first week of Wimbledon, and I'd
been practicing with him off and on since the Queen's. We might
have had our differences, but we weren't stupid. We knew hitting
together made us both better.

After my match with McNamee, I bump into Mac in the locker
room.

"Hey, I'll see you tomorrow and we'll hit some balls, OK?"

"No, no, no. I don't think we should hit anymore," he says to me,
looking uncomfortable. I can guess why. It probably just dawned on
him that he might have to play me in the finals.

"What?" I say. "We've been practicing together for three weeks.
You think it's going to make a difference now? Well, if that's what
you want. See you around."

*Connors is a one-dimensional player, whose only stroke is his two-fisted
backhand.*

I don't know how many times I heard or read that about myself
over the years. It used to just make me smile because anyone who
said it knew nothing about tennis. As I've said, I had adapted and
adjusted elements of my game over the years to try to find a way
to win. The 1982 Wimbledon final against Mac was no different.
I was climbing out of a four-year slump and was about to face the

best player in the world at the time. To be the best, you have to beat the best.

My game was in place—I knew it, even if no one else did—but that wasn't going to be enough. Mac was going to attack me every chance he got, looking to take the ball out of the air to counter the unpredictable bounce of the Wimbledon grass. I had to come up with a way to pin him to the baseline. The answer was clear: change my serve by putting more juice on it, flattening it out, hitting it deeper. If he managed to get his racquet on it, my forward momentum would allow me to get to the net quicker. He wouldn't be expecting that. If I could rattle Mac and keep the match close, I could beat him. My confidence in the improvements I'd made in my game would only grow.

There was a certain amount of risk, since pushing too hard could produce too many second serves, which he would pounce on. But I was going to force the action just the same. If I lose, I lose. But it will be on my terms.

The stats tell one story—13 double faults, no aces. That's three free games I handed Mac. Add in his 19 aces and that's more than a set.

The score tells another story.

No aces for me only meant that Mac managed to make contact with my first serves; it didn't mean they came back at me. I had a 60 percent success rate on them; Mac only had 54. If he did manage to make a return, I rushed the net to punch volleys away. I gambled and it worked.

On that Fourth of July, we gave the fans the longest match in Wimbledon history at the time. We were battling it out in the trenches, working hard, making mistakes, but producing many moments of outstanding tennis. The fans appreciated our effort and were cheering, clapping, shouting encouragement, jumping out of their seats, and generally making such a ruckus that the umpire was repeatedly forced to ask for "Quiet, please." But that wasn't going to happen. New York had come to London for the afternoon.

With Mac leading two sets to one, the match hinged on a tie-breaker in the fourth. Only three points from defeat, I made my move and took the breaker, 7-5. In the fifth, I broke early and held on to win my second Wimbledon title.

I leaped in the air, arms raised in triumph. As I walked to the net to shake Mac's hand, I remembered something Newk had told me: "The second time [you win Wimbledon]—that's when it sinks in. That's when you realize it was no fluke, that you deserve your place in history."

As the crowd rose to give us a standing ovation (the only other time I've received one of those, I was on my knees after Richard Lewis's ball hit me in the nuts), I waved to Patti to come down onto the court with me. I wanted us to share the moment. She'd led the way there, always believing in me. As I gave her a kiss in front of 14,000 spectators, I knew we'd won the title together.

I wish I'd remembered and respected those feelings in the months that followed.

The next morning, before we headed back home, I had one important stop to make. Ladbrokes. This time there were no sniggers. The manager greeted me with a big smile.

"Congratulations, Mr. Connors. Your check is waiting for you."

Just what an old gambler likes to hear.

I decided to take some time off after Wimbledon—yeah, to cash in, I admit. That's how we made the real money back then. Winning a Slam was the high point, but it also opened financial doors, which none of the top players walked away from. You'd be nuts if you did. It wasn't going to last forever.

Unlike earlier in the summer, I was the hot ticket for promoters running exhibition matches. So, naturally, my price doubled and they were still beating down my door.

In July, Borg and I played at Industry Hills, California, in a four-man, two-day exhibition with Vitas and Sandy Mayer. In the final, I beat Borg for the first time since the 1978 Open final, in five sets over three and a half hours in 100-degree heat, to pick up $50,000.

Later that month, it was Richmond, Virginia, where over four sets I won again, coming away with $40,000. Then, with the US Open coming up, it was back to business. My time off hadn't seemed to hurt me any, but the mechanics of my new serve did. After spending my whole career up to Wimbledon tossing the ball behind me, I tried tossing it more forward, and it threw my back out of whack. In Columbus, Ohio, I won my 95th tournament, defeating Brian Gottfried, but a week later I had to withdraw from the Canadian Open at the semifinal stage with pain in my lower back.

It didn't look like I was going to be able to play in the ATP championship, in Mason, Ohio. But with my doctor's help, stretching exercises, and a big dose of patience, I made it through to the semis, where Ivan Lendl beat me in just over an hour. It wasn't my back. As I've said before, if I stepped on the court, it meant I was well enough to play. Lendl was better than me on that day, that's all. Now the Open was only a week away, and Mac was the favorite.

Some people said that I tanked in Ohio to give Lendl a false sense of security. I didn't. I never tanked, ever. But Wimbledon and the US Open meant more to me than anything else in tennis, and as they approached, I sometimes found myself distracted and looking ahead. It's not like I didn't care about the tournament I was playing in, I just didn't have my usual concentration. That said, I'm not suggesting Lendl wouldn't have beaten me no matter how hard I had focused.

Winning Wimbledon wasn't enough for me. After 1975, I had responded to those who said I was washed up by transforming my game. Flushing Meadows was the perfect place to complete my second reinvention. With Mac seeded first, me second, and Lendl third, I was going to meet one of them in the final, and it didn't matter to me which one.

You want a fight, son? You can have it. My blood's pumping now.

The fourth set of the 1982 US Open final, Connors versus Lendl. I'm up two sets to one, 4-2 on his serve, 15-15. My return of serve is a net cord. Lendl moves in for the return. My lob's quite a bit short, and Lendl has the whole court for a put-away. Next thing I know his smash is coming directly at me. I'm hot, I'm tired and dying for a beer, and putting up with his target-practice antics didn't help my mood. Lendl's well known for trying to hit his opponent with the ball, and while I didn't take it personally, if I offended anybody when I told him to fuck off get over it. I won my fourth Open title 6-3, 6-2, 4-6, 6-4.

My second Slam of the year made me more in demand as Borg and I took up where we'd left off before the Open.

Montreal in October, a straight-sets victory and $80,000.

Seattle in mid-November, two sets to one and $75,000.

San Francisco a week later, a fifth victory in a row over Borg, $75,000.

These events were usually only two- or three-night stopovers, which wasn't good for three-year-old Brett. There wasn't enough time for him to settle into a routine, so Patti and I decided that she would stay home while I traveled with the guys, Johnny or Lornie, sometimes both. It was like the old days, meeting up with my buddies, staying out late, and enjoying the perks of fame. I told myself that I'd earned all this and that it wouldn't last long, anyway.

Then I started to believe the hype that comes with winning, and it wasn't long before I made the biggest mistake in my life.

16

HOUSE DIVIDED

I n 1983, I was the biggest name in town. I was king of the tennis mountain. I thought I could do what I wanted. And I wanted my life to be as fun and free as it had been before Patti and the baby.

When I was home, I acted like I was above all the everyday things—car trouble, dinner preparations, arrangements for Brett now that Adela had left us? Not my problem. *I shouldn't have to deal with this crap. I'm a Wimbledon and US Open champion.*

It didn't occur to me that at home I wasn't the best player in the world but a husband and father. I left it to Patti to deal with everything and spent my time resenting her and pushing her away.

Mom didn't help. When we went to visit, she would cut my wife out. We'd arrive and Mom would say to Patti, "Hi, glad you could come," and that would be it. At mealtimes, if Patti offered to assist Mom in the kitchen, all she would get was "If I need any help, I'll ask for it." When it came time for us to leave, Mom would say nothing more to Patti than "See you later." Patti tried not to let it bother her but it was obvious her feelings were hurt. And, again, I let it go.

Back at home my mood was getting worse and I spent most of my time planning my next escape with my buddies, where I could really be "me." All during this time, Patti kept a positive attitude, trying to make the best of a difficult situation, hoping, I guess, that I was just going through a phase.

After so many years of me fighting my way back to the top, Patti was just giving me time to get whatever it was that was bothering me out of my system. I didn't tell her I didn't want to work it out. I didn't tell her anything.

I was happy playing the champion, being in demand and naming my price. A certain amount of selfishness is required for an athlete who wants to compete at the highest level but until now I had always checked that me-first attitude at the door of my home. I took Patti and Brett to Vail, Colorado, for Christmas and gave Patti an expensive pair of diamond earrings. Guilt jewelry? Probably. It was strange, but we had a good time on that trip. We hadn't brought any friends with us, I had no flights to schedule or matches to play, and for a few days I was the contented husband and father I'd been before.

But at the beginning of 1983, with the winter indoor season approaching, my mood darkened again as I tried to ignore the guilt and invented justifications for my behavior.

Patti and I should have dated longer, enjoyed ourselves more, got to know each other better before we married and had a son. It all happened too fast.

Patti just doesn't get tennis. She never has. She's holding me back.

Hell, I'm holding her back. She could have had a great career by now.

I can't drag Patti and Brett around the world with me forever. It's not fair to them.

On and on it went. I should have been saying all of that to Patti; instead I just let it bounce around in my head while I glared at her.

Early January, I made a decision. I sat down with Patti at home in Turnberry and told her.

"I'm going to travel with the boys for a while," I said. "You and Brett don't really like going to all those winter indoor tournaments. I think this is for the best."

"Oh, OK, if you're sure. But you know I enjoy coming along, right?"

I didn't answer her. Patti had been traveling with me for nine months out of the year for the last four years, and now I'm telling her she is no longer welcome on the road.

My first match was an exhibition in Rosemont, Illinois, after which I could have gone home before the Masters at Madison Square Garden. But I didn't. Lendl beat me in the semis in New York, and from there, after only a quick visit home, I was off again, to Toronto for another challenge tournament, which was quickly followed by Memphis, where I won a record sixth US Indoor championship.

One of Patti's favorite tournaments came next, the Congoleum Tennis Classic, in La Quinta, California, near Palm Springs. When I didn't invite her and Brett to go with me, that was the moment, Patti says, she knew something was very, very wrong.

There was a reason I didn't want her at the next tournament in La Quinta. I wasn't alone and some of my friends knew about "her." I always claim to have no regrets about my life, but that's not strictly true. I regret cheating on my wife and my son, and I always will.

The affair was bad enough, but allowing it to become an open secret, with so many people aware of it, but not my wife, was unforgivable.

I lost to Mike Bauer at La Quinta, because, as I said at the time, "I couldn't keep my mind on my business during the match."

No shit, Jimmy.

Patti had announced that she and Brett were going to visit some friends in LA where I would meet them after my match. Patti was still completely in the dark about this other woman, and I wanted to keep it that way. When I arrived in LA, I told her we needed to talk.

"Things have changed," I said bluntly as she sat opposite me in shocked silence. "I don't want the same things I wanted before. I want a divorce."

Patti started crying. "I don't understand. What's happened? I know I haven't been traveling with you, but I thought that's what you wanted. Did I do something wrong?" There was a long pause and then she asked, "Is there someone else?"

"No, it's not you. I still love you and Brett. It's me. I've changed, and that's all. I don't want to be married anymore. And there's no one else," I lied.

Later, Patti said that she had believed me when I said there was no other woman. She just thought that, given Mom's coolness toward her and the fact that we had married so soon after we'd met, that I had really changed.

We spent that night together without touching, and Patti sobbed all night.

Brett cried when we left the next day. He didn't want to be with me, because I'd been gone for so long and Patti had always been the one constant in his life. Now I was taking him away.

I said I'd tell you my story, and this is part of it. I've never cheated you on the court, so I'm not going to cheat you in this book. The truth isn't pretty, but it's what happened.

The other woman was on the same flight I took back to Belleville to attend the opening of my brother's new restaurant, The Center Court. We weren't sitting together, but we were going to the same places. To Mom's house. To Johnny's opening. Meanwhile back home, Patti's heart was breaking and she was beating herself up for something that wasn't even her fault.

Brett and I stayed with Mom while we were in St. Louis, and so did my new friend. We in separate rooms, but she was still sleeping in the same house.

I was supposed to take Brett to the airport in St. Louis to meet Patti so she and her mother could pick him up and take him to Vail for a few days. I didn't go. I sent Johnny and Mom instead. It was the final act of betrayal on my part. I knew I had caused Patti pain but I couldn't even begin to imagine the depth of her suffering

It didn't take long for Patti to find out the truth. The day Patti picked up Brett from the airport, my little boy, in total innocence, said, "Mommy, did you know Daddy has a girlfriend? I saw them hugging at Grandma's."

It makes me sick just thinking about it even now.

Patti always deals in reality, and she knew it was time to protect our son and herself from whatever insanity I was going through. She hates lies, and I had lied to her. She also knew that Mom would be dealing with the business end of our divorce and that Mom would be looking out for *my* best interests.

Patti contacted a secretary who worked with Mom to schedule my business trips and was able to get flight numbers, hotel bookings, names, everything that proved I hadn't been traveling alone. Then Patti asked a friend, a photographer who lived in LA, to get a photo of the two of us. It wasn't hard. Subtlety has never been my strong suit.

My next step was to reduce the amount of money available to Patti, giving her a small amount every month. I canceled her credit cards and kept a record of Patti's absences when I called to speak to Brett. I wanted ammunition to use in court. "Patti not home," "Patti not home," I wrote as if she was being a bad mother, even though I knew Patti's mom was there, looking after Brett while my wife had deliberately arranged aerobics classes or tennis lessons so I could talk to Brett without her in the room.

The press got wind of our separation and the fact that I was seeing someone else. They called Patti at home and followed her whenever they could. Everywhere she went people would look at her and whisper. The strain took a toll on Patti, and that had an impact on Brett. I learned later that Patti would arrange play dates for Brett, but when his friends came over he'd slam the door in their faces. Concerned, Patti took him to a child psychiatrist, who explained that since Dad had left him, Brett couldn't stand to be away from Mom. Nor did he want anyone else in the house. That's when Patti knew she had to take action to try and get Brett's and her life in order without me.

I went to Turnberry to see Brett after the Alan King Classic at the end of April, which I won for the fourth time. Patti told me she'd arranged for a limo service to pick me up at the airport. A friend of hers owned the limo service, and when I got off the plane the driver was waiting for me, carrying a card with my name printed on it. As I walked toward him, a man came up to me.

"Are you Mr. Jimmy Connors?" the guy asked.

"Yes," I said, thinking he just wanted an autograph.

He handed me an envelope. "Consider yourself served."

Patti had started divorce proceedings. Included in the papers was Patti's custody claim for Brett, with a court order blocking me or anyone else taking, enticing, or removing Brett from Dade County. I just stood there, my bags at my feet, hundreds of people milling around, going on with their lives, as I watched mine fall apart.

"Do I at least get a free ride to the hotel?" I asked the limo driver. He opened the car door and I got inside.

"Do you know where my family is?" I asked him.

There was no answer.

I spent the week at Turnberry with Brett while Patti stayed with her mom. I loved being with my son; I had missed him, but I failed to realize that spending an extended period of time with him, then suddenly leaving, would only confuse him even more. The day after I left, Patti told me, Brett said to her, "Next time Daddy comes home you stay, too, OK?" Hearing him say those words broke her heart all over again, but Patti never hides from the truth. She would deal with the situation, even if I wouldn't. She knew she had to be gentle with Brett and that it would take time for him to understand, and she then would have to pick up the pieces.

"Brett, Mommy and Daddy are going to get a divorce, and that means we are not going to live together anymore. But Daddy still loves you and Mommy still loves you. It's just that you will be spending time differently with us from how you have been."

"OK," he said, but Patti wasn't really convinced he understood.

After Wimbledon and the French, during July 4th, I visited again. Patti picked me up at the airport with Brett, and after giving me a kiss the first thing he said was, "Daddy, how come you don't love my mommy anymore?"

It was like someone had shoved a knife right into my heart. Did he really think that? I loved Patti, but was Brett really asking if I'd stopped loving them both?

"Brett," said Patti, "don't bother Daddy with those questions right now. OK, honey?"

Was Patti turning my son against me? On a deeper level, I knew Patti was incapable of anything like that. But, still, I glared at her all the way to the hotel where I was going to stay. Isn't it funny how far you'll go to not take responsibility for the damage you do to the people you love most in the world?

David Schneider and I are driving back to Turnberry across Alligator Alley from his place in Fort Myers, Florida, where I had spent the night. It's a long drive, about 150 miles across the Everglades, and for the past hour he's listening to me complain about Patti.

"This is bullshit, Schneider. She's telling me when I can and can't see my son. Fuck that. I told her I'd take him away and she's got lawyers saying I can't."

"No, you can't, Jimmy. And the fact that Patti won't fold is messing with your head. You know she's right and you don't like it.
Look, man, I love you, but I love Patti, too, and I don't want to hear
you talking about her like this anymore."

David had already told me more than once that he didn't like
how I was acting. And he wasn't the only one of my friends who felt
that way.

In reality, I had backed Patti into a corner and she'd come out
fighting, showing the same instincts that served me so well on the
tennis court. I was trying to rally my buddies to my cause, and they
weren't buying it.

We didn't have a lot of friends in Florida, because we had spent
so much time traveling. When I decided I didn't want to be married
anymore, Patti was forced to rely on a handful of people for support.
Eddie Dibbs and his wife would visit her and make sure she was doing OK; so did Father Charles, the priest who had baptized Brett.
Father Charles was staying in an apartment at Turnberry because of
the kindness of the owner, Donny Soffer. Why was I depending on
others to take care of my family? What a dick.

Once Schneider and I got back to my hotel in Turnberry, I asked
him if he wanted to get a drink at the bar.

"Sorry, Jimmy, can't do it."

Then he drives away, leaving me on the front steps of a hotel full
of people I don't know.

Roland Garros. I've just lost 6-4, 6-4, 7-6 in the quarterfinal match
against Frenchman Christophe Roger-Vasselin, who is ranked 130th
in the world, as the crowd screamed, "Roger! Roger!"

Afterward, I'm in one of my favorite restaurants in Paris, sitting
across from Lornie talking about tennis. This doesn't feel right. And
it has nothing to do with tennis.

At Wimbledon, Kevin Curren of South Africa defeats me in the fourth round 6–3, 6–7, 6–3, 7–6, after serving up 33 aces. It's the first time I've failed to reach at least the quarterfinals of the tournament. In the post-match press interview I call the match "a bad day at the office." In reality it was a tough loss on the number 2 court, which was known as the Graveyard of Champions. Can you say *karma*?

I'd ended the affair. It had been a mistake from the beginning but I can't go back and undo it. I'll have to live with that for the rest of my life.

Later that night, I'm at the Playboy Club, once again sitting across from Lornie and talking tennis. Still. This really doesn't feel right. But then nothing has felt right for a long time.

Then this overwhelming feeling comes over me and it doesn't take me long to realize what it is: I miss my wife.

After Wimbledon I called Patti and asked if it was OK if I came to Turnberry to see Brett. It wasn't my agreed-upon visitation arrangement, but Patti never once refused to let me see our son.

Patti and Brett picked me up at the airport in Fort Lauderdale, and we decided go to a Chinese restaurant, Christine Lee's, for dinner. After a few glasses of plum wine, I stumbled my way through to what I really wanted to talk to her about. I call that Plum Wine Courage.

"Do you think we can make this work?" I asked.

"Make what work?" asked Patti. Later, she told me she thought I was asking if we could work out things between us financially in the divorce.

"Us. This crazy circus?" I said, indicating Patti, Brett, and me.

"I don't know. I don't know if I even like you, let alone love you," she said.

I didn't know what else to do except hug her. I wanted to be with my family, and you know me well enough by now to know that I would fight to the death to win them back. I stayed in Florida for two days before returning to Belleville. I had to figure out some way to show Patti I was serious about trying to fix our marriage.

"Listen, I've got to go to South Africa for some exhibitions in a couple of days," I said to her. "Would you like to go and keep me company?"

There was silence. In that moment, I allowed myself some hope.

"OK."

"Really?"

"Yes. Mom can look after Brett. But, understand, if I do, it's as a friend only."

Beggars can be choosers. I'll take it.

We decided that we would meet in New York and fly out from there.

I'm waiting by the departure gate at JFK and the London flight has just been called. The plane from Miami landed half an hour ago. I start to think that Patti has changed her mind.

I look at my watch. I'm going to have to board and the rest of my life is starting to look pretty fucking lonely. I understand that, if Patti shows up, she's just testing the waters to see if she can even stand being around me. I know we can eventually be friends, but what I'm holding out for is that she'll love me again.

And now here she is, walking across the concourse toward me.

That was a good moment. A very good moment.

After a quick stop in London, the press is out in force in Johannesburg, waiting for us when we touch down. Word has gotten out that we are traveling together.

"Did you tell them?" Patti hisses at me as we make our way through the explosion of flashing bulbs. "Because if you did and didn't warn me, I'll kill you. I'd have brushed my hair and put some makeup on!"

She's always known how to make me laugh.

We go straight to a private plane that takes us to Sun City, which is owned by Sol Kerzner, who built the big Atlantis resort in the Caribbean. Sun City looks like Vegas, with spectacular hotels and casinos, and Sol books all the big acts, like Rod Stewart and Elton John.

In our hotel that night in Sun City, we have the conversation I've been dreading. I've been hoping I would never have to talk about it, but I know if I'm going to have any chance of getting my wife back that this has to happen. Now.

"Why did you do it, Jimmy?" Patti asks.

"Do what?" I say, stalling for time.

She just looks at me.

"I don't know," I say. And I really didn't know.

"Tell me honestly about that woman," Patti says.

"She's just a friend, nothing more." This is the lie I've stuck to since Patti filed for divorce and I was going to stick with it no matter what. She never believed it for a moment.

"What do you mean, 'Just a friend'? We've been married four years and I've never met her. She's not just a friend, and I want the truth. Right now. This is it, Jimmy. There are no second chances. Either you tell me the truth and admit it to my face now or I'm on the next plane out of here."

She's looking right at me and asking me to be the man she married, not the man I've become over the last few months. I take a deep breath. I can hardly get the words out, because I start crying. "I'm sorry, I'm sorry."

"Did you love her?"

"No."

"What was it, then?"

"I don't know."

It isn't much of an answer, but Patti understands. She nods, holds my hand, and says, "OK, Jimmy, let's talk about what the future might look like. But before that, I'm going to have to speak to your mom and straighten out some things."

"I understand you have to do that. But you should also know, after Wimbledon, when I was dropping my bags off at Mom's house, she said to me, 'Jimmy, go back to Florida. Go see your wife and son. That's where you should be.' In her own way, Mom was telling me that she and I have both made mistakes and that we need to try to fix them if we can."

It took a while for Patti and Mom to make peace, but eventually, in later years, they would form a close bond that would last until Mom's death.

That night in Sun City, for the first time in a long time, we talked to each other openly and honestly about what had gone wrong, and what I allowed to go wrong by keeping my feelings to myself. We made a deal that whether I was in a tournament or not, we'd face whatever issues came up in the moment and try to resolve them. We've stuck to that ever since. I still turned into that "other person" whenever I stepped onto the court, but instead of letting things fester and slide, either Patti brought me back to earth or I dragged myself there on my own. Thirty-three years later it still works.

On one of the days we spent in Mala Mala, Patti decided that we needed some exercise and the safest place to do some jogging was the small airstrip. We were happily jogging along when we saw a jeep coming toward us. It was our ranger and our guide and they were carrying rifles.

"Mr. Connors," the guide said, "you shouldn't be jogging out here without a guide." Then he pointed behind us. Patti and I turned around to see three lions crossing the airstrip. I guess they needed a little exercise, too. And maybe a little snack to keep up their strength.

From Mala Mala, we went to Durban for another match, then on to the beautiful city of Cape Town for yet another. This was still during apartheid, and we would encounter signs like COLORED BATHING BEACH and WHITE BATHING BEACH. Patti was offended by the cruelty and injustice and didn't hesitate to voice her opinion, "You guys are going to regret this. The blacks outnumber the whites, twenty-five to one. You haven't provided education or social services and this is going to come back and bite you in the ass." As usual, Patti was right.

South Africa will always be a special place for me. With my head full of myself, and so much else going on in our lives with tennis and Brett, I'd forgotten until that trip that having Patti as my partner and lover was my life. I would never forget again.

Back home we took it slowly, but we both knew we were back together for good, and after Thanksgiving Patti withdrew her petition for divorce.

Although I may never fully understand why I cheated on my wife, what I do know with absolute certainty is that without Patti's understanding and forgiveness, my life would have taken a very different course.

The thought of any other outcome now is unacceptable. If Patti hadn't come running across that concourse at JFK, we wouldn't have had the incredible joy of having our daughter, Aubree, our second child.

It's the semis of the ATP championship, at Mason, Ohio, third set, late evening, and it's still sweltering. Earlier the courtside temperature topped 115 degrees, and tempers are short. Not the best conditions for a match between Mac and me. We've both been trash-talking, complaining about calls, and generally getting on each other's nerves.

There's been a heckler in the second row on Mac's back all night, and Mac finally snaps.

"Come on, Jimmy, you can beat this punk," the guy shouts, and Mac turns on him.

"Fuck you. And your girlfriend, too."

Never bring the girlfriend into it; it only means trouble. The guy is big and now he's out of his seat and heading for Mac.

I jump the net and stand between them.

"Come on, let's just cool down," I say to Gigantor.

"Jimmy, I'm rooting for you, but he disrespected my girlfriend and I'm not going to take it."

I glance behind me and Mac's giving the guy the "Fuck you, buddy" treatment as he walks backward in full retreat.

"Come on, Mac, why not just apologize to the man's girlfriend?"

The stadium has gone quiet. I think half of them hope the guy gives Mac a pounding. (Personally, I'd pay to see that!) "Mac, do you mind? Let's face it, the two of us together don't stand a chance against this guy."

Reluctantly, McEnroe nods and approaches.

"I'd like to apologize to your girlfriend. But fuck you."

That works for me.

I look at the guy, hopefully. "You got to accept that, right?"

"Sure, Jimmy. Until the match is over."

I really should have let the guy kick Mac's ass. Instead, Mac kicked mine 6–4 in the third.

It's Flushing Meadows, September 2, 1983, and my 31st birthday. I don't have a match today, but I've gone to the stadium to pick up some racquets. Patti suggests we get a bite to eat while we're there. We're about to go into the player's lounge when a pretty young woman wearing glasses and dressed in a business suit, runs up and grabs my sleeve.

"Mr. Connors, Mr. Connors, I love you. I love you. Please can you get me a ticket to come and watch you play?"

Oh boy, after everything that's gone on with Patti, this is just what I need. The young woman now has a death grip on me and I can't get away. "Sorry, I have my family here. I don't have any extra tickets. I am really sorry. But thank you for your support. I've got to go now."

Patti and I enter the players' lounge, which is packed with about 200 people, and the young woman follows us inside, hanging on to my arm.

"Please, Mr. Connors, please. At least try and get me a ticket," she says.

She's not giving up and she won't let go and I can't just shove her away. I look over at Patti and raise my eyebrows as if to say, "What do I do now?" She just shrugs and mouths over to me, "Who is she?" This is a familiar question, but I have no idea.

The young woman finally releases my arm and reaches into her bag. What the . . . ? A gun? Is she going to kill me? No. She's pulling out a tape recorder. Does she want an interview? She doesn't say another word; she just puts the tape recorder on a nearby table and presses play. Oh, God, what now? Music?

Bow-chica-wow-wow.

She's taking her hair down and pulling off her glasses. Now she's removing her jacket! Shit! She's a stripper! Patti's going to freak out and I've already caused enough trouble for a lifetime. Sandy's wife looks shocked. The bra is coming off! I'm about to have a heart attack. Then I glance over at Patti. She's doubled over with laughter.

It's been a rough year and she thought a stripper would lighten the mood. What could I do? I sat down and enjoyed myself.

My life at the US Open that year was going pretty smoothly. I had my family back. I was doing a job I loved and I'd only dropped a single set, in the first round and made it to the final. There was just one little hitch: Someone really did want to kill me, and it wasn't the stripper.

I had been called into the director's office, where a member of the NYPD met me.

"Mr. Connors, we have received a credible threat to your life. We don't know who it's from yet, we're investigating, but we are taking this very seriously."

Knowing me, you can probably guess that this isn't the first time I'd been threatened, and I usually didn't give it too much thought. But this time it's different; I have a family now. I sit down with the police officer and discuss the options. It's the US Open, my championships, and I'm defending my title, but I've got to put Patti and Brett's safety first. I tell the police and the Open officials that I'm not pulling out, but if anything should happen, they have to look after my family. I'll figure out my own getaway. I might be a moving target, but Patti and Brett would be sitting ducks. The police agree to surround them with plainclothes officers and reassure me they will monitor the situation during each of my matches and add increased security on the gates and in the stadium.

As far as my game was concerned, the thought of my life being in peril wasn't going to be a big problem. Once on the court, I've always had the ability to switch off distractions—yes, even death threats (yeah, I sleep with one eye open). So I went through the entire tournament unaware of any potential danger while the ball was in play, then went back to worrying about Patti and Brett in the warm-ups and at changeovers. Patti and I agreed that we wouldn't let it disrupt our lives. We'd be careful, but otherwise we'd go on as we always had. In the end, nothing happened at the Open, but we felt a little uncomfortable for a few months afterward, knowing the person who made the death threat hadn't been caught and was out there somewhere.

The fact that someone in the crowd wanted to kill me didn't actually bother me as much as my little toe on my right foot did. I'd hurt it earlier in the tournament, and by the end of my semifinal victory over Bill Scanlon, it had become swollen and infected.

On the morning of the final against Lendl, I could barely walk, let alone play. I cut a hole in my sneakers to reduce some of the pressure, which helped, but unless the doctor could do something immediately I knew there was a risk that I'd have to pull out.

I only had one option. The doctor shot a powerful painkiller into my foot, which numbed the pain but put my foot to sleep. You know what it's like when your foot falls asleep? It's like your leg stops at your ankle. Even when I rubbed my toe on the hard court as it poked out of my shoe, I didn't feel a thing.

When you rely on your footwork as much as I did, especially against a guy like Lendl—superfit, four inches taller, eight years younger, with a big serve and a long reach—having a leg that stops at your ankle might be a problem. I was going to have to chase balls across the baseline all afternoon with a dead foot. Oh, well.

Look, at my age the chances of challenging for titles were getting fewer and fewer. Lendl was coming up quick; so were a couple of Swedes—Mats Wilander (he'd already won the French) and a new kid named Stefan Edberg. And Mac wasn't exactly ready to call it quits. Realistically, the odds for me weren't good, so I had to take any opportunity I could.

It was brutally hot inside Louis Armstrong Stadium. During the second set, which I lost in a tiebreak, I had to leave the court. I said I had an upset stomach, but really I had to get another injection in my foot because the first one had worn off. Without another one, I wouldn't have been able to continue the match. And the second one had to last because you couldn't leave the court twice.

In the third, with set point on his serve, Lendl choked. A double fault brought the score back to deuce. He didn't win another game.

He fought hard to the very end, saving two match points before a crosscourt forehand won me the championship for the fifth time.

I acknowledged the absolutely incredible New York fans as they cheered and chanted, "Jim-eee! Jim-eee!" I walked very slowly to the net to shake Ivan's hand, not because of my painful toe, but because I wanted to milk this moment for everything it was worth.

It would be eight years before I was able to experience this feeling again.

I think, of all my wins, this 100th was probably the sweetest. I wanted to have that US Open title just one more time.

As I listened to the applause in my stadium, from *my* New Yorkers, I knew that I had turned a corner. I still had work ahead of me to rebuild my relationship with Patti, but it was work I was looking forward to doing. Life was good.

I would never win a Grand Slam final again.

17

ROAD WARRIOR

C ome on, Connors. We're late already."

"No, I can't go yet."

"Come on! Everyone's waiting for you. Let's hit the road."

"Screw you, G. I'm not going anywhere yet."

It's January 1984 and I'm sitting in Nasty's apartment in Manhattan during the Masters. Gerry Goldberg and Ilie are here, together with their wives and Patti. We've got dinner reservations and they want to get going. I'm not moving. Why?

Because Bill Laimbeer, of the Detroit Pistons, is on the free throw line, time has expired, and he's shooting two. I need them both to win my bet.

I'm leaning forward in my seat, staring intensely at the TV screen, palms sweating, heart racing.

"Connors! The car is waiting downstairs. You can find out the score later."

It's not about the score. It's about this moment, as addictive as any drug.

Boom! The first one's good. If he'd missed, I'd be screwed and could walk away, the money gone. But now . . .

The ball's in the air.

He knocks it down! It's over. Winning or losing a couple of grand doesn't affect me one way or the other. But the rush, man, that *is* what it's about.

I walk out the door feeling an emotional letdown. My adrenaline is suddenly gone. All I can think is what an asshole I am for waiting for that schmuck to sink a free throw just because I've got a bet on it.

Although Patti and I were becoming closer than ever before, my gambling, which had always been a little excessive, was starting to slip out of my control.

John McEnroe won the 1984 Wimbledon final in 80 minutes, beating me 6-1, 6-1, 6-2. I was getting my ass kicked in front of 15,000 people and millions more on TV. I tried different things that might rattle Mac enough to get me back in the match. Nothing worked. Mac simply played better than me. On days like that you just say screw it and move on to the next tournament.

But this particular match stands out to me for a couple of reasons—other than getting crushed in one of the shortest finals ever. One, it turned out to be my last appearance in a Grand Slam final. Two, it was the first I'd played with a midsize racquet.

I'd hung onto my T2000 through my 1983 US Open victory, even though almost everyone else on the tour had long since been using the new generation of oversize or midsize graphites. But I couldn't ignore the fact that by sticking with the T2000 I was giving too much away.

Wilson had officially stopped making my racquet years before but had kept unofficially making them for me. Once I made the decision to give up my T2000, I had a word with Wilson to see what they could do for me. Generous as ever, they applied modern technology to my requirements and produced a racquet that became known as the Pro Staff.

I found the transition tough, I went from a racquet with lots of movement to a frame that felt as stiff as a board. Wilson said the new racquets had been made exactly with the same specs I had before, but they weren't. The difference in material and the way it played and felt in my hand had no resemblance to the steel racquet that I had used throughout my whole career. The ball didn't fly off the racquet; it required too much effort on my part to generate the pace that I was looking for.

I had been using my same strokes for so long that changing them was out of the question; they were part of my muscle memory. So I worked hard to integrate the new racquet into my existing game. In January 1985, at the US Indoors in Memphis, I alternated between the two racquets in my semifinal loss to Edberg. I stuck with the Pro Staff for my next tournament, the Pilot Pen Classic at La Quinta, where I lost in the quarterfinals to Greg Holmes. So much for the Pro Staff experiment. There was nothing wrong with the racquet; it just didn't work for me, and I went back to my T2000.

I knew Wilson wasn't going to produce any more T2000s, so for the next two years I used up the 10 or so frames I had left. Eventually, I had to accept that my T2000 couldn't compete with the new technology, and I went with Slazenger for their Panther Pro Ceramic. And I thought the Pro Staff was too stiff! This one was even tougher for me to play with, and even though I worked with Slazenger to try to make it better, it just didn't fit. I wasted a lot of time that I didn't have trying to find a racquet that suited me. I finally settled on Prince's single-throated Mono during my time on the Champions Tour. It's the racquet I still use today, the fastest I've come across since the T2000. Of course, I wish I had found it sooner—some results could have been different.

A word about technological advances in tennis: I think the racquets players use today make a lot of them look and play better than they actually are. Add to that all the other advantages available now, like the high-tech machines to build strength and fitness, scientifically tested diets to increase stamina, line calls that are far more accurate than ever before (which can be regularly challenged without risking a warning or penalty point—jeez, that's no fun), slow grass, fast clay, trainers allowed on court when the players have an itch, permission to disappear to the locker room for a "comfort break" as many times as they want—man, they have everything they need. Anything else we can do for you? Room service?

I'm not denying the greatness of guys like Federer, Nadal, and Djokovic, but some of the other players have reached exceptional levels of expertise that they wouldn't have attained without technology unavailable to my generation. It amounts to this: Today players are given every opportunity to advance in the game without having to know the basic fundamentals and technique, like using your imagination, working the whole court to your advantage, and shot-making skills. The players today are all taught to play the same way, with power being the main objective. The new equipment allows them the luxury of playing one way, and getting by with that. But that's just my opinion. I've been wrong ONCE before.

In 1984, Mac and I spent a lot of time together. Not all of it was fun.

Losses in Dallas in April (final, straight sets), Roland Garros in June (semis, straight sets), Queen's Club in June (semis, straight sets), Toronto in August (semis, three sets), and of course Wimbledon were topped off by defeat at the Open, again in the semis.

At least in New York I took him to five sets in what a lot of people regard as a classic match, but really, so what? I got beat; that's all I cared about and I was starting to get really pissed. The explosion wasn't far off.

Throughout the year Mac and I had also had the pleasure of each other's company as Davis Cup teammates.

I'm pretty sure he enjoyed it about as much as I did.

I had signed with Donald Dell's ProServ agency in 1982 after a year with IMG. Donald saw the Davis Cup as an exercise in brand-building as much as anything else. He thought flying the US flag would be good for business and I went along with it. I really shouldn't have, but I liked Donald, so I took his advice.

After my bad Davis Cup experience of 1972 and the disappointment of losing in Mexico in 1975, I'd only played one other tie, the quarters in 1981 against Czechoslovakia, where I won both my matches (including a straight-sets victory over Lendl). I should have left it right there. Let's face it, having Mac and me on the same team in 1984 was never a great idea.

Mac had won the Davis Cup four times already, and if I'd been thinking straight, I would have wished him good luck and watched the matches on TV. Instead, I joined up and there were problems from the get-go. He was whipping my ass (and pretty much everyone else's), and that didn't sit well with me.

We were barely talking to each other at our first match, in February in Romania. The others just tried to keep out of our way and hope for the best. The captain, Arthur Ashe, didn't help matters by ignoring us and letting our issues fester. It made for a tense atmosphere, not exactly ideal for team competition.

To top it off, we were given instructions on how to treat Nasty! He'd already played over a hundred Davis Cup matches for Romania, we all knew him, and he was a friend but we were supposed to see him as the enemy. I wasn't allowed to talk to him and they even banned his wife, who was from the US, from our locker room. I mean, come on. That's one of the things I really didn't like about Davis Cup. It was OK for the team to set itself apart to a certain extent, but to ignore one of my best buddies off the court? Seriously?

So big surprise. I ignored the rules. To me, this was a nice vacation where I could visit with my old friend Nasty and play some tennis while I was at it. Patti, Gerry Goldberg, and his wife were with me on the trip, and in the evenings we'd go out to dinner with Nasty and his wife. We also went to Nasty's home, where he and his family entertained us in grand style so we'd have a memorable experience in his home country.

Nasty had so many obligations that he wasn't able to perform at the level he wanted, and we won the match comfortably. In the fourth rubber I got to play my good friend in a match in front of his home crowd. And, boy, did he put on a show. His shot-making was like the Nasty of old, and the warm way he treated his fans and drew his countrymen into the match made me realize why he was the superstar that he had become. Of course, it meant that 8,000 people weren't rooting for me, only this time I was happy to let Nasty enjoy the spotlight.

Next up was a quarterfinal against Argentina, played in Atlanta, where I showed up at the last minute so I didn't have to hang around the team any longer than necessary, followed by the semis against Australia.

The finals took place in Sweden—and I should never have gone to that match.

I had a lot going on in my life outside of tennis. Patti, Brett, and I had just moved from Florida to a ranch in the Santa Ynez Valley, above Santa Barbara, California, a place that was ideal for raising our children. Yes, children. Patti was very pregnant with our daughter, Aubree, but on her due date I was scheduled to be in Sweden.

I should have bowed out. I could have said, "Look, I have family obligations and I need to be home. I'm happy to let someone else take my place." But when I raised the possibility of skipping the match, back came the emotional blackmail.

"You gotta play, Jimmy. We need you. Think of your country."

Tennis or family? Family or tennis? It's an issue I've struggled with over and over in the second half of my career. This time, I made the wrong call, and instead of staying with Patti, I went to Sweden.

I'll admit I didn't have the best attitude. When I said I'd go, I was ignoring one of Pancho's rules. "You don't play if you are injured. If you play, you are not injured." If I was going to be there with the team, I should have been prepared to be there with the team 100 percent.

It went downhill from there.

There had been a schedule change for the first practice session that I wasn't told about, so when I arrived on the court, I was the only one there. I was pissed. I mean, really pissed. My approach has always been that when it's time for tennis, it's time for tennis. When Ashe finally showed up, I let him know how I felt about the situation. With my racquet I wrote FUCK OFF ARTIE in the clay. I made sure he noticed before scrubbing it out.

Sweden in December is cold and wet, so we were indoors on a newly built court, which suited the Swedes a whole lot better than it did us. It was probably the slowest clay court I've ever played on. My opening match was against Mats Wilander, A French Open champion and one of the world's best clay-court specialists, and I knew before I even stepped on the court that it wasn't going to be my day. I wasn't disappointed. Along the way, my attitude had deteriorated and the result wasn't pretty: smashed racquets, verbal abuse, point penalties, game penalties. It was a bad scene. I should have been defaulted immediately; maybe that's what I was hoping for, but this was the Davis Cup final and that didn't happen.

We lost 4-1 and I was gone before the end, after Mac and Peter Fleming lost their doubles to give the Swedes an unbeatable 3-0 lead.

Leaving when I did was about the only smart thing I did in Sweden. I was able to miss the now infamous closing-ceremony dinner, where Jimmy Arias talked throughout the playing of "The Star-Spangled Banner" and Mac and the other guys left before Hunter Delatour, the new USTA president, had given his speech. After seeing his own country's players walk out on him, Delatour hit the team with both barrels (yahoo!), calling our behavior and attitude in the competition unpatriotic and claiming we were an embarrassment to our country. For years I've been trying to tell them I shouldn't play Davis Cup. If only they had listened.

Then it got ugly. There were calls for Mac and me to be banned from Davis Cup, and the sponsors, Louisiana-Pacific Corporation, threatened to withdraw their support unless a code of conduct was imposed on the players in the future, which it was. Eventually we had to make public apologies, and as far as I was concerned, that was it. Since Two-Mom's death, the Davis Cup felt jinxed for me. I'd never play it again and I'm sure no one was too upset.

Back in Los Angeles, Patti and I got ready for the birth of our daughter. Her official due date was December 25, a Christmas baby, but we knew Aubree would be delivered by C-section, as had Brett, so we could choose Aubree's birthday. We didn't want Brett to be separated from his mother on Christmas day, so we picked December 20.

On December 19, Dr. Lloyd Greig met Patti and me at the hospital, where she was signed in and taken up to her room. Then Doc and I left to watch a Lakers game, on which I'd placed one of the biggest bets of my life. Brenda Richie, Lionel's wife, arrived at the hospital that night with a bottle of wine and a backgammon board to keep Patti company.

"I can't drink, Brenda," Patti told her. "I'm having a baby in the morning."

They stayed up and played backgammon until 1:30 in the morning. I arrived later that morning and they took Patti into the operating room.

With Brett, there had been some complications, so I had stayed by Patti's head during the surgery, but with Aubree, I was down there—up close and very personal—watching the entire thing.

"Now I know you inside and out," I told Patti later.

Aubree Leigh Connors was born at 9:51 a.m., December 20, 1984. She was a fragile little thing with, nothing like Brett's impressive set of lungs. Aubree just let out these tiny cries that sounded like a kitten mewing.

"Is she OK?" I asked the doctor over and over, even though they kept reassuring me that she was healthy and fine, a perfect, beautiful little redhead. And I fell in love with my family all over again.

During the 1970s, the exhibition matches and special events that Nasty and I played became our main source of income. Tennis was still in its rapid growth phase, and the various associations still hadn't realized that they would also have to offer bigger prize money. Even though it slowly went up, it didn't happen in time for the guys of my generation.

From a financial point of view, the Slams—particularly Wimbledon and the Open—were important; win one of those and the price you could command for exhibitions went through the roof. Tennis was my love and I respected it, but it was also my job. Exhibition guarantees—payments and expenses to sweeten the deal—started appearing around the early to mid-'70s. We were committed to playing a dozen or more tournaments, plus the Slams, but we could choose from among over 80 sanctioned Grand Prix events on the tour, but which ones? That's where the guarantees came in.

The ATP and USTA were against guarantees. In 1983, they tried to make an example of Guillermo Vilas by fining him $20,000 and imposing a year ban after he supposedly received money to play at a tournament in Rotterdam. Mac, Lendl, and I came out publicly in favor of guarantees, which might have helped Vilas, because although his fine was upheld when he appealed, his suspension was dropped.

Of course, I never saw a problem with guarantees; to me, it was no different from paying Sinatra to play a concert. People wanted to hear him sing, they bought tickets, and the promoters and venues all made money. Why should tennis, or any other professional sport, be different? We're all in the entertainment business, aren't we? I never understood why the authorities made a stink, but they did. We just kept it quiet and they turned a blind eye. Or did they just accept it? The fans got to see the guys they wanted, the tour continued to be exciting, and everyone was happy. No big deal. But, look here: Just because I was getting a big guarantee didn't mean that winning the tournament wasn't still my top priority.

Today players don't need the guarantees (even though they still get them), because they earn so much in prize money and endorsements. The schedule allows them to take weeks off at a time. In my era, we had to cash in while we could. Win a Slam and within a day you'd be back on the road, making a living.

I didn't want to admit it, but by the mid-'80s my career had peaked, and I was on the down elevator. I figured it was time to build up my retirement fund and let me tell you, I had some fun doing it.

Over the next seven years, through 1990, I was on an airplane, flying all over the world to grab any opportunity I was offered. It took its toll, but it was worth it. I was able to experience new cities, cultures, food, and I was being paid to do what I loved. By the way, I was also still active on the main tour throughout this period. Out of the 13 Grand Slams I entered between 1985 and the end of 1989,

I made five semis and three quarters and remained in the world top 10 through 1988.

Exhibitions were real matches. Players like Nasty, Vilas, Mac, Vitas, Borg, and, later, Yannick Noah all wanted to win. Our reputations were on the line, so there was no chance we were going to cruise through the matches. But the fans were also paying to be entertained.

I remember a four-match tour with Petr Korda and Goran Ivanisevic in Prague and Budapest and ending up in Italy. When Ivanisevic had to pull out because of an injury, we called on Noah, the former French Open champion, for the last match. The event was being televised and the promoters had sold twice as many tickets as the stadium would hold. There was almost a riot when half the fans didn't have seats, but they packed them in anyway. Standing room only. The crowd was on top of us, and the atmosphere was buzzing. Just the way we liked it.

Noah was a wreck when he flew in that afternoon. Tennis wasn't his priority, and playing at that level was something he wasn't used to doing at that point. And when he saw the size of the crowd and the number of cameras, his nerves started to take over.

In the locker room Noah pulled a bottle of Courvoisier out of his bag and took a drink.

"Better take it easy on that stuff, Yannick," I cautioned.

"Don't worry, Jeemy. It's just to calm me down."

By the time we started to play, Noah was tipsy. Watching Yannick in the warm-up was something to behold. He was a mess.

"Listen, Yannick," I said. "Don't worry about the match. It's all good."

On the first point he serves, I send back an easy return and he follows up with an approach to the net. I make like I have to stretch to reach his shot and deliberately set it up perfectly for an easy volley, which he puts away. Thank God. Noah relaxes immediately.

"OK, Jeemy," he slurs at me from across the net. "I get it. I'll be OK now."

Well, sometimes that's how it goes. We have to make it work. That's what we were getting paid for.

Needless to say, one of the downsides of an exhibition schedule like mine was jet lag. Once, after finishing a match in São Paulo, Brazil, my friend Bill Lelly, who traveled with me, and I were getting ready to go home when we got a call from Onni Nordstrom, the former NHL player and now a sports agent and promoter.

"Can you guys make it to Helsinki by tomorrow night? We've got a tournament and Boris Becker's opponent has just pulled out. We'll pay for the flights. And what else will it take?" We made a deal in five minutes.

Hell, yeah. So we hopped on the plane for a 7,000-mile flight, crossing God knows how many time zones.

When we arrive in Finland at 11 o'clock that night, I go up to my hotel room and find a feast waiting for me. Nasty, who was also playing, had brought foie gras, caviar, and smoked salmon, from Paris. My kind of welcome.

The next morning, I hit some balls, attended a couple of corporate events in the afternoon, went to a cocktail party that evening (now dead on my feet from jet lag), and still managed to play a couple of matches over the next two days.

Another time, I agree to an exhibition match in Ecuador against the local favorite, Andrés Gómez. It's near Christmas, my game's a little rusty, and I think that the best-of-three set match will start preparing me for the year to come. The president of Ecuador is going to be in attendance.

However, on the flight down with my friend Gerry Goldberg, when there's no turning back, the promoter tells me, "Oh, by the way, this is three out of five sets." Oh, boy. Suddenly, my mood takes a sharp downturn. And it doesn't improve when the crowd goes crazy for Gómez, the local hero, and the line judges are helping him out any chance they get. *And* the temperature's over 100 degrees and humid. I'm hot and tired and playing on red clay. I swear at the officials, throw my racquet around at all the bad calls, and grab my crotch whenever I win a point, just to piss people off. Not my brightest move.

At a changeover, I hear Goldberg shouting at me, "Cool it, Connors!"

When I sit down, he fills me in.

"Lay off the crotch," he says, "or you're going to jail. The head of security has just had a word with me. You're offending the president of Ecuador. Listen, they're gonna put us both in jail if you do it again!" Well, at least I'll have some company.

And to answer your question, no, I didn't do it again. That's all I needed: to be in an Ecuadorean prison in my tight white shorts.

I think the hardest thing for me during this period of combining the main tour with exhibitions wasn't jet lag or the threat of Ecuadorean jail but the challenge of trying to balance tennis and my family life. In 1985, the reality of just how difficult that was came crashing home to me.

Pop had been in an assisted-living facility near Mom in Belleville. He'd been in good shape, still driving, still taking his daily walk to the cigar store, but at Christmas his health took a serious turn for the worse, so I made a plan to take baby Aubree and the rest of my family to see him in early spring. If his health kept deteriorating, I couldn't stand the thought that he wouldn't have had a chance to hold his great granddaughter. But I was in Europe getting ready for the French Open and Wimbledon when I got the call from Mom.

"Pop's passed, Jimmy. It was peaceful."

"I'm coming home, Mom. Tomorrow. First flight I can get."

"No, you're not. Pop made me promise to say this before he left us. He said, 'Tell Jimmy not to come back for the funeral. I don't want him interrupting what he's doing just for me. Promise me you won't let him, Glo.' That's exactly what he told me, and that is what's going to happen. You finish your business there. I'll take care of everything else here."

I felt brokenhearted and alone. Pop had been such an influence in my life and on my career, and wasn't that just like him to say, "Finish your business"?

So I wasn't there when my Pop died, and I wasn't at his funeral, and even though that's what he wanted, it still hurt. It was another two months before I stood at his graveside to say goodbye and thank him for everything he'd done for me.

Between the exhibitions and the tour, I was away from home for long stretches, for up to half the year. It was hard on Patti, but she never made a big deal about it. When I'd call and ask how things were going, she'd always say, "Fine, Jimmy, no problems." The work she did during those years allowed me to concentrate on the tennis.

But it was the same old story: When I was home, I wanted to be playing tennis, and when I was playing tennis, I wanted to be home. I'd arrive back in Santa Ynez and feel like I didn't fit in, because Patti and the kids didn't stop whatever they were doing the moment I walked through the door. I felt like a visitor in my own home.

I knew my family was always happy to see me, but they had an established routine of mealtimes, homework, soccer practice, dance lessons, tutoring, and their friends. I had to get with the program or go back on the road, and it was always a little unsettling.

My homecomings turned into a good opportunity for the kids to dance around Patti's rules and get me to do what they wanted. Patti would have said no to something, but then the kids would hit me up. "Can we go to a movie, Dad?" "Can we go to McDonald's?" I'd feel guilty for being away, so I'd give in. "Yeah, sure, let's go." After a few days of this I'd be off again, leaving Patti to pick up the pieces. I'm no dummy.

On occasion, I would take Brett out of elementary school early for summer so he could come along for some of the tournaments. Aubree was too young, and she stayed home with Patti while I traveled with Brett to Europe.

He was a natural traveler, but there were still times when he gave me a few early gray hairs.

I was playing a special event in Frankfurt and 20,000 German fans were cheering their homeboy, Boris Becker. Brett seemed perfectly happy soaking up the atmosphere, and I figured the worst that could happen was that I'd lose the match. Then, at a changeover, he was gone. His seat was empty and the bottle of water he'd been drinking was knocked over next to the chair.

I panicked. I called over my friend who was supposed to be watching Brett.

"You haven't seen my son, have you?"

"Oh, my God, I don't know. He was there a minute ago."

I was frantically looking everywhere at the same time they were telling me that my match was about to start. The event was being televised, so I went back onto the court to play, putting my faith in the German authorities to FIND MY SON! Two games later, on the changeover, they had located him—under my bench on the court, taking a nap. The travel had finally caught up with him.

A few years later in Argentina, Brett learned about work when he had to get down on his hands and knees to save a match that Guillermo Vilas had arranged way out in the country, west of Mendoza.

We were shocked at the venue when we arrived. It was a big tin barn. Right next to it was an old bus, which I had the horrible feeling was our locker room. Nothing but the finest for you, Jimmy.

"Are you sure this is the right place, Willy?" I ask, using my nickname for Guillermo.

He shrugs his shoulders and nods.

It's freezing inside. This is winter in Argentina and the "stadium" doesn't have heating. Instead, the organizers placed huge metal drums in each corner of the barn and started fires in each of them. The smoke is billowing up onto the roof.

Again, only the best.

Guillermo and I go out to hit some balls as the crowd starts to filter in. Luckily, they hadn't built the stands too high or fans would have been passing out from smoke inhalation.

I move to hit a return. Did I just feel something move under my feet?

I go to serve. There it is again. Man, the court is shifting. I call Billy Lelly over. Brett follows.

"Something's up with the surface, Lelly. Can you take a look?"

It's 10 minutes before showtime.

Lelly pokes at the corner of the court. Sure enough, it moves. He looks underneath. The sections have been glued together, but they've forgotten to attach it to the ground. It's just sitting there on concrete. Play on this and one or both of us is going to break a leg. Guillermo just shrugs.

Brett and Lelly get busy with some tape they've found, scrambling around on all fours doing the best they can to stabilize the court as the spectators start to get restless. By the time they finish the place is literally rocking as the crowd stamp their feet and whistle. And it's getting smokier.

We start the warm-up again. Guillermo can't keep two consecutive balls in play. He's out of condition, out of practice, and the crowd is out of patience.

I have a quick word with Brett and Lelly.

"Find some tacks or something. You've got to let the air out of the balls. Slow them down as much as you can so Guillermo can hit a few or we'll be murdered in here."

My eyes are stinging from the smoke and my throat is getting sore. Funny what you'll do for a few bucks.

I make sure we have a few rallies and somehow we get through the match. I can't tell if the fans are satisfied or not because I can barely see them through the smoke as we make a quick getaway.

When we get to Buenos Aires, Guillermo has a confession to make.

"Now, Jimmy, the reason I brought you out here, and I know you're not going to mind this, is that I have to win here in my country's capital."

"So," I say, "I get to win in a barn where we're almost invisible, but you take all the glory in the big city, in front of 10,000 fans—is that it?"

Guillermo shrugs his shoulders. He's good at that.

What can I say? It's not like it's a high-stakes match and Willy has assured me that it won't be televised or anything. So I play along. For two and a half hours I run him all over the court and make him work harder than he has in years. I never hit a winner, only make him hit shots. If he's going to win, he has to pay. He wins the first set and has me 5-4 in the second when I can see him struggling, starting to cramp. Now I've got him right where I want him. Suddenly he runs over to Lelly, holding up his hand, which looks like *T. rex*'s claw.

"Billy, Billy, pull my fingers apart, I can't do it. Put my racquet in my palm and then close my fingers around it. Please." Finally he's doing something besides shrugging.

This is too much fun. I decide to win the next game, then back off and let him take the set 7–5. I can't stop laughing as I walk to the net to carefully shake his hand. I've never seen a man move like that in my life, crouched over and twisted in pain. But he's smiling. He's won and the crowd is happy. And I enjoyed inflicting pain on him. After all, he's my friend. That's what it's all about.

Next day at the airport, we're waiting in the lounge for our flight home when I happen to glance over at a TV. It's a tennis match. I take a closer look. It's a rerun . . . of . . . of Connors versus Vilas, shown live last night! Am I a sucker or what? How's that hand, Willy? Still cramping?

18

TORMENT

Mellowed.

I didn't like that word when it was used to describe me in the 1980s and I don't like it now. Growing older, having your own family, that's all part of it, but even then you don't change who you are deep down. I grew up having to battle to be the best, while all the time the press and the establishment were trying to shoot me down. I learned you either fold or fight. Turns out that fighting is more fun. That belief hadn't changed by 1986. Mellowed? Screw that.

Boca Raton, Florida. The semifinal of the Lipton International Players Championships, Friday, February 21, 1986. Me versus Lendl, fifth set, Lendl up 3–2 and serving, 30–0.

Lendl hits a slice volley; it's sailing over the baseline. It bounces out and I hit it away.

I don't hear the line judge's call. Maybe I just missed it. It's noisy here.

"Forty-love."

I glare at the line judge. "No, no, no! You're wrong. Admit you're wrong."

I get nothing back.

Jeremy Shales is in the chair. He's been shafting me the whole match, giving me nothing and thinking he's the show. It's not the first time, and I'm not putting up with it anymore. That one was blatant. I charge over to him.

"You are overruling, right?"

"The ball was good, Mr. Connors. Play on."

"You're kidding me! The ball was *that* far out." I show him: six inches at least.

"Play on, Mr. Connors. The score is 40–love."

I'm snarling at him now, my blood boiling over in the steamy atmosphere. I can hear people shouting at me from the stands. What do I care? I'm standing up for my rights.

"No, you're wrong," I shout at Shales. "The ball was this far out. I'm not playing under these conditions. Get the supervisor out here."

"Mr. Connors, you have 30 seconds to resume play or face a penalty point."

"I'm not going to play under those conditions. Get the referee out here. And the supervisor. Call 'em out here. You're the one wasting my time. Call 'em out here." The crowd is booing louder and now I'm not sure if they're for me or against me. I really don't care at this point.

"Point penalty, Mr. Connors. Time violation. Game, Mr. Lendl. He leads 4–2, final set."

"You're the one wasting time. Get 'em out here!"

Just then Ken Farrar, the Tennis Council's supervisor, and Alan Mills, the referee at Wimbledon, come out. They must have been watching from the side. The crowd starts to cheer. Seems like they're on my side.

I approach Farrar. "I've been playing for three hours and 41 minutes, and if I'm going to stay out here and grind it out, then this is too much. That was not a judgment call. I didn't even play the ball it was so far out."

They try to calm me down. Like that's gonna work. I see Lord God Almighty sitting up there in his chair looking at his stopwatch.

This is nuts. Turning back to Farrar and pointing up at Shales, I yell, "He has a job to do, and he isn't doing it. This whole situation is fucked. I don't want to play anymore, not if this is what it's like. Are you gonna do something about it?"

"Jimmy," Farrar says quietly, trying to reason with me, "you don't want to go out like this. Let's get back to the game."

"Game penalty, Mr. Connors. Delaying the match. Mr. Lendl leads 5–2, final set."

The crowd is now begging for blood. They are booing, swearing at Shales, and some of them are throwing things. I can see Patti, who's shouting the loudest of all.

I am not backing down. No way.

"Game, set, and match, Mr. Lendl, by default."

You know what? I don't give a shit. I slam my racquet into my bag and sling it over my shoulder. As I do so I glance across to where Patti is sitting. I can't help smiling.

She's leaning forward out of her seat, a Coke in her hand, which she now launches at the umpire's chair. Really? Well, I guess so. She was taught by the best. Despite all the crowd noise, I make out what she screams at Shales: "You bastard!"

Lendl's victory brought him level with me in our career head-to-head, 13 matches each. More significantly, it was my eighth loss to him in a row. I hadn't won since the Seiko Super Tennis tournament, in Tokyo in October 1984—my last tournament win up to that point, coincidentally. Number 105. The press was writing me off again. Like I wasn't used to that.

The Lipton default cost me $25,000 in fines and a 10-week ban. How did I feel about that? The things you have to do to get some time off, right? Anyway, the suspension I received was an opportunity for me to play a couple of special events and half a dozen exhibitions. I made a hell of a lot more money than I would have playing the tournaments.

What did piss me off was the way Shales had umpired the match. I really didn't think it was good enough. He wasn't purposely targeting me initially (although I believe he was later, in the heat of the moment); he was simply incompetent. And he wasn't the only one. I never argued with an umpire I didn't think deserved it. We would be busting our guts out there with no instant replays to protect us. It's no surprise that the players with hot tempers lose it from time to time. I think the authorities knew they weren't delivering in the professional manner they should have been but refused to admit it. I'll leave you with this statement from Butch Buchholz, tournament director at Boca Raton, which he made just after my default: "The officiating has been better than last year, but it's an area we can improve. Eighteen years ago we got people out of the stands to call the lines. We're now past that stage." Not exactly a ringing endorsement.

Going into Wimbledon four months later, I feel as good as I have in years. Definitely on a par with 1982. The enforced layoff has worked in my favor, making me hungry for competitive tennis. My conditioning is no problem; the exhibitions and special events have looked after that. As I hit balls with David Schneider in Holland Park the week before the start of the tournament, I honestly believe a third Wimbledon title is within reach.

"Jesus, Connors, I haven't seen you move this well in years," Schneider comments.

No one else seems to think that. The talk in the papers is focused on how I've slowed down around the court. In press conferences the same questions are repeatedly thrown my way. "How long are you going to stick around, Jimmy?" "It's almost two years since you won, Jimmy. Are you done?"

The fact that I had to pull out of the Queen's final with a groin strain only added to the speculation.

"Is your body trying to tell you something?"

I just smile. "I enjoy the battle and the fight. But no one is going to have to tell me when I can't play any longer. There comes a moment when you know you've given everything you have and there's nothing left. When that time comes, I'll know." As Two-Mom would say: Keep an element of mystery about yourself, Jimmy.

I leave them scribbling furiously, preparing my tennis obituary. I know the time hasn't come; nowhere near it, in fact. If they want to believe otherwise, that's fine by me.

The odds offered on a Connors win are too good to resist. This year I'm going bigger than ever. I'm not in this to go out and have a fancy dinner, I'm in it to do some serious damage. With a couple of grand laid down in a string of betting shops, I'm ready.

"You feeling good, Jimmy?" Ken, my driver, asks a couple of days before my first match. Since I arrived in London, he's been driving me around to my practice matches and to the bookies.

"I'm thinking of getting in on some of this action," he says.

"Yes, son, I'm feeling very good."

At the press conference after my first-round match against Robert Seguso, the questions are the same.

"Will this be your last Wimbledon, Jimmy?"

"Will you be back next year?"

Only this time I'm not smiling. I've just been beaten in four sets.

I knock their questions straight back at them. "Why? You want me out of tennis? That's your problem over here. You don't know what you've got 'til you lose it. Why don't you just let me make my own decision? That's my worry, not yours."

Back at the hotel and Schneider is shaking his head. We've both just taken a big hit.

"I'm not so mad about you or me, Jimmy," he says to me, "but our driver, Ken—well, he's in the soup line. Don't know how he's going to explain that one when he gets home."

Oh, man, that sucks. I'd forgotten. Sometimes I should just keep my mouth shut. Looks like Ken's gratuity just got a lot bigger.

A year later—1987—and I'm back in London. That's something you could have bet on (and I wish did). The drama, the crowds, the excitement—it's all part of who I am. I'm not tossing that aside lightly. As long as I feel capable of winning, I'll keep coming back.

That's what I feel right now. But I'm the only person on Centre Court who thinks that. It's the fourth round and I'm playing Mikael Pernfors, from Sweden, a guy who is 11 years younger than me and was a runner-up at Roland Garros a month ago. And he's leading 6-1, 6-1, 4-1, and I'm getting an old-fashioned ass-kicking. The crowd lost interest a long time ago. I think at this point they just want to see me put out of my misery and I don't blame them. I've been struggling out here at 34; should be preparing for my afternoon nap instead of playing on Wimbledon's Centre stage.

What they don't know is that something miraculous just happened. It was invisible, but it definitely occurred.

On that last return, I anticipated Pernfors's shot. That's the first time it's happened in the match. I knew where the ball was going and I got there and passed him down the line. It's not that I'm suddenly trying harder. Quite the opposite. Maybe I've been too clever, attempting too much, putting too much pressure on myself, and now I've relaxed. It's like Mom always says, "Jimmy, don't try and be any better than you are."

That one shot has suddenly brought the court into focus. I can see it all clearly now. This isn't over yet. What is it inside you that makes you want to stay in there and fight instead of rolling over, like most people would, and saying it just isn't my day? For me, I could call upon what I learned from Pancho at the very beginning. He always said it's pride. Always walk off with your head high, no matter what the results, knowing that you have given everything that you had to give. It was much easier for me to find inspiration to plant my feet than it was to come up with reasons to surrender.

Two hours later, just before eight o'clock in the evening, I fire a match-ending two-fisted crosscourt backhand beyond Pernfors's reach. Over the past 10 years, since the boos of 1977 faded into history, the Wimbledon crowd has given me a hell of a lot of support and encouragement. With that shot, I like to think I gave something back to the loyal fans who had stuck around. I throw my arms high in victory as the spectators rise to their feet.

A year later, in July 1988, I won my first tour event in almost four years, the Sovran Bank Classic, in DC, beating Andrés Gómez in straight sets in the final. I confess it was a relief. Although I closed the previous year at number four in the ATP world rankings, the defeats in the semis at Wimbledon (Pat Cash) and again at the Open (Lendl) frustrated me. By the time I arrived in Washington, I'd slipped to eighth in the world, not where I wanted to be or where I felt I should be. Sure, I was 35 years old, but I was determined to shove phrases like "antique" and "old man" down the press's throats. The win over Gómez was a good way to answer my critics.

However, I couldn't deny forever that age would eventually overtake my desire to fight on. In my mind, I still had a number of combative years ahead, but maybe, just maybe, it was time to prepare to reinvent myself again. The call from Merv Griffin in October provided the perfect opportunity.

I'd known Merv for many years. He was the creator of the megahit TV game shows *Jeopardy!* and *Wheel of Fortune*, a regular visitor to the La Costa Tennis Club, in San Diego, and pals with Pancho and Lornie. After a few minutes of catching up on friends and family, Merv cut to the chase, "I don't know if you have read about it in the press, Jimmy, but Pat Sajak is stepping down as daytime host of *Wheel of Fortune*, so we're looking for someone to replace him. What do you think about trying out?"

This is so cool. I'm stunned but flattered. Merv Griffin thinks I've got what it takes to host one of the most popular shows on TV!

"Just say when, Merv. I'll be there."

I arrived at the studio the next day, excited at the prospect of where this might lead. During our previous conversation, Merv and I had discussed how the hosting gig could work alongside my tennis. I'd been up front with him, explaining that while I was very interested in the job, I wasn't looking to retire in favor of a career in front of the cameras. Turned out it wouldn't be a problem. They recorded five shows a day, a week's worth of broadcasts, and they were willing to fit the taping around my schedule. Whenever I had a free week, which I could make happen by turning down exhibitions, we could crank out five weeks' worth in one session. In the studio they ran through everything—how to walk out on the set with co-host Vanna White, introduce the contestants, ask them questions to put them at ease, all the things I'd watched so often on TV. I was offered a script but refused, confident that I could wing it. We ran through a number of takes, and I think I did pretty good for an amateur. Sure, there were a few rough edges, but those could be ironed out. Most important, I'd felt relaxed and enjoyed myself.

A week later the producers called with disappointing, but not life-threatening news. Pat Sajak had decided to re-up as the daytime host until the New Year. Until then, they explained, plans for his daytime replacement were being put on hold. And so, I guess, was my TV stardom.

Shortly after the audition I was off to Toulouse, France, where I

battled through more foot discomfort to record my second tour victory of the year. In the semis, I was pitted against my friend Andrei
Chesnokov with whom I practiced all week. While hitting with
him, I had noticed that his tennis shoes were worn out. The soles
were flapping so bad that he had to wrap tape around them to keep
the shoes together. I kept wondering how he was going to be able to
play the tournament in those things but I had my own foot problem
to worry about.

Shortly before we went out to play our semi, the concierge delivered a box to my hotel room. Lelly, who was traveling with me,
received it and put it aside for me to open later. It was only after I
beat Chesnokov in straight sets and Lelly and I returned to the hotel,
did either of us notice that the box was supposed to have been delivered to Chesnokov. It was the new pair of tennis shoes that he was
supposed to have worn in the match against me. Oops.

After beating Andrei, I played my old nemesis, McEnroe, on
Sunday, October 15, in the finals and came away with a 6-3, 6-3
victory—my 108th tournament title.

From Toulouse I went to Tel Aviv, and had one of the most
incredible experiences of my life. Gerry Goldberg had arranged another private tour, and we took a helicopter to the Dead Sea, where
we ate lunch at a beach resort, then spent a couple of hours floating
in the salty water. As we were heading back to Tel Aviv, we spotted
a Bedouin tent in the desert and asked the pilot to land. We didn't
know what to expect, so the pilot left the engine running as he approached a Bedouin to ask if we would be welcome.

They treated us to some special hospitality, inviting us into their
tent and bringing out some ancient cups that looked like they hadn't
been used for quite some time. They cleaned out the cups and served
us tea. I felt like I was an extra in *Lawrence of Arabia* until the Bedouin's son came into the tent wearing a pair of Jimmy Connors

Converse shoes! I really, really didn't want to leave my new fans but I had a match to play that evening. Always take care of your business, Jimmy.

I beat Israel's Gilad Bloom 2-6, 6-2, 6-2 to win the Riklis Grand Prix event. The prize money was $20,000, and I donated it all to the Israel Tennis Center, where we were playing and Gerry was on the board. I didn't know it at the time, of course, but that win, my 109th victory on the main tour, was my last.

The discomfort in my left foot didn't worry me too much at the time, but over the following few weeks, what had started as an ache turned into a sharp pain, which required surgery by November. That left me convalescing for three months, unable to move around very easily and certainly in no condition to accept Merv Griffin's renewed offer to host *Wheel of Fortune* and tape five shows a day come January. The slot went to Rolf Benirschke, the San Diego Chargers' kicker, and I was left to imagine how upset poor Vanna must have been to miss out on my suave one-liners.

My foot injury set me back significantly in terms of match fitness. I didn't return to competitive tennis until early February, when I lost in the second round in Chicago to teenager Michael Chang, quickly followed by a quarterfinal loss to Kevin Curren in Memphis.

To have any prayer of getting back to where I thought I should be, I realized some radical thinking was required. Off-pace and off-target, I needed as many matches as possible to sharpen my game, so I decided to hit the clay circuit of Europe once again, playing both singles and doubles, a tactic I hadn't employed for years. It was punishing playing on those painfully slow surfaces, which meant grinding out every point. That was the whole idea, I guess, to build fitness and consistency, but it wasn't a lot of fun.

In Monte Carlo, I fell to Italian Paolo Canè in the second round (Spain's Sergio Casal and I went out in the first round of the doubles), then performed a similar disappearing act a week later in Munich, this time at the hands of Argentine Martín Jaite, in the singles, and again with Sergio in the second round of the doubles. These defeats took me out of the world's top 10 for the first time since computer rankings began, in 1973.

OK, this was not going according to plan.

Publicly, I joked about relishing the prospect of becoming a dangerous, unseeded floater in the Slams if my position dropped any further, but privately my form worried me. With no disrespect to Canè or Jaite, it was clear I required more than a good workout if I was to save my season; I needed to be battling the best players around and my early exits from tournaments was making that impossible.

Salvation arrived in the form of an exhibition in France, made possible by the fact that I had never signed with the ATP. Directly after my defeat in Munich, Billy Lelly took a call at our hotel, asking if I'd be free to play against Becker and a couple of young Australians in a bullring in Lille, France. For any ATP member, the answer would have had to be no, because of a rule prohibiting players from participating in two events in a week. No such restriction applied to me. Give me a day to fulfill my obligations to the organizers in Munich, glad-handing a few corporate sponsors, that sort of thing, and I'm there.

Turned out to be a good call. The arena they'd constructed suited my game far better than the clay in the previous two tournaments, and Becker pushed me hard. My game improved almost immediately, resulting in a better showing in Hamburg a week later, where I made it through to the quarters.

I wasn't the most popular guy in town that week, although that was hardly new territory for me. Some of the players were pissed at me for managing to squeeze in the extra, well-paid event that they had to refuse.

"But guys," I would explain, "I've always said there's a big bonus in being independent."

"Screw you, Connors," they'd reply sweetly.

My trek across Europe continued in Rome with the Italian Open, which I'd never won and hadn't participated in since Nasty and I lost in the doubles final of 1975. There was a reason I hadn't been back.

Once, Nasty and I were playing a pair of young Italians in one of the early round doubles matches on an outside show court, the crowds were giving us some trouble while they rooted for the home-town favorites. Nasty, who speaks fluent Italian, wasn't taking it lightly. He was giving back better than he got. The match was close, and as we took the lead in the third set the crowd's abuse turned ugly. They started throwing coins, drinks, food, shoes, babies— everything they could at us in an attempt to spur on their country-men. It didn't happen.

Now, knowing that things were going to be tense, I had moved my bag to the other side of the court so I could make a quick get-away, if necessary. Nasty, on the other hand, thought everything would be fine, so he left his bag near the crowd. As soon as we won the match, the angry fans stormed the court, and headed directly for us. I grabbed my bag and took off running. I'm pretty fast when I need to be, and I thought Nasty was behind me, but just as I turned to look for him, he passed me, the mob hot on his heels. We made it to the locker room just in time and bolted the door. We were held in there until they cleared out not just our court but the whole stadium. We eventually left accompanied by armed guards.

I was always willing to improve myself, and those hot-blooded Italians made an art form out of throwing a tantrum. And to this day it's one of the things I admire most about them. Rome remains one of my favorite places in the world, even though to this day when I

walk down the street I still look over my shoulder for a flying piece
of rotten fruit. In addition to their fiery temperament, the Italians
also have long memories.

My performance in the singles improved as I reached the third
round after a marathon two-and-a-half-hour match with Massimo
Cierro, from Naples, played on what I think is best described as
thick soup, following heavy rainfall. We eventually finished at 11
o'clock at night with my legs like Jell-O, which showed the next day
in my 1-6, 1-6 loss to Sergi Bruguera, a young Spanish kid half my
age. Literally. And I felt every one of the 18 years that separated us.

None of this preparation did me much good at either the French
or Wimbledon. A kid from New Jersey, Jay Berger, beat me in the
second round at Roland Garros, and in London, Iowan Dan Goldie
did the same. The only bright spot came in the doubles in Paris,
where I was playing with Vitas. Vitas had been on the receiving end
of some pretty harsh press concerning the state of his fitness, so he
had both of us walk out onto the court for our first-round match
on crutches. We won a lot of friends that day. The same couldn't be
said for points. The red clay of Paris took its toll as we fell to our
first-round opponents, but this match with Vitas was one I would
never forget, because it was the last time that Vitas would have the
opportunity to play on such a big stage.

I still had the US Open in my sights; playing well there could sal-
vage my year. I destroyed French and Wimbledon runner-up Stefan
Edberg in the fourth round, 6-2, 6-3, 6-1, silencing a lot of people
who thought I didn't have a chance including the moron who a
couple of days earlier after my victory over Andrés Gómez shouted
out from the stands, "Let's go, old man!"

Worse, I cramped badly after the Gómez match, requiring two
and a half hours of medical attention and intravenous drips before
I could even leave the stadium. The smart money next day had me

withdrawing. Who were they kidding? Had they forgotten what tournament it was?

Against Edberg, I played some of the best tennis I had in a long time, maintaining a level throughout the match that I'd only been able to reach occasionally over the past couple of years. The New York Mets were playing across the parking lot at Shea Stadium, where they kept flashing my scores against Edberg, and I could hear the cheers every time I was in the lead. Did I just make that up? Doesn't matter. This was *my* tournament. The fans at the Open demanded more from me than any others in the world.

The previous year, 1988, at the same stage of the tournament, the quarters, I'd been beaten in straight sets by Andre Agassi. Afterward he came out with a smart-ass comment that I didn't appreciate: "I didn't think Jimmy had that much in him."

(Really? You obviously changed your mind a few years later, Andre, when you came asking for coaching assistance. Let me refresh your memory. We met up at Southern California's Sherwood Country Club and spent a morning hitting balls together with John Lloyd. I'd have been interested in working with you back then. You had bags of talent, but you weren't making the most of it. So it never panned out. Maybe you didn't like my price. I don't know. Remember that, Andre?)

When I heard what the 18-year-old Las Vegas native had said and how he predicted before the match that he'd beat me easily, I just shook my head. Kid, maybe you should have considered winning something bigger than Charleston or Stratton Mountain before running your mouth.

In the press conference, I fired back: "Well, hell, I used to spend a lot of time in Vegas, and I am old enough to be his father. Stranger things have happened."

Now, in 1989, I wanted to take him down. I almost made it. A combination of flat Coke and Gatorade helped me through the second set, when the heat in the stadium caused me to feel nauseated and dizzy. In the fifth, 20,000 raucous New York fans helped me storm back when I was 0-4 down. I pulled back to 4-5 and sensed him beginning to choke, but I didn't quite have the legs to finish the job. He held on, no thanks to anything special he came up with. My energy levels just dropped too far for me to push my 37-year-old body over the line. That's all. Shit happens.

I'd first met Agassi when he was four years old, in Vegas during the Alan King Classic. His father used to string my racquets when I came to town for a tournament. He was one of the best in the business. He loved tennis, and I got to know him pretty well. I liked Mike Agassi, still do, so when he asked me to hit with little Andre, I happily agreed. Even at that age it was clear he had something, and I said so to his father, paying his son an honest compliment. According to Andre, his dad was annoyed because he hadn't been seeking confirmation of his son's talent. Funny how he had such a vivid memory of something that happened when he was only four years old . . .

Agassi was never my kind of guy, but why should he be? He was from a different generation. He had that whole "Image Is Everything" approach going on, and it worked for his era, no doubt about it. He brought a lot of people to tennis, which was a good thing, since the sport needed him at that stage in its history. Years later, it turned out that the image was nothing but an act. Tennis gave Agassi everything—his fame, his money, his reputation, even his current wife—and he went on to knock it in his book. All that playing up to the fans who had provided him with an exceptional living—it was a bluff. For me tennis was all about standing out there and being honest, not pretending to be something I wasn't.

People admire Agassi for fighting his way back after dropping way down the rankings in 1997. I get that, but you can also look at it like this. He should never have let himself sink so low. He had a huge talent but when things got tough for a while, he put his head in his hands and let it beat him

I was there at Flushing Meadows in 2006, coaching Andy Roddick, on the day of Agassi's last match, when Benjamin Becker ousted him in the third round. Agassi walked into the locker room and everyone stood clapping. Not me, not my style. I wasn't trying to deliberately disrespect him; I just didn't care about him, and he didn't affect my life in any way.

At the 1988 Open, even Donald Trump couldn't get a ticket to sit in one of the boxes, so Gerry Goldberg invited him into mine to watch my quarterfinal against Agassi. After the second set, it was pretty clear who was going to win. Trump got up, left, and reappeared seconds later in Agassi's box. I guess he knew where the cameras would be.

19

RESURRECTION

The following February, in 1990, I decide to play my first tournament of the year, an indoor event in Milan. In the first round I'm up against Markus Zoecke, a big-serving German guy I've never heard of. It's not a match I like to think about too often. It's 5-5 in the third when he hits his first serve long. I go to flick the ball away with my racquet and—*snap*—my left hand is flapping as if there's nothing but skin keeping it attached to my arm.

I shake it off and keep on playing. I'm finally beaten 7-5 in the tiebreaker in the third set.

After the match I was taken to the local hospital to have my wrist checked out. I don't know where the hell they put me; was it the ER or an operating room? All I know was that over in the corner—now, all you OCD people reading this will surely feel my pain—was a pile of bloody rags. Was someone just shot? Oh, my God. This place isn't clean. Not only did I lose the match; I was gonna die from some infection. I turned to Lelly: "Get me out of here. We're going back to Belleville!"

After the match I took the first flight home to start on a round of visits to specialists, trying to work out what was wrong with my wrist and what I could do about it. Rest, rest, rest. All the wrist specialists in New York and everywhere else told me the same thing. No one seemed to have a clear idea what the problem actually was.

In January, Patti and I had moved our family to Connecticut

from Santa Ynez. Not one of my smartest decisions. I was 37 and thought it made sense to be within hopping distance of the European tournament circuit. I could take the Concorde back and forth to the US to see my family two days a week—it was all part of the guarantees—and the only thing it cost me was the flight time. I'd uprooted the kids and the dogs and moved into our new house during an East Coast winter. Unlike Patti and me, Brett and Aubree loved the snow, even though they were sick every other weekend (California kids). By June we were back in California.

In the middle of all of this, a multi-year saga with my brother Johnny began. The tangled deals and contracts and, most painfully, the lawyers who became involved are too crazy and complex to go into unless my publisher would like a second volume of my life story. Suffice it to say that I was at the heart of it and I didn't understand it, and I still don't. What mattered most were the consequences. They cut deep into my family, opening wounds that took years and lots of heartache to heal.

Through it all, I kept asking myself, "Why didn't Johnny just ask for the money? Why didn't he just say, 'Look, Jimmy, I'm in on a deal. I need funds, do you mind?'"

I'd have said yes. He's my brother, I love him, and he's the guy I looked up to as a kid, followed around, modeled myself after. Of course I would have agreed.

What matters most is that my brother and I are good friends again, and I enjoy spending time with him, even though sometimes I want to blow my brains out just thinking about what happened over the course of a 17-year period when our relationship was so fractured it appeared impossible to ever rebuild.

The first signs of trouble arose around early 1990. Until that point, Mom had been running my business on her own, but it was getting to be too much for her. She had asked Johnny to step in and help out, an idea I agreed with at the time. Mom didn't need the hassle of tracking the prize money, endorsements, and guarantees. She'd done more than enough for me over the years, and if she felt the time had come to take a backseat, Johnny was the obvious one to drive the gravy train.

While he was helping Mom, Johnny had the opportunity to launch a riverboat casino in East St. Louis, as part of a package aimed at reenergizing the area and supplementing state finances. The mayor's office was looking at the possibility of changing the laws to allow no-table-limit gambling on the Mississippi, and it looked like a license would be granted, effective January 1991. Johnny was at the center of the action.

Johnny is smart and streetwise, knows how to hustle and make things happen. So when he left my business to concentrate on this new potentially lucrative venture, I didn't think anything of it.

Only thing was, I noticed that my bank balance wasn't going up as much as it should have, considering the amount of money that was coming in. We decided to dig into the accounts to work out what the problem was, and that's when we discovered that Johnny had been dipping his hand into the cookie jar big-time.

Why didn't he just ask me for a loan? I think it was pride; he wanted it to look like he could pull off the deal by himself. He needed seed money, which I figure he meant to pay back when the riverboat was up and running and turning a profit. Kind of like he wanted to be able to say, "Hey, Jimmy, Mom, look what I've done." But everything blew up before any of that could happen, and that triggered years of unnecessary upset and pain.

Mom took it hard. She was proud of the way she managed my business, and when all of this came out, she blamed herself for getting Johnny involved in the first place and for not keeping a closer eye on things. No matter how many times I told her that none of it was her fault, she was never able to shake the guilt she felt.

It was an ugly situation that ended up in years of separation from my brother. First, Mom was pissed at Johnny, then he got pissed at her, and when he did that I got pissed at him. Pretty soon everyone was pissing on everybody, including Patti and the kids, who heard all the yelling and screaming on the phone almost every day.

Then I made a disastrous mistake. On Mom's recommendation, I hired this lawyer from Belleville to sort out the mess. I had too much on my mind, and if my career was going to keep going forward, I had to trust the attorney. (Did I just say that?)

After Patti and I moved back to California from Connecticut, I was feeling restless so I packed my bags and headed to Europe to play a couple of events. Racquets, shoes, shorts, shirts. And a bottle of Novocain and a syringe. If you have enough of that stuff in you, nothing hurts, even a wrist that's shot to pieces and getting worse the more you play.

I lasted two tournaments, failing to win a single match. Now, I was really mad. Back to moping around, popping painkillers, feeling sorry for myself, and wondering what I was going to do with the rest of my life. What was left if tennis abandoned me? I got so caught up in my own misery that I even forgot to pick up Aubree, then five years old, from grade school one afternoon, leaving her waiting and anxious in the schoolyard. And even though she laughs about it to this day, she won't let me live it down.

Eventually Patti had enough and called our local orthopedist, Dr. Rick Scheinberg, a friend and avid tennis player who had previously performed surgery on my foot.

"You've got to come over and take a look at Jimmy. He's not good."

Dr. Scheinberg didn't take long to make up his mind. "You, tomorrow morning, nine o'clock, at my place. Be ready for an operation. I'll tell you now: If you're not there, if you wait even a day longer, you're going to be finished. There'll be nothing I, or anyone else, can do to save your wrist."

He performed the operation without general anesthetic, by cutting off the blood supply from my shoulder. It's called a Bier block. Within seconds my whole arm was dead. It was explained to me that I could only stay like this for an hour and a half without risking permanent damage. The doctor didn't know exactly what he was going to find when he opened up my wrist, and there wouldn't be a second chance. Going back in at a later date and poking around would only weaken whatever repair he'd managed the first time. Whether 90 minutes would be enough to save my career, we'd both have to wait and see.

How did I feel? How do you think? Scared shitless. This wasn't how I wanted it all to end.

With a sheet tented up over my arm, I was unable to watch the doctor operate, but I was alert and talking to the doctor and explaining to him how to do his job. (Yes, you're right, I took too many pills before I saw him.) Finally, I let him get down to business and do what he had to do. Time was running out.

The damage was worse than we thought. One of the tendons on the inside of my left wrist, which essentially held my entire game together had been frayed bare against the bone and was hanging by a thread, waiting to snap.

My doctor figured I only had days to spare before it blew, taking with it any hope of me ever picking up a racquet again. In the 90 minutes that my arm was numb, he had to reconnect the tendon, rebuild the shattered sheath that protects it, and sew everything back in place in such a way that my wrist would be capable of withstanding the repeated assaults of a five-set tennis match.

I am not a good invalid. I hate hanging around doing nothing. I need to be active, getting things done. But with my arm in a full cast all I could do was sit around and feel sorry for myself. Patti would come home from shopping and find me curled up in a ball on the sofa, staring into space like a zombie. I was in terrible pain, and it wasn't physical. Dr. Scheinberg came to check up on me, and he wasn't there to hand out sympathy.

"Jimmy, get your ass out there and start training. I don't care what everyone else says, I didn't operate for you to screw it up by not being ready to play. I thought you were a fighter."

That did it. I've never walked away from anything in my life. I didn't plan on starting now on account of a goddamn cast on my arm.

That's when David Schneider called to say he was coming for a visit. Actually, I think Patti called him because she was sick of my moping.

I was in the full cast for eight weeks so my wrist would stay immobile, then a half-cast to below my elbow for four more weeks, which allowed me the luxury of squeezing tennis balls in my weakened hand. A couple of weeks of building the muscles back up and the cast was practically just for show, protecting my wrist but allowing me to just about pick up a racquet. Baby steps.

"When that comes off, then we'll know. If your wrist lasts a month after that, it will last forever." OK, doc. Thanks.

On my backyard court, I started off almost as a beginner. My kids would come out and gently toss balls to me, and I would gently pat them back. Dink. Dink. Dink. I also started on the backboard for three or four five-minute sessions a day. Slowly, my confidence returned. By early 1991 I knew I had to test myself in match conditions, and do it quickly. The world of tennis has a short memory, and my ATP ranking of 936 suggested I was all but forgotten.

A new generation of sluggers had ridden into town: Agassi, Sampras, Courier. They hadn't even been in high school when I won my first Wimbledon, and here they were cleaning out what they saw as the old guard: Becker, Lendl, Edberg. Where did I fit in? And the new racquets they used sent balls flying at you harder and faster. Was I too far out of touch already? Clinging desperately to past glories? That's not how I wanted to be remembered. (By the way, my wrist got hardly any press at all, while today a player gets a hangnail and becomes front-page news.)

For all that I had achieved in the game, I had a sense that the next few months were going to define my career—for better or worse. It was a risk, but I had to find out if I could still cut it.

It's fall 1990 and I'm throwing up at the side of the Santa Barbara City College track.

It's not a good look for anyone, but for a 38-year-old man in a rubber sweat suit with his arm in a cast, it doesn't get much more uncool.

"What the fuck are you doing, Jimbo? Why don't you just quit? Who needs this at your age? It's over. You're finished. Why are you doing this to yourself?"

I look up at Schneider, standing over me. He came out to California a few days ago. I picked him up at the airport in my Porsche and drove with the window down and my cast sticking out, taking a mountain pass one-handed, juggling the steering wheel, the gearshift, and the clutch.

"You're nuts, Connors. You know that? Bloody nuts."

I love Schneider. He's a true friend. I don't have many, only a small circle of loyal buddies I've known for years, and that's the way I like it. Loyalty is important to me, and it cuts both ways. I don't want just anyone having a look inside my private life. Too many people have screwed me in the past, but once you're in with me, you're in for life. David is one of those guys I can count on one hand.

He's come all this way from Florida just to help me get into shape. "You're a loser, Jimbo," he tells me early one morning when I'm struggling to get out the door and go for a run. He knows the buttons to push. This time, though, I don't think he's playing mind games. He's worried about me.

"David, I can't quit," I tell him, catching my breath and feeling the stomach acid burn the back of my throat. "I feel like a warrior with no war. I've got to fight one more time."

That's what it comes down to, that's why I'm killing myself out here—to pursue the dream of one last fight, one last heavyweight clash at the US Open. The jogging, the sprint drills, the stamina building and lung-busting runs up the steep hill in the nearby Chumash Indian reservation—all of it is necessary. You see, I'm not finished with tennis, even if it looks as though tennis is finished with me.

My comeback began down in Florida, where I had a few practice matches with some buddies I knew from my time living there. That got me moving on a court again, but I needed tournaments to see exactly how far I'd come and still had to go. You would think I'd have been welcomed with open arms, the old warhorse preparing for one last charge, all that. Come on, that's got to be an angle for some sharp-eyed promoter to exploit. OK, I admit I was asking for up-front payments because I have never believed in selling myself short, but this was a sure thing! The publicity would be huge!

Nope. Nobody wanted to take a chance on a broken-down tennis player whose best days were so far in the distance you'd need high-powered binoculars to catch sight of them. The Connors show was over. Barnum & Bailey had folded up their tents and moved on to where the younger guys played. I'd been discarded.

The only call I got during that time was from Billie Jean King and her partner, Ilana Kloss, who asked if I was interested in playing Team Tennis.

"Billie Jean, thanks for the offer, but I've just had wrist surgery and I'm sitting here in a full arm cast."

It didn't seem to bother them at all. They were willing to take the chance that I would be able to play some kind of tennis. You can't buy loyalty like that, especially from a great champion like Billie Jean. It just drove me that much harder to stick it up everybody's ass.

I made my way into four tournaments without winning a single round, but I wasn't worried. After each loss I could feel the old drive building steadily inside me. By the time of the French Open, I knew I was back on track, if not quite firing on all cylinders. Not yet.

The clay in Paris back then played incredibly slow, which meant hitting more balls per point than I had for a long time. I'd won my first two matches by staying faithful to my game, hitting it early, flat, close to the net, on the lines, basically attacking the ball instead of hanging back. And now I was playing Michael Chang, who was a mere 20 years younger than me.

The mercury had risen to over 100 degrees as I walked out onto the red clay of Roland Garros to face Chang, an opponent who was prepared to be there all day if necessary, to run down every ball. It's kill or be killed. That turned out to be a bit too close for comfort.

We traded the first two sets, he took the third and then in the fourth I hit the wall for the first time in my life. I had no idea where I was or what I was doing. I was done—fatigue, dehydration, everything. At one of the changeovers, as I looked around the stands, I turned to Lelly, who was sitting courtside. "Why are all these people here?" I asked. Just a little out of my mind.

Doing things half-assed doesn't fit my personality, and I hit that wall running so hard I managed to force my head through to the other side just long enough to hear a voice tell me, "Not yet, Jimmy. Not yet." A couple in the crowd made a move to leave.

"Don't go," I called to them. "This isn't over yet."

I broke Chang to go 5-4 up and held on to even the match at two sets each.

"Allez, Jeemeee! Allez, Jeemeee!"

After three hours 31 minutes, I faced my second fifth set in as many days. Wounded and exhausted, I dragged myself out of my seat. I knew I'd gone as far as I could. My back was seizing up, my vision blurred, head spinning. Kill or be killed? What asshole said that?

All through the months of hurt and sweat that had brought me to that moment in Paris, I'd only thought about one thing, the tournament that defined me, the US Open. New York in September.

To keep going against Chang would be insane, jeopardizing everything I'd been working toward. If I screwed up, if I injured myself, that would be it for the summer and probably forever. Yet I didn't have a choice. The crowd wanted more.

I thought, "Come on, Michael, let's see what you've got."

Chang serves the first point of the fifth set. I attack it with my backhand, sending the ball screaming down the line, clipping the baseline, leaving him with no response. *Now* I am done. Slowly I walk forward to the umpire Bruno Rebeuh's chair.

"It's my back," I tell him. "I'm trying my ass off out here. I did all I could, but I just can't play anymore. Believe me, if I could, I would." The scores stand at 4-6, 7-5, 6-2, 4-6, 0-15. If you've got to quit, then do it when you're ahead.

Bill Norris, the ATP trainer and one of my friends on the circuit, helped me off the court. Bill had been around forever. I knew him well, and I knew he'd look after me. As we walked off, the Parisians came to their feet, cheering and clapping. That place rocked. They knew what they'd just witnessed, and I like to think they were saying *merci*.

The rain came down pretty much constantly throughout the first week of Wimbledon, creating a huge backlog of matches, but my wrist had held up to that point. No matter what the weather, you were expected to show up as scheduled. And wait. Trapped in the locker room. Needless to say, clock-watching did not suit me.

Still, there were some light moments. Brett, now 12, had come with me to London, and he was in the middle of a card game with Sampras and Richey Reneberg when Richey shouted over to me, "Connors, your son is up three hundred dollars on me. What am I supposed to do? I don't have any cash."

Brett had a solution. "Hey, don't worry. I'll take your racquets." That's it, son, always pick up your winnings.

I won in straight sets against the Finn Veli Paloheimo—who later told the press I was the best player he'd ever faced—and my buddy Aaron Krickstein.

For the very first time in Wimbledon's history, they opened the gates on the middle Sunday. "People's Sunday," they called it, with tickets printed the night before and sold on a first-come, first-served basis. The real tennis fans!

The atmosphere couldn't have been more different from the usual stuffy Wimbledon experience. Unlike at the US Open, the All-England Club tennis fans are there to watch and enjoy the tennis with their usual restrained attitude. Don't get me wrong, they love the sport as much as they do in New York and Paris, but Centre Court is more cathedral than coliseum—a place for the subdued appreciation of skill and endeavor rather than the frenzied cheers and catcalls thrown down from the Flushing Meadows stands.

But on that middle Sunday in 1991, a transformation occurred. From the moment Gabriela Sabatini stepped out to face Andrea Strnadová for their third-round encounter until the last point later that evening, not a seat was empty. Corporate hospitality had given way to sports fans, and they were there to make themselves heard.

There was shouting and singing, and the wave even rippled around the stadium all afternoon. I loved it, especially the wild support that followed every shot I made, and that was just in the warm-up. As I walked off Centre Court that afternoon, after Derrick Rostagno beat me in straight sets, the crowd rose spontaneously to give me an incredibly generous send-off. It moved me. As in Paris, I felt as though the tournament was bidding me farewell.

On the flight home I thought about my Slams so far that year: two third-round appearances, feeling and playing better after each match. But I knew I wasn't where I needed to be. The match against Chang proved that I wasn't in the shape to deal with back-to-back five-setters. I wasn't recovering quickly enough.

I call my dentist friend Joel Woodburn, who recommends the Cooper Clinic, in Dallas, where they'll put me through a series of tests to assess my body-fat ratio, the lactate levels in my blood, and a variety of indicators that will allow them to customize a diet regimen to improve my recovery time. OK, I'll give anything a try . . . once. Given my normal eating habits—a Pepsi and Snickers bar in the morning and a BLT at lunch—I'm guessing they might be able to help. The explanation they give me makes sense.

"Mr. Connors, look at it this way. As you are now, you start out at one hundred percent, play a match for four hours, during which your fitness levels naturally drop by fifty percent. That's fine; your opponent will be facing the same thing. The problem is, before your next match you're only recovering to seventy-five percent, which means that when you drop again you're operating at less than half capacity. The other guy will have the edge, and even if you do get through that, the next one will be a near impossibility. What we're looking to do is to get you back up to one hundred percent after every match, or close to it."

They put me on a carbo-loading diet: blueberry muffins every day, pretzels, raisins, and a supercharged drink before and during my matches.

Given what happened in the following weeks, I'd say they got it about right.

Over the summer I played Team Tennis with John Lloyd, as the captain of the Los Angeles Strings. I had some tough workouts and some good match practice, and for once I was a team player. Of course, we were the most hated team in the league, not only because we were a big draw but also because we weren't afraid to show we were having a little fun. But at that point, I couldn't care less what people thought. I had only one goal in mind: get to New York.

The US Open has always been my stage and the crowd my people. The rubber sweat suit, the track work, and running up that hill—it has all been for this. If I can win a match or two, I know the crowd will do the rest for me. If I can build momentum, I really think something good will happen. It's time to get the show on the road.

My old T2000 racquet had long been overtaken by technology, and by 1991 I was using an Estusa racquet, which I painted fluorescent purple at the French and Wimbledon. For New York, I wanted something with more attitude. Style never beats substance, but let me tell you: When I produced my neon-yellow racquet for the first time, I felt like I was holding Excalibur. If I didn't play decent tennis with *that* color racquet, they'd run me out of town.

Connors versus McEnroe again, in the first round, only this time it's Patrick, the little brother who doesn't quite have Mac's whole game, but he does have 15 years on me and is dangerous. Walking out under the stadium lights, flashbulbs popping all around, I don't have *that* feeling—the anxiety in the pit of my stomach, the tingle in my fingertips. I feel OK, but I can't find that instinctive sense of belonging, which I've been used to for so many years here. I'm nervous. Maybe it's because I didn't play last year? Does anyone care I'm even here? Obviously so. They've scheduled me on Tuesday night, so they were expecting a big sell-out crowd. No pressure.

Seems they're right; the place starts out packed. But I'm getting my ass kicked and those loyal New York fans are beginning to desert me. The box-seat holders gave up on me after a couple of hours, hitting the exits in time to make their dinner reservations in Manhattan. At least that lets the diehards climb down from the bleachers and fill the courtside seats, but I'm guessing they're here to see the last stand of an ex-champion. It won't be long now, guys. You'll still be able to catch a beer before the bars close.

The corporate guests weren't the only ones who found they had better things to do with their time than watch me slip into the sunset. Even my good friends Nasty and José Luis Clerc left when things weren't looking good at two sets down. When Nasty returned home that night to his wife, he said, "What a shame it was about Jimmy."

"About what?" his wife asked. "Look at the TV. He's serving for the match right now. And where have you been?" For the first time, Nasty was speechless—and busted.

And it wasn't just my buddies who bailed. Patti and the kids had returned home to California for the beginning of the school year and sat suffering through the first two sets on TV. By the start of the third, Brett couldn't take anymore. He went over to his friend's house to play video games. Patti drove him there. If I could have, I would probably have left as well.

I'm two sets down, 0–3, 0–40, when *that* feeling returns. Where it comes from, I don't know, but, man, am I glad the electricity has been switched back on. Fuck this—I'm not letting Patrick McEnroe beat me in my own backyard. This is where I live. This is my stadium. I'm not ready to say goodbye.

The air around me is changing. I don't know how, but the crowd seems to sense something happening. Now I get it. All the hard work, the fight to regain my fitness, the need to be out here one more time—none of it has been about me or my family or Mom. I've won enough for them in the past. I've won enough for myself. This is about winning for the fans. It has been from the moment I was throwing up on the City College track.

I hold my serve to make it 1–3 in the third and the stadium erupts. Now I can't miss. Nothing Patrick throws at me is good enough. The fans are giving me everything they have, and they're demanding everything I have. I've never experienced anything like this before. I doubt I ever will again.

I pump my fists, I point at the crowd, I thrust my racquet toward the sky, swearing in frustration and screaming in delight. Nothing is going to stop me.

"How can you miss them all?" I yell at the umpire after another bad call. "Get the referee out here. You can't do your job."

Patrick's not giving up; he battles to the end. At 1:35 a.m., four hours 18 minutes after we began, I serve out the match. That insane New York energy surging from the fans has fueled my comeback. Turning to each of the four stands, one by one, I let them know how much I owe them, how much I've always owed them. Then I look into a camera to send a message home: "Hi, Brett and Aubree. You guys better be in bed; you've got school tomorrow. Ah, hell, if you're not, that's OK."

The regular TV broadcaster had also given up on me, switching the match to a different channel. A friend telephoned Patti at home to tell her. "Turn the TV back on, Patti. Jimmy's coming back. It's into the fifth." She found that hard to believe, but she took a look and immediately called Brett.

They were watching me come back from the dead one more time.

In the following rounds, I faced two good players, the Dutch qualifier Michiel Schapers and 10th-seed Czech Karel Novacek, but for me it was back to business as usual with straight-set victories in each. After overcoming Novacek to reach the third round, I sensed people were thinking that the madness had to end.

Not me.

I draw Aaron Krickstein in the fourth round, on my 39th birthday. Aaron's a buddy whom I've practiced with at my house and a player I respect. He's never beaten me, and I've defeated him once this year already, at Wimbledon. While I know the New York hard court suits his game, going into the match I'm confident that if I can jump on him right from the start and take control, he won't be able to hold on.

Wrong.

I lose the first set 3-6, expending a lot of energy in the process. He showed up with a game plan—to let me be the aggressor while he stayed back, keeping the ball in play, moving me around, wearing me down—and I haven't dealt with the aggravation well.

To survive, I have to pull in the reins in the second set, change tactics, adjust my game, come to the net more, and shorten the points. For a while it works. I'm cruising at 5-1 in the second set, when Aaron somehow grabs the momentum and pushes me to a second-set tiebreaker. I've expended too much energy, and getting to the tiebreaker has drained me. Falling behind two sets to love would be a disaster. The tiebreaker is full of drama. I'm ahead, then I'm behind, and at 7-7, I bury an overhead on the line. The linesman calls it good and Krickstein's complaining. Umpire David Littlefield overrules. "Very clearly out," he's muttering. You gotta be kidding me! I charge toward the chair, screaming.

"He called the ball good! You couldn't see the goddamn ball. Get your ass out of the chair. You're a bum. I'm out here playing my butt off at 39 years old and you're doing this?"

Down set point, I bury a backhand volley that levels the score 8-8 and I'm thrusting my racquet and pointing my finger repeatedly at Mr. Littlefield. He sits there motionless. (When I watched the match later on television, the commentator Pat Summerall came up with a line I love: "I don't think he's saying he's number one.")

Forehand volley. 9-8. More pointing. More thrusting, and again Mr. Littlefield registers nothing. But he gets the message. Oh, yeah, he gets it. So does the crowd. No one is taking this away from me. No one. The place is going nuts.

Double-fisted volley. Second set, Connors. I'm swinging my racquet like it's a guitar, Springsteen's Telecaster, *Born in the U.S.A.* But I'm exhausted.

The fight to hold on in the tiebreaker has worn me out, and I'm being forced to let the third set go. I hate doing it. But there isn't any option, not if I'm going to win this match.

I'm not tanking. You know by now that's not my style. It goes against everything I stand for. If I thought I could win this set, then shit, that's what I'd be doing. I don't want to be out here any longer than I have to be. But my legs are gone and I only have one choice: give 100 percent and lose in four, or hold something back and have a chance of winning in five. So when the ball comes back at me more than twice during any point, I let it go. It's called taking a breather.

The intensity of noise in the stadium is overwhelming. Even

now, after that third set, no one has left, not one person. And they're being rewarded. We're in a shootout, and neither of us is about to blink.

This is what I live for, what I've worked my whole life to achieve, to be in this place, in these circumstances. As I've grown older, I have become what you might call a "situation player," capable of bringing out my best game when I need it most, on the biggest stages. Throughout most of my career I have always played the key points as good as anyone, maybe even better, wherever I am—Paris, London, New York, or Little Rock. One hundred and nine tournament victories to this point and a win average of .824 tells the whole story. Now I'm in one of the greatest "situations" I have ever experienced. My best game isn't going to be good enough. Two sets to one down, with the momentum against me, I've got to find a way to get back into it or I'll be packing my bags.

I'm up 4-2 in the fourth, first point of the seventh game, and my return is called long. No way. Man, this sucks. I pause a second, waiting, not really expecting anything. And nothing comes, not from the chair at least. No overrule and the crowd doesn't like it. They're jeering. I slowly walk toward Littlefield, stopping just close enough so he can hear.

"That ball wasn't going fast enough for you not to see it." Sarcasm. Love it. "Listen, kiss me first before you do anything to me next time. Just kiss me."

The fans. That's what I keep coming back to. They are driving me on. I take the fourth 6-3 and I have a chance to break back at 2-4 in the fifth, but my approach is called long. Players know the moment the ball leaves the strings whether a shot is good or not. This one is good. Once again I wait for the point to be reversed. Once again, it isn't.

We've been out here for four hours. If Aaron holds serve, I'm facing a 5-2 deficit.

"You . . . you . . . motherfuh—" The word is halfway out when I snatch it back. "You are an abortion." Yeah, yeah, I know, not my proudest moment, but I guess it could have been worse. Hell, it has been worse.

After a series of deuces, Aaron holds.

Back to the crowd. At 2-5, they're demanding more drama, and I am going to give it to them. I hold serve and now the pressure is on Aaron.

He is two points away from victory. Deuce in the ninth game, on his serve. These are the big points, my points. Attack, attack, attack. Crosscourt winner. Backhand volley.

By now, I'm exhausted but not tired. There's a difference. I don't want Aaron to see me huffing and puffing. If he begins to think he doesn't need to hit his shots quite so far from me he'll stop taking risks and the ball will remain in play longer. That could screw me.

"Isn't this what they paid for? Isn't this what they want." Now we're in a fifth-set tiebreaker and I'm talking directly into a courtside camera. I mean what I'm saying. I have total respect for the people in the seats around me and I am not going to disappoint them.

The end comes in typical serve-volley style, from me, a supposedly second-tier, one-dimensional baseliner. Deep serve, move forward, punch the volley, anticipate the return, bury it.

The noise again—it's . . . it's . . . I can't describe it. It just is.

Victory.

These people, these fans, when they eventually stumble out of Louis Armstrong Stadium they will be as emotionally drained as I am. They have given so much of themselves. I guess they wanted me to stick around as long as possible. After this, maybe they're thinking there isn't going to be anymore.

Before they leave, I'm blessed with a 20,000-strong chorus of "Happy Birthday."

Life can't get much better.

Since that match, I haven't seen Aaron once. Not once. Wait. Is he avoiding me?

I couldn't go back to the locker room right away; sitting would have brought on total, full-body cramps. Instead I walked around the small adjacent grandstand by myself. I didn't want to be with anybody. There must have been about a thousand people just sitting there watching, plus those dining in the overlooking restaurant. No one bothered me.

Finally, Mike Lupica, of the New York *Daily News*, came out. "You mind if I just walk with you, Jimmy?"

"OK. Walk, but don't talk. I need to concentrate." I needed to concentrate so I wouldn't cramp. Left foot, right foot; now repeat. I like Mike but if he was looking for a scoop, he wasn't getting one.

I was worried about my heart. Once I'd cooled down and my body had sucked in the fluid that was waiting for me, I felt fine, but I still couldn't leave. I had to hang around and piss into a fucking cup, for the fourth time in a row at the tournament. Everyone in tennis knows I have never had anything to do with drugs, but now they think they have to test me? At my age? Come on. On the other hand, after seeing me play this well at 39, can you blame them?

When I get into the locker room, I have a couple of calls to make. First to my family, then to Mom. Of course Mom couldn't leave well enough alone.

"Jimmy, I would prefer that you never call anyone *that word* again."

I go all innocent. "What word, Ma?" That's a battle I can't win.

Mom told me later she had televisions on throughout the house and wandered around, room to room, unable to settle and watch. If a game went against me, she was convinced it was her fault for staying in one place too long. She circulated through the house for four hours 41 minutes. The only call that she would take was from David Schneider, and at the time they said to each other, "What does Jimmy need to be doing this for?" I'm the only one who can answer that.

As for Patti and the kids, halfway through the match they drove to the chapel at our old Mission Santa Inés and lit a candle. I spoke to Aubree the next day. She was in second grade and had received some shocking news from a friend that morning.

"We saw your dad on TV. He's famous."

Up until then, I had just been her dad, who was away a lot playing tennis. "Hey, Dad," she said when we spoke on the phone, "did you know you're famous?"

"I am? Wow! I didn't know that."

20

NOT DOGGING IT

First things first. Take care of business.

After the US Open, which turned out to be the best 11 days of my career (I made it to the semis before Jim Courier ended my comeback in straight sets), I had to deal with the legal mess surrounding the investment Johnny and I had made. We were involved in the original riverboat casino, the Alton Belle, which opened in November 1991, then its replacement a couple years later, the Alton Belle Casino II. The company eventually grew, went public, and expanded to riverboats in six different states. The lawyer I hired to represent me made some interesting choices, to say the least.

It's a sad, complex tale of multiple lawsuits that lasted 11 brutal years. OK, another fine lesson I learned. No wonder I wanted to keep everyone at arm's length.

I fought it and won. This last battle in this prolonged affair was a lawsuit that one of my lawyers brought against me claiming that an "indemnity clause" in one of our agreements required me to pay the costs incurred in a deal that didn't even involve me. Here's an excerpt of the ruling from Judge Evans of the Seventh Circuit Court of Appeals. Reading it was the only time in this sorry saga that I smiled.

Jimmy Connors is known throughout the tennis world for many things: his fierce two-handed backhand, his numerous Grand Slam singles titles (eight, on three different surfaces), and his fiery competitive spirit, to name just a few. Connors has been engaged in an equally long-running battle off the court—or rather, in court—against his former attorney. The indemnity provision does not apply to this matter, and even if it did, we would find it unenforceable under Illinois public policy. Game, set, and match to Connors.

Johnny and I barely spoke for years. It took Mom's passing in 2007 to bring us back together again. He's my brother, and in our grief, I realized I couldn't turn my back on him. The time had come to say fuck it and move on.

I never retired from tennis, not officially. I kept on playing through 1992 before I quietly slipped away. I wasn't interested in some grand, dumb-ass farewell tour, even though, if I think about it now, it would have been worth a small fortune. I knew there would be no tears from either side when I left. When your time is up, you should make room for the next group of guys coming through. I'd entertained enough crowds and played some great tennis over the years. If people remember me for that, I'm good.

I continued to play Team Tennis with John Lloyd and the LA Strings, but, after failing to reach the playoffs that season, I moved to the Phoenix Smash in 1993 along with Lloyd, Mary-Lou Daniels, and Carrie Cunningham. We were joined by Ellis Ferreira, and together we were quite a draw, with crowds of 7,000 regularly packing into our indoor arena. It was tennis's version of the Wild West as we interacted with our rowdy fans and caused more than a little mayhem.

Under Lloyd's leadership, we grew into a tight, close unit. Courtside, the team members who weren't playing would horse around, ordering pizzas, chicken wings, and beer (I think my liver doubled in size), but on court we gave our all. Soon we were the most hated team on the circuit because of our antics and past reputations. That's right. Us against them. Again.

In April 1993, we lost to the Newport Beach Dukes in the play-offs, but we had left our mark on Team Tennis. Although maybe it was just a question mark.

I had no shortage of offers to play exhibitions, the most lucrative being my Challenge Match with Martina Navratilova in Vegas for the Battle of the Sexes II, almost 20 years after the original, starring Bobby Riggs and Billie Jean King. Fourteen thousand people were jammed into the stadium for the televised one-off match. This time the purse was half a million dollars to the winner. Even though we were both offered big guarantees on top of the prize money, I didn't want to lose to Martina. I still wanted to win and I loved the rush from a high-stakes bet.

I'm with my posse of Goldberg, Schneider, Vitas, and Lornie, along with Bobby Riggs, who's doing the TV commentary, when I stopped to see the bookie at Caesars Palace from the practice court.

"I wanna lay a bet. Me to win, straight sets, losing no more than eight games."

The bookie calculates the odds and they sound good to me.

"How much do you want to stake, Mr. Connors?"

"A million bucks."

"Consider it done, Mr. Connors."

Nuts. Absolutely fucking nuts, but here's the reason I'm telling this story. Every time I played tennis somebody was paying me; this time if I lost I had to pay them. With my money, in the bank, taxed. And it would have hurt, which, of course, was the thrill of it. Betting on myself was the ultimate gambler's high. I was out of control and I didn't realize it, though that bet should have been a big-assed hint. Viva Las Vegas, baby—even when you're losing, you can convince yourself you're one throw of the dice away from winning again. All I can say is thank goodness for tennis. Patti didn't know any of this at the time, and that was a good thing. She'd probably have passed out—after knocking me out.

For some reason, I didn't take into account that Martina wanted to win the match as much as I did. She's never been capable of taking any match lightly, and that's why she's such an incredible champion.

The rules gave me just one serve and gave Martina use of half the alleys. By the start of the fifth game of the first set, I was down 1-3. "This is tough, G," I told Goldberg, sitting courtside. "I didn't think it would be like this." During the previous week of practice, Schneider had been encouraging me, saying how great I was playing, and I believed him. It was only as we were getting ready to leave my hotel suite to walk down to the court that Schneider pulled me aside and said, "Look, I dropped a big wager on you, so you better be ready, Jimmy. This isn't going to be as easy as you think it is." Fine time to tell me that after kissing my ass all week.

As the fifth game was about to begin, there was a commotion in the stands. Lornie is out of his seat and rushing to the exit with a worried expression.

Up in the commentary booth, it turned out, Bobby Riggs was having trouble breathing, and a message has been passed down to Lornie, a close friend of Bobby's, to get up there immediately. When Lornie arrived, Bobby could barely talk, and we assumed he was having a heart attack.

"Bobby, we've got to get you to a hospital. Right now."

"Hold on, Lornie," Riggs said, grimacing. "Give me a minute. I've got to see how Jimmy's doing."

So Bobby had put some money on me, too.

By now I'm in lockdown mode on court, hitting the ball straight down the middle, hard and deep, but taking no chances. I start turning the match around. Riggs begins to calm down, and his breathing returns to normal. I must be ahead.

"What happened, Bobby?" Lornie asks, relieved that the crisis seems to have passed.

"I've got a fortune on him for straight sets, and I got so nervous at the start. It looked like I was screwed!"

I win the match 7-5, 6-2, and as I walk through the doors of Caesars with Mom, a guy approaches. His face is familiar; he's in charge of the sports book and he's become a friend.

"Jimmy, will you please come with me?"

Mom asks, "What's happening? Where are we going?"

"Come on. I think you'll enjoy this."

My friend takes us behind the cashier windows, where they've already counted and stacked my winnings. He shakes my hand. "Thank you for your bet, Jimmy."

For once, I leave Caesars Palace with a few bucks in my pocket.

In the days, weeks, and months after I finally accepted the reality that I was off the tour for good, I went through a really tough time, tougher than I thought it would be. For so many years, time had been measured by events and tournaments, not days and months. January was the Masters, May was Roland Garros, June was Wimbledon, September the US Open. That's not a normal way to live, and when that's gone, it's unsettling. Tennis had been my life—my escape from Belleville, from everyday problems, and my outlet for anger. Now it was gone. Just like that. Waking up every day at home, I couldn't shake the feeling that I should be in Paris or London or New York. I became a different person.

I got mad at the kids over nothing. I knew they loved having me around, but I didn't know how to cope with this new life. They began to joke with me that they had liked it better when I was gone half the year. I don't think they were kidding.

When I was on tour, Patti and I had worked out how to adjust to my stepping in and out of our family's life, but now I was there all the time. What was my role? Where did I fit in?

"Jeez, Jimmy," Patti would say, "don't you have somewhere to go?"

I didn't. I had to find my way back into the world, the real world, and sitting home drinking my days away wasn't a very good strategy.

I've been asked in the past whether I ever saw a psychologist for help during this difficult period of being a warrior without a war. The answer has always been no. But that's not exactly true.

I had *six* in-house shrinks.

My dogs.

I'm a dog guy, always have been, always will be. I love all animals, but dogs are my heart. Big ones, small ones—doesn't matter. I've had them all my life, and I love them all.

Goldie was a golden retriever we got when Patti was pregnant with Aubree. She was a special dog—beautiful, soulful, and sympathetic. When she got old and her life was winding down, Patti and I would spend the night outside on the ground lying next to her, just listening to her breathing. She didn't want to be in the house, because it was too hot, and we didn't want her to be alone when she passed. The night she died there was a big red ring around the moon that ever since we've always called a Goldie Moon.

In 1986, when Brett decided he wanted a puppy, we got Mackie, our West Highland terrier. Mackie was built like a fire hydrant but had the soul of a samurai. We referred to him as "a little barrel with legs." When he was older, he had some health issues and suffered seizures. During one of those episodes he stopped breathing, and as we were rushing him to the hospital I held him on my lap with tears rolling down my face. I wasn't ready to let him go. "Stay away from the light, Mackie," I told him over and over again. "Stay away from the light." Once we got to our vet, Dr. Bob Dean, Mackie recovered like nothing had happened. We were fortunate to have Mackie for another year after that. He died when he was 14.

We got Skylar, our crazy husky, in January of 1997, and she was a handful. She was Patti's find, one of the most beautiful dogs we'd ever seen. Patti had always wanted a husky but had no idea how high-maintenance they are. For instance, Skylar had a habit of eating my Calvins; we used to joke that whenever she did her business we could see the Calvin Klein label. No wonder huskies are such survivors in the Arctic; they'll eat anything. She was athletic, silly, and completely entertaining. She loved chasing tennis balls on the court and she loved her family. We lost her on June 2, 2010.

Sophie, another golden retriever, came along in February of 1998, and she is one of the sweetest dogs we've ever had. We call her our "special child." She was the runt of the litter and the last one out. She liked to sleep on top of my head even as she got older. Now that she's a senior citizen, she's slowed down a little, but she brings us joy every day.

Then came Tobey. We were at one of our local street parties, looking to find a hot dog for lunch, and instead we ran into Tobey, a small fat golden retriever with whom we fell in love immediately. Tobey became my little buddy. His eyes were almost human, and so was his empathy; he could sense when any of us got upset, and he was the first one to try and cheer us up. Tobey left us on September 28, 2012, and I'm still not over it.

Then there was Buddy, a shepherd mix. It was our good luck that he chose us as his family. Patti and I were walking the dogs one day and we saw him watching us from the property line of another ranch. "Ooh, he looks mean," Patti, said. Later, he found out where we lived, planted himself on our front porch, and stayed with us forever. He was our watchdog, keeping all intruders out, even though he was really a gentle fellow. Boy, I wish I'd had him around when I was on tour. Our Buddy passed on December 16, 2012.

The house is becoming very quiet now. They were my companions, and I loved coming home to a house that resembled a dog pound. My dogs and I have grown old together. It was my pleasure to take care of them after all the years they took care of me. I still walk around the house and look for them where they would always lay down. Their places on our bed are empty now, but we still make room for them.

Those were my shrinks.

My dogs helped show me the way when I lost my motivation. *Get your fat ass out of bed, Dad, and let's get some exercise.* All the runs, the walks on the beach, the swims in the ponds, and the roaming in the river proved to be lessons in positive thinking and living in the moment. My puppies would run alongside me, never refusing me, never complaining, and never judging me, allowing me to clear my mind and deal with the daily pressures. After miles and miles of therapy with my pups, I would be able to untangle my thoughts enough to talk to Patti.

I can honestly say that my pups' unconditional love and loyalty saved my life. My memories of them are ingrained in my mind forever. No matter how impatient or cranky I got, they forgave me. Even writing this now, I have tears in my eyes. I'd give anything to have my dogs back with me.

I'd been playing with the idea of an over-35 tour for a while. I always felt that my buddies had retired too soon and left me out there on my own. The time was right to pull them out of retirement and experience a little of the pain that I knew came with throwing an aging body around a tennis court.

I wanted to play those guys again—Borg, Clerc, Vilas, Gerulaitis, Lloyd, Dibbs, Stockton, Gottfried, all of them—because we'd combined great matches with fun for so many years. If I got this right, we could all have a second career.

I had a simple pitch when making the first calls. "Listen, we've got a chance to play some tennis, make some money, and become famous again. Are you in?" Not one guy turned me down.

Now, this wasn't a new idea; many great players before me had tried it, but it hadn't worked out. My dogs and I figured it out. To be successful we'd need corporate sponsors. Without them, there's no tour. And they had to get their money's worth, which came down to how the guests were treated by the players.

All the guys on the tour were champions, and they had presence and personality. The Champions Tour didn't work because of me; it worked because of the generation of players I grew up with, who understood what we were trying to do.

We had cocktail receptions and events for sponsors and fans who had devoted countless hours of their lives to watching all of us play tennis. We circulated among our guests, introducing ourselves, making small talk about backhands and forehands or anything else they might be interested in. If it came down to answering the same old questions over and over again, we did it with smiles on our faces, like it was the first time we'd been asked.

We were in the people business. That was the business end. The guys all had to be in shape. No one was going to pay to watch a bunch of broken-down athletes looking pathetic on the court. A few of the players showed up 40 pounds overweight and I sent them away. "I'm not looking for an easy 45 minutes and then you're out of there. You have to be able to maintain a good standard for an hour and a half. If you can't, I'm not interested." Whenever that happened, they hit the gym hard and came back in better condition than they'd been in years. Tennis players want to play tennis.

At first, there was a big difference between some of the players and me, because I'd just come off the main tour, and most of the guys hadn't played a real match in years. Mom always told me that the game she'd given me was built to last. "The problem, Jimmy," she would say, "is that you'll be playing your best tennis when you're too old." She was right about that. By 1993 I could keep the ball in play all day long, but my legs couldn't compete with the young guys. My game was so well honed, I could hit a dime crosscourt, but you know what they say about experience: By the time you get it you're too old to do anything with it.

At the beginning it was important to show the fans what we had left. They wanted to see that we could still deliver the kind of tennis for which we had all become famous. We were able to control the ball in such a way that if an opponent was out of position we'd take just a little off our shot to allow them to reach it, without spectators noticing. Because we were that good.

Once we decided to set up the Champions Tour, I partnered with ProServ executive Ray Benton on the business side. For sales and marketing I got Karen Scott (now Happer), my contact at ProServ Australia, who had looked after me when I played events like the Sydney Indoors in the 1980s. Karen had married Marshall Happer, the Pro Tennis Council administrator who'd spent years fining and suspending me. Yeah, I kept him busy. But it was nothing personal on either of our parts. When Karen agreed to join the team, I had to reassure the guys that if they saw Marshall around he wasn't about to cost them money!

The one mistake I made was to allow Benton to keep the tour's base of operations in DC, where he resided; by doing that I eventually lost control of the big picture. Nuveen Investments became our main sponsor, and thanks to them we pulled in various car companies, hotel chains, and banks. Against all odds we put on three events before the end of 1993: Hilton Head, South Carolina, where

Stan Smith was based; Sherwood, outside of LA, where Roscoe Tanner was; and Marty Riessen's New Albany, Ohio. From the beginning, all three ex-pros understood the value of what we were bringing to their clubs, and they were happy to accommodate us. After those three events, almost every match was sold out. We had eight tournaments in 1994 and by 1996 the number had grown to 22 tournaments worldwide.

Our headline was "Small Stadiums, Big Names." Our biggest venue was Pebble Beach, with around 7,000 seats, while places like Riviera, in LA, or the Boca Hotel, in Florida, handled 4,000. All of our locations had golf courses easily accessible, and golf became a big part of our corporate entertainment.

Our events would usually run Tuesday night through to a Sunday final. During the day we offered a choice of individual clinics, playing in a pro-am, where five guests plus one of the pros would form, say, Team Connors and take on Team Borg in a match or a round of golf.

The matches took place in the afternoons and evenings. The deal was that if you were playing in an early session, you didn't do any of your shtick until later, but if you were playing at night you'd be working during the day. If you lost the first round you stayed on all week to fulfill your social obligations.

At 7:30 in the evening the guests would take their seats and showtime would begin. I was usually on second, so that I could stay at the pre-match cocktail receptions as long as possible. It was my name on the tour and I was willing to do whatever it took to make it successful.

For the main sponsors, we erected big skyboxes in the corners of the courts, complete with a bar and seating for up to 40 people. If I was on court, Lloyd might be sitting with the guests in one of the boxes and Borg in another, and if one of them couldn't make it,

Vitas, Clerc, or someone else would step in. Then, when I was done I'd drop by to see how things were and discuss the match while my opponent did the same thing in another box. We worked hard, but that's why it succeeded.

Camaraderie between the players in our group was important. We were well paid, and we knew that we had to rely on, and trust, each other for that to continue.

Our flagship event, the Citibank Champions tournament, was first held in 1994, hosted by Westchester Country Club, in New York. On the morning of the finals, Vitas called Karen Happer at home. He was already out of the singles and doubles.

"Karen, Vitas. Hi, hi. I know I'm not playing today, but do you want me to come over? I'm at my mom's place at Oyster Bay. Do you want me there for the corporate stuff?"

"Yes, I'd love you to."

"Great, great. See ya."

She put the phone down and two minutes later it rang again. Vilas.

"Karen," he drawled, "it is Guillermo."

"Hello, Willy, how are you?"

"I'm a little bit tired this morning. I went to the Rolling Stones concert last night. But tell me, do you want me to come today?"

Most of the guys were like that, totally with the program from the very beginning.

Back in the 1970s, Borg, Roscoe Tanner, Peter Fleming, and I were just acquaintances. On the Champions Tour we became friends. But all the players we recruited had to—*had to*—be on board with our main aim: to entertain. As the number of events expanded, so did our pool of players. At its peak we had close to 25 guys to call on, and it was during that expansion period that Ray Benton suggested we add Brad Gilbert, the coach and recent author of *Winning Ugly*. I had my views about it, but I put it to the vote of the group.

The result was unanimous. A 16-0 rejection. That only happened once, and he still blames that on me, but we've grown older now and become friends.

The quality of tennis improved quickly after those first few tournaments—and with it the competitive edge. Especially when the prize money started to increase. In a short space of time, the big events evolved from staged showcases to hard-fought contests.

We created our Grand Finale, which was held every March in Naples, Florida. Using the WCT structure, players earned points throughout the year depending on how far they progressed in each event, with the top eight coming together for the Nuveen Masters.

We had the first Grand Finale in 1995, where Borg and I met in the final. Every session had been a sellout, and the fans had been treated to old-time tennis at its best. Borg wanted to beat me as badly as I wanted to beat him; there was nothing staged about that match. I eventually won, 4-6, 6-4, 7-5. The following year Andrés Gómez took the title, defeating José Luis Clerc again in three sets, and in 1997 I won again with a 6-2, 6-2 victory over Mel Purcell after defeating Mac in the semis.

For the first couple of years of the Champions Tour, Mac had buried us in his TV commentary, calling us dinosaurs. Then, in 1995, we offered him a check to play a few events, and suddenly we were the greatest show on earth. Gotta love Mac. He's nothing if not consistent. Did I want Mac involved? Sure, he was a huge draw. He made his first appearance in Moscow in April that year, beating me in the finals. His feelings toward the Champions Tour changed, and he soon became a regular and valuable asset.

At marquee events like Westchester or Naples, Mac would go out and kill his opponents, which was understandable since all the guys were trying their hardest to win. Unfortunately, he'd do the same thing in the early rounds of the smaller venues. Come on, Mac. That wasn't nice. This isn't Wimbledon. Apparently, he just didn't get the memo.

Was history repeating itself? It sure felt like that during 1998. By mid-August Mac had won three titles, including Citibank, and topped the Nuveen rankings.

Since we'd both been off the tour, we were easier with each other, but bitter rivalries don't just die. There's always unfinished business that—given the right circumstances, such as two Irish left-handers going after the same prize—can get ugly in a hurry. Which is exactly what happened during the final of the Champions Tour event in Dallas in September.

It's hot as hell. I want to win. He wants to win. He's complaining about bad calls. I'm joking with the fans. And we've only played five games in the first set.

Mac makes a return of serve. I make a step toward it, then stop. It's going wide. The line judge calls it wide. The umpire nods and announces the point in my favor.

Mac explodes. "So you're just going to sit there," he yelps, "and let Connors intimidate you?! That's all he's doing, trying to intimidate you!"

"And you"—now he's pointing at me—"you are a fucking cheater! That's the only way you can win!"

"Really?" I fire back. "You think I need to cheat to beat you? That's the furthest thing from my mind. But, listen, Mac—if you want it that bad, then you can fucking have it. Take the match and stick it up your ass."

I don't say another word, but as I walk toward my chair, I pass Eddie Dibbs sitting in the front-row. I wink at him, then pick up my bag and leave the court.

The crowd goes stunned. They haven't even seen half a dozen games yet.

Just as I'm about to disappear out the back, I hear someone in the stands shout at Mac, "See what you did, you asshole?!"

"Fuck you," Mac yells and flips the guy the bird. That doesn't go down well with the crowd and now the natives are restless.

In the locker room, I'm sitting having a sandwich and a Pepsi when Mac and his agent, Gary Swain, come in. I can still hear the fans going nuts out there.

"Come on, Jimmy, you gotta get your ass back out there," Gary says, and he's leaning right into me as he says it. I'm not in the mood.

"I'm hot and I'm thirsty and you'd better get the hell out of my face."

Then Mac says, "Come on, Jimmy, let's get back out there."

"With all due respect, Mac, I'm sitting here quietly trying to eat. It would be better if you just give me some space."

Billy Lelly's standing behind me, and he starts to say something, but I cut him off.

"Billy, son, I'm not doing it. This fucker here"—and I point to Mac, and now I'm just stirring the shit—"can't get by with that. I'm not going back out there. I'm stiff and I'm done."

Of course I'm going back out. I'm just enjoying myself first.

I stretch this out for another few minutes before agreeing to play on. Mac steps onto the court first, and the boos rain down from the crowd. I appear and the fans cheer.

I'm not really back into the game, though. Mac takes the first set, and starts celebrating like he's just won Wimbledon. Will he never get over that?

That just pisses me off.

I win the second set and we're into a super tiebreaker to decide the match. The first to 10 points wins.

The tennis is intense and exactly what the crowd had come to expect from us.

I'm a mini–break up, it's match point, and I'm hovering at the net. I volley, he tries to pass me, I dive full-length, and the ball comes off my racquet for a winning drop volley.

The crowd erupts. Mac and I don't even glance at each other. Mac exits to the left and I exit to the right. Just like the old days.

Mac and I might not have changed that much on the Champions Tour, but Borg sure had.

On the main tour, he'd kept to himself or hung out with his own circle of friends. After quitting the main tour, he went through some tough years in his personal and business life. When he joined the Champions Tour, he was in shape, playing high-quality tennis, and a pleasure to be around. Björn had come out of his shell.

When Patti and I went to dinner with him, he'd have six beers lined up in a row before we'd even ordered. They'd be gone before the appetizers arrived, but it never seemed to affect him. He stayed sharp and fit right through the years of the tour. Well, most of the time.

We're down in Chile for a match organized by Hans Gildemeister, we're due to play on a court they had constructed right on a beach. It's a couple of hours from our hotel, but we've got plenty of time to get there. Now we're waiting for Björn in the hotel lobby when we should have left 15 minutes ago. I see one of Borg's people walking across the lobby. "Any sign?"

"Sorry, Jimmy, no. I've called his room and knocked on the door. Nothing. Maybe he's gone out for a walk?"

"You mean to clear his head," I say. "He was pretty messed up last night." Ten minutes later and still no sign of Borg. I'm getting anxious. Then the elevator pings, the doors open, and Borg emerges, looking, as they used to say in the Wild West, rode hard and put away wet. In other words, he looked like shit.

We shove him into his limo as he mumbles, "Morning." Yeah, Björn, it's morning in Tokyo. He smiles, saying, "Thanks for waking me. I'm looking forward to the match."

We're off. Hans has arranged for a police escort, and we drive like bats out of hell, making it to the court just in time. The passenger door of Borg's car opens and he crawls out into the hot sun. The car ride hasn't done him any favors.

Somehow he makes it through the warm-up, and we're into the first point, and I'm thinking I'd better take it easy on him.

I send up a lob, perfect for a smash. I look at Borg as he sets himself. Suddenly he's back with us. Thank God. He's a class act, playing to the fans, pointing to the ball as it comes down, cocky, full of confidence.

He swings. Fresh air. The ball lands on his foot and rolls into the net.

He's looking at me, I'm looking at him, trying not to laugh. We're not far apart.

"Hey, Borgy," I call quietly over the net, "you're not lookin' so good, son. How about we get this over quick?"

A weak nod is all he can manage. There's such a thing as being too far out of your shell.

By 1997, I could see that the Champions Tour had begun to move in a direction I wasn't comfortable with, and I decided to sell my stake to IMG. I didn't agree with some of the decisions being made from our Washington head office. I didn't like the subtle change in attitude that I thought I saw in my partner, Ray Benton. It wasn't an overnight thing, but I could sense that Ray was beginning to believe he was the show, that he made this thing work and the guys on court should be grateful for that.

There were other issues. First, Ray and his team began to move away from elimination tennis to a round-robin format. They argued that the change would give fans the opportunity to see their favorite players at least three times. My feeling was that if I didn't win, I didn't care about playing any more matches in that event. If you're out, you're out. I know Borg and many of the others felt the same. We liked the knockout format. They were going to dilute the tournaments with potentially mean-ingless matches. Second, Ray and his people proposed lowering the minimum age from 35 to 30. They would be introducing a new younger generation—wow, doesn't that sound familiar? This tour was started for my generation of guys, and when I saw them being pushed aside, it was time to tear it down. The younger guys, it seemed to me, weren't used to working cocktail par-ties and doing all the extracurricular stuff required to keep the Champions Tour unique and successful.

There was a core group of sponsors, friends by then, who'd sup-ported us for a long time. If the players were going to be forced into a format they didn't want, one which I believed would ultimately drive them away, I felt strongly that I had a duty to make our spon-sors aware of my concerns. I couldn't abandon everyone who had worked so hard with me to nurture and create a thriving business without letting them know how I felt. After that, it was up to them. But, for me, I was done.

What amazes me is that when the Champions Tour was at its peak, tennis's decision-makers didn't realize what a good thing they had. We were playing to a different demographic, and if the authorities had been smart they could have used us to attract those fans to the main tour. For instance, imagine an event in the 1990s featuring Borg, McEnroe, Connors, Nastase, Clerc, Orantes, Stockton, and Vilas staged at Wimbledon on the outside courts during the second week of the tournament. Fans would have flocked there, bringing more money and interest to the game.

Why did the geniuses in blazers ignore the opportunity to showcase the excitement and skill—and controversy—of the guys of my era? My guess is that, deep down, they were afraid that we would steal some of the limelight away from the main-stage players.

But wasn't the point to make tennis bigger and better?

Wait. Maybe I just answered my own question.

I have so many great memories of the Champions Tour—and one sad one that will stay with me forever.

Seattle, Friday, September 16, 1994. It's eight o'clock at night and I'm with my family in my hotel room. I get a knock on the door and it's Vitas. He wants a quick word.

"Jimmy, would you mind if I take off."

"Where you going?"

"I'm going to fly back to New York because I've got a charity event on Saturday. I'll fly overnight, stop off and see my mom and change my clothes, then go out to Long Island to do the event."

I'd played doubles with Vitas on Wednesday. He was scheduled to play golf with the sponsors the next day, but he had strained his back during his match with me, and it was still bothering him. "I'll be OK to knock a few balls around, Jimmy," he had told me. "I just can't manage a full match. Or 18 holes." That was fine by me. I knew Vitas would never try and get out of his obligations. If he said his back was causing him problems, then it was. There was nobody better at taking care of business than Vitas.

"Listen, son, it's too late to head east now. You'll be exhausted. Why don't you hang here a bit? I could use your help, and then you can leave early tomorrow after a good night's sleep."

That's what I wish I'd said. If I had, maybe my friend would still be alive today.

21

A FRIEND REMEMBERED

V itas Gerulaitis was 17 and I was 19 when we first met, after he
joined the Riordan circuit.

We hung out a lot together through the '70s and '80s. When I won the US Open in 1978, I went out for a celebration dinner at Maxwell's Plum, in Manhattan. Vitas drove up and parked right in front of the restaurant, and let me tell you, he was hard to miss: Vitas was the only guy around tennis—or around most places—who drove a yellow Rolls-Royce. He got out of the car with two cute young girls who couldn't have been a day over 18, waltzed in, and sat down to congratulate me. He was the only one who did that. He was all class.

What the public saw was the real Vitas: the dazzling smile, the free-spirited guitar-playing rocker, the over-the-top playboy lifestyle. Yet he was also one of the most decent guys I've ever known, and everyone liked him.

Although he had his own crowd that included Borg and Mac, Vitas and I were close, and it was a no-bullshit friendship. It was an open secret that Vitas had a big problem with cocaine, and it led to his retirement from the game at the end of 1985. Without the discipline of tennis to hold him in check, Vitas's habit intensified dramatically. It's the reason I asked him in 1989 to travel with me to Europe for five months. I might not have been his closest buddy, but you don't abandon people when the going gets tough. As much as

I hated drugs, we were buddies throughout the good, the bad, and the ugly of it all.

While we were in Europe, we were basically together from the time we woke up in the morning to the time we went to bed at night. He was rarely out of my sight. I wanted to do everything I could to help him kick the drugs and get back to tennis. We hit balls together during the day, and he was slowly getting back in shape. He took a lot of criticism from the press about his weight during this time, and they ran cruel stories about how he wasn't in decent enough shape to practice with me. That's why he came up with the idea of coming out on crutches when we played at Roland Garros, as a response to everyone who saw us as long past our prime.

Being together in Europe helped both of us, even though I knew how tough it was for him. He was an addict, but he battled it. He was never a quitter. That's another reason I liked him so much.

I used to say, "Vitas, I can't babysit you for 24 hours. We're friends and I'm trusting you." It worked, because during those months he was clean, to the best of my knowledge, and it looked like he was getting back on track.

Back in the States, it was a different story.

It's the early 1990s and I'm waiting for Vitas to come to Santa Barbara to join me at a Pebble Beach golf tournament when my phone rings.

"Vitas, where are you?"

"Oh, I just landed in LA."

"How you getting up to Santa Barbara?" I ask. "You can take a plane or drive or I'll come down and get you, whatever."

"Wait, wait a minute," Vitas tells me, and then I can hear him asking someone for directions to Santa Barbara.

"Pal, you're in Dallas, Texas."

I start laughing. "Vitas," I say, "you're a long way from Santa Barbara, son."

"Oh, my God," he says. "It's all right. I'll just hop a plane and come on in."

Even though it was funny, I was afraid to ask if he was wasted.

It turned out that he was back in deep. Most of the "hangers-on" had deserted him in 1992, and when things started to spiral out of control, I was one of his friends who got the call.

Vitas had been on a coke binge while staying in a condominium at Turnberry Isle, in Miami. Donny Soffer (who owned Turnberry), Vitas's friend Stanley Ross, and Janet Jones Gretzky (Wayne's wife) had called in an intervention doctor to try and get Vitas into rehab before he did some real damage to himself. Vitas had once been engaged to Janet, and they were still good friends. She had given him an ultimatum: "Our friendship or the coke."

Patti and I were just coming off a boat from the Bahamas when we got the call.

"Jimmy, we need help with Vitas."

Patti and I went to the hotel suite where Donny, Janet, Stanley, and the rehab doctor were waiting.

"Where is he?" I asked

"He's over in his apartment in Tower 2."

When he opened the door a crack, I could see that his curtains were closed and the lights were off. Vitas looked like he'd been run over by a tractor-trailer.

"Hey, Jimmy."

"Let me in," I said as I pushed my way into the apartment.

The place was a mess. He had Styrofoam boxes of takeout food that looked like they'd been rotting in there for days. Janet, Stanley, Donny, and the rehab doc wandered in right behind us, and Vitas became a little defensive.

"Well, to what do I owe this honor?"

"Listen," I said, "we're all here, because we love you. And I don't want to pick up the paper one day and find your name in the obituaries. So sit down and listen."

Vitas heard everyone out about how concerned they were and after a couple of hours he just said, "OK. I'm ready to go." All of us admired how brave he was and what it took for him to stand up in that moment and recognize that it was time to get help. He had a strong support system and he understood that taking that first step, hard as it was, could save his life.

Janet called Wayne and told him she was going to go with Vitas to the rehab facility, and he said, "You go down there, Janet, and take care of him."

Vitas stayed in rehab for six months, and while he was there, both of my kids wrote him letters and cards every week. He always wrote them back and thanked them for their encouragement, telling them how he was doing and how much he missed seeing them.

Vitas came out of rehab—clean, sober, and looking good—and right into the 1993 Champions Tour. Vitas and Borg had been my first two phone calls when the Champions Tour began to take shape. I knew how important they would be to making the tour successful, and they were.

For the two years that he played on the Champions Tour, Vitas was clear-eyed, and back to his old charismatic self. Golf—a game he loved playing and excelled at—became his new addiction. He was also pursuing a broadcast career that could easily have launched him as one of the country's top TV tennis commentators. He was a natural. For the first time in many years, Vitas Gerulaitis's future looked very bright.

Then that night in Seattle in 1994, I let him go back to New York.

Vitas did just as he said he would after leaving the Champions Tour cocktail party. He flew overnight to New York, arrived home early the next day, dumped his bags, packed another one, said "hi" to his mom, got in his car, and drove to Southampton, Long Island, to attend a charity event. Then, because he was exhausted, he went back to the home of his friend Marty Raines, where he was staying. He told Marty that he was too tired to go out to dinner and needed to take a nap.

"I think I'm just going to stay in," he said. "I'm going to watch some football and take it easy." He asked Marty if he wouldn't mind sending over a sandwich to the pool house where he was resting.

The next day he was supposed to participate in the charity event. He never showed up.

I've asked myself too many times to count, "What would have happened if I had just said, 'No, Vitas, I want you to stay in Seattle until Saturday. I need you to play a few holes with the sponsors. You're the only one I can count on."

I was in the finals of the Champions Tour on Sunday, and afterward Patti and I took Aubree and Brett to a nearby theme park. When we returned to the stadium to pick up my tennis bag, a young woman approached.

"Jimmy, I need to talk to you," she said.

Thinking it had something to do with the tour, I told Patti to take the kids and go on back to the hotel.

"What's going on?" I asked the young woman.

"Look, Vitas is dead."

"What?" I said, refusing to believe what I'd just heard. I asked her to repeat it.

"He's dead, Jimmy," I couldn't move. I just stared into space, trying to comprehend the news.

"Come on . . . ," I said.

She just nodded her head.

"Was it drugs?" I asked.

It wasn't. What none of us knew at the time was that Vitas had died from breathing carbon-monoxide fumes from a swimming pool's new heater.

I felt like I was in a bad movie. I leaned against the wall, slid down to the ground in disbelief. We'd been together less than 48 hours ago. It was like someone had just kicked me in the nuts.

At one time I might have been expecting a call like that about Vitas, but not now. He had really beat it. He fought through everything to get clean from the drugs. If you put it in tennis terms, Vitas had come from two sets down and a break in the third to make his way back.

My friend Vitas was only 40 years old when he died. He was very close to his mom and his sister, he was a good son and brother and always looked after his family. Patti and I went to his funeral, at St. Dominic Church, in Oyster Bay, Long Island, and joined 500 other people—including Mac, Borg, Billie Jean King, Tony Trabert, Jack Kramer, Bill Talbert, Fred Stolle, and Mary Carillo—to mourn our friend. Out of respect for Vitas, the governor closed the Long Island Expressway when they took his casket from the church to the cemetery.

Vitas brought a lot to tennis—not just his athletic style of play but also his rock-star sex appeal, which added a new dimension to the tour. He was wild and flamboyant but also a great champion, winning the Australian Open in 1977 and reaching the finals of the French Open and the US Open. He was a Davis Cup participant and winner of 25 Grand Prix tournaments. Is any of that recognized by the tennis establishment? No. Vitas had a Hall of Fame career, but apparently he didn't have a Hall of Virtue career, but who does? It shouldn't be the case but his outstanding record and major contribution to the sport have, sadly, been overshadowed by his issues off the court.

I miss him still.

22

OPEN HEART

n 1997, the committee of the Tennis Hall of Fame, in Newport, Rhode Island, approached me about becoming an inductee. I turned them down.

"I appreciate the offer, but the thing is, I'm not done playing yet."

And I wasn't. I was still active on the Champions Tour, and I'd agreed to sign up for Team Tennis with Kansas City for the next year. Retirement was a long way off.

The committee kept after me for several months. I appreciated their gesture—becoming a Hall of Famer was a huge honor—but I didn't seek the accolade, and I'm not the kind of guy who wants to stand around and relive my past glories. I was either out there to play tennis, because I had something left to give, or I was finished. However, the more I thought about it the more I realized that accepting my place in the Tennis Hall of Fame would give me a chance to publicly recognize all those people who had made my career possible.

So in 1998 I accepted the committee's invitation. I wrote my speech on a flight from Kansas City to Newport on Saturday, July 11, 1998. Everything I said then continues to be true to this day, and parts of it are worth repeating now:

> As everyone probably knows, because it has been written about far more than I would like, I was quite a loner over the course of my career. But standing here alone is not right. If I

could, I would put some seats to my left and to my right. In the seats on my left, I would put my mother and my grandmother. They taught me the game, allowed me to play, and gave me the opportunity to reach for my dreams.

My grandmother was around for all the hard work of the first 15 years, but then left us when I turned pro at 19, in 1972. I know she's looking down, and I hope I've made her proud. Her seat is next to me. My mother was left to take over the task of furthering my career. I don't know if she always liked her inheritance, but she was able to wear three hats over the course of my life—as a coach, as my mother, and as my friend. For her to be able to balance all that, and still, after almost 46 years, for us to be able to sit down and talk to each other, is quite something.

She took a lot of criticism over the years for how she handled me, but it never really bothered her. She understood what she wanted to do with my career and for that, and for everything she has done for me in my life, there can never be enough thanks. You have all my love. Thank you. Have a seat.

To my right, I want to put my immediate family—my son, Brett, my daughter, Aubree, and my wife, Patti. My kids do not play tennis. By their choice, and perhaps a bit by my design, they have their own ideals and goals. They have grown up to be the kind of kids that make me, as a father, so proud.

My wife, Patti, well, I don't think she knew 20 years ago what she was getting into. It was said and written over and over that Patti Connors was a saint to put up with Jimmy Connors, and that is probably the only darn thing the press got right in all that time.

The way I played tennis was very selfish. I had one thing on my mind, and that was to try to be the best. For those 20 years, Patti went along and made it possible for me to do so. The way she handled everything when I was gone from the family, taking care of both my children, taking care of the house, and then, after doing all that, finding time to be my wife, is truly amazing.

In 2005, I gave an interview to the *Sunday Times*, in the UK, and was accurately described as having "severed all ties" with the sport. The reporter, Paul Kimmage, asked why I'd chosen self-imposed exile, and I told him, "For the last five or six years, the most important thing in my life has been my family. It was nothing against tennis; tennis was my love and passion, but after thirty-odd years of it, I needed a break."

That was all true, but not the whole truth.

I was at home in August 1998, and Patti and the kids and I were having dinner when Patti said, "Jimmy, I think I need to go to the hospital and get an EKG, because my heart is really racing."

Patti, Aubree, and I went to the ER, where they saw that Patti's resting heart rate was 120 and diagnosed her as having atrial fibrillation. They strapped her into a machine that was supposed to put her heartbeat into a regular sinus rhythm. We were there until 3 a.m., when her heartbeat came back down to normal

In addition, Patti had been losing weight for some time and having episodes of dizziness and nausea. It took a few weeks of anxiety and uncertainty before they identified the source of her problems, and in October she was diagnosed with Hashimoto's disease. They found nine good-size nodules on her thyroid. A week before she was to have surgery, we got our little puppy Tobey. Patti underwent the operation to have her thyroid removed, and luckily none of the nodules were cancerous. But she'll remain on daily medication for the rest of her life.

Then, in January 1999, I got a call from Mom's doctor, and he told me that she needed open-heart surgery.

"Listen, before you do anything, I need to call some doctor friends of mine to discuss this."

"Jimmy, your mother won't make it until tomorrow night. She needs a triple bypass and it has to happen in the morning."

I started to panic. "But I have to make those calls. I've got to speak to someone."

"Jimmy, you have to understand. Any delay at all and your mother will not live to see the end of tomorrow. Do you understand what I am saying?"

I did.

Patti was in LA for the day and I called her.

"I have to go back to Belleville, Mom's got to have heart surgery tomorrow morning," I told her.

"Well," said Patti, "you're not going without me." I wouldn't have expected anything less from her.

Patti raced home from LA to Santa Barbara and we made it just in time to see Mom before they put her under. That would have been impossible if I hadn't owned a private jet, a Westwind, purchased when I established the Champions Tour. I would have been unable to fulfill my obligations to the sponsors and events without it. But the jet was never more important than on that day in January.

Mom looked so small and frail when they wheeled her into the operating room. It broke my heart. Then, when I saw her in the recovery room, it was as though she had collapsed in on herself, like all her vitality had escaped with the surgeon's first incision. Worse, she was so cold. Patti rubbed my mother's arm as she slowly came to. "Grammy, it's me, Patti. Can you hear my voice? Are you in pain?" I had to leave the room.

For the next four months, I slept on the couch next to my mother's bed in Belleville. She was too weak to feed herself without my help. She'd given me everything. Now it was my turn to be there for her, to do what I could to build up her strength, to do whatever it took for her to recover.

In time, we tried to get Mom to move to California, but she didn't want to. We even rented a house for her next door to ours, but still she refused. For her, home was home. She had her friends and her students and it was familiar and safe.

By the summer Mom told me to get back to my family, because she was feeling better. "Go home, Jimmy. Look after Patti. Play some tennis. You can't stop just because of me. It's not right."

That was Mom, practical as ever. It reminded me of the time when she was in her late fifties and was robbed at gunpoint in Belleville. She'd parked her car behind a row of stores and had gone across the road to the shoe store. It was getting dark as she left the store, and a guy was waiting for her when she got back to her car. He held a gun in front of her face. Mom stared at him for a moment before speaking. "OK, buddy. You can have my money, but you're not getting my license or my credit card. It's too much of a pain in the ass to have to replace those things." Thank God the idiot went for it.

In the summer of 1999 I played a handful of events while dividing my time between California and Belleville. Then, in November, Patti had to have another surgery. The doctors had been monitoring a growth on one of Patti's ovaries, and as it continued to grow, they made the decision that it needed to be removed.

In the pre-op room at Cedars-Sinai hospital, Patti and I waited for our friend Dr. Greig, to arrive. We were concerned but not too worried.

A doctor we didn't recognize came into the room and introduced himself as one of Patti's physicians.

"I'm your cancer doctor, Mrs. Connors. We need to be one hundred percent sure during the operation."

Cancer. For a second it felt like all the air had been sucked out of the room. I felt sick. Patti and I had seen the scans and we knew how big the growth was, and if it was cancer, it was going to be everywhere.

This can't be happening.

What would I do without her?

Patti says the blood drained from my face.

When they took Patti into the operating room, I ran to the bathroom and threw up.

Tests confirmed it was a benign tumor, but in that moment in the pre-op room I'd been more scared than at any other time in my life. That's when I decided I was done with tennis.

I'd already made plans to play a couple of events in 2000, and people were relying on me to fulfill my obligations. I talked with Patti and then Mom and we agreed that I would honor my commitments, but after that I would be finished. Honestly, it was a no-brainer for me. Patti and the kids needed me, and so did Mom. My hand was called, so I played it.

Over the next couple of years we still couldn't get Mom to move to California, but Patti, Brett, Aubree, and I spent a lot of time with her in Belleville. She had recovered from her surgery, but she was never able to get back on the courts. The surgery had taken too much out of her. The combination of her osteoarthritis and rheumatoid arthritis also started to take a toll on her.

On one visit to Belleville, Patti sat down with Mom for a talk.

"Gloria," she said, "I want you to know that I realize and understand that it's because of all your hard work, everything that you did with Jimmy, that we have a wonderful life. You made this possible. Thank you."

Mom never once said to me that she was responsible for the life I'd been able to lead. But I think it meant a lot more to her to hear it from Patti. It's just sad that it took so long before Mom opened up enough for Patti to be able to say those words. So often over the years, Patti had told me that she understood Mom better than Mom realized.

"I know what she's protecting, Jimmy. I get that she poured her life's blood into you. I want her to know that I see that and I love her for it. All I've ever wanted is to be part of her life. She just won't let me in." What matters most to Patti and me is that it happened in the end.

I guess I had too much time on my hands.

We moved from the ranch to Santa Barbara in April 2001. With the kids growing up and leaving home soon we didn't need as big a house and property, not to mention the headaches of maintaining a ranch. As much as Patti and I loved the big skies and sitting outside by the pool late at night watching the stars, the ranch was pretty isolated, and we had to be aware of Patti's heart condition. Her thyroid operation had dealt with the immediate problem, but she continued for years to have irregular sinus rhythms, and both of us would feel more comfortable closer to bigger medical facilities.

I had backed off on the gambling during the time I was taking care of Patti and Mom. Well, not completely. After everyone was back on their feet and we'd moved into our new home in Santa Barbara, the urge to gamble returned. I had bet heavily all during the Champions Tour, and sometimes my habit became out of control.

It's Vegas, mid-1990s. I've just won the event and I'm at the blackjack table with Goldberg. I'm down and I'm pissed. I open the cover of my tennis racquet and dump my winnings on a square. I know how much it is: $70,000.

When the dealer goes to count it, I tell him, "Don't touch the goddamned money. Leave it there. If you win, you take it. If I win, then you can count it and pay me."

I'm dealt a 10 and a 6. The house has the same.

"Hit it."

A 4. I'm on 20.

The dealer turns over his hand. He has a 16 and he must hit. It's a 5 for 21. He sweeps my money away.

Goldberg and I stand up and leave. At the main entrance I turn to him.

"Fuck it, G. What am I going to do now?"

"What do you mean?"

"I'm broke. Can you lend me money for a cab?"

I'd just lost 70,000 bucks, and although it didn't feel great, I'd played the game and lost; that's how it goes. If he'd dealt me 13 and I'd drawn a 10, I'd have been pissed. Who wants to lose before the game even begins? But for him to have 16 and draw a 5 to narrowly beat my 20, well, that kind of action is worth it. But, man, I wish I had all that money back that I pissed away over the years.

Pretty soon the craziness came home with me. I'd spend whole days doing nothing but watching football and basketball, reading six different papers, trying to figure out the patterns, looking for the edge, then making the calls.

"I like Boston minus four and a half."

In the evenings I'd sit watching the games. I can tell you, not all our TVs made it through intact. Some I kicked in; one I even threw out the window. I was looking for something to replace the tennis, but it shouldn't have been this. I knew gambling on someone else wasn't my thing. My best results have always come when I'm betting on myself or making my own decisions. If I have the dice in my hands or cards in front of me, then I'm responsible. But if the quarterback throws a bad pass or a guy misses a basket, that's out of my control.

But I needed the fix again. That's what it had become, a fix that I wasn't even enjoying.

Patti had had enough, and in a two-minute conversation she slapped some sense into me.

"We go out for dinner with the kids and you spend more time on the phone calling the sports lines to find out the scores than you do with us. Is that really how you want to spend your time?"

I needed help, so I attended Gamblers Anonymous. Once. That's all it took. For five years after that, I didn't make a single bet. Except at golf. I mean, come on—it's golf.

I like the game, but let's face it: It's not tennis. It can be tiring, sure, but it's not the kind of exercise I'm looking for. I want to work up a sweat. Golf is more of a mental pursuit, an opportunity to learn how to concentrate better while trying to figure out the technical side. Waiting 10 minutes between shots? Well, you know enough about me to understand that 10 minutes alone in my own head can be disastrous. Adding something to the mix though, even if it's just a beer at the bar, gives me a reason to play.

I accept that I'm a gambler and I don't want to change. Pop was right all those years ago. I like it too much. But I know at this point in my life that I can keep it under control. Maybe everyone thinks that, but everyone's not me. I'm back on sports-betting again, but only with a group of local buddies. It's a form of socializing for me now. Do I occasionally hit the tables? Yeah, I do when I'm traveling, but gambling doesn't dominate my life anymore. I won't let it. Remember any time I had to overcome anything, I always went back to what I knew best: exercise and pushing myself so that I could exorcise my demons. Exercise to exorcise.

Mom's health started rapidly declining in 2003. She never strolled or meandered. She moved quickly, and that had been her lifelong pace.

Before the illnesses took over, she'd tell me over the phone, "I'm going to the tennis courts, Jimmy. I'm hitting some balls with a friend."

Then it became "I'm going to hit five balls against the backboard."

Soon all she could manage to do was walk to the courts to watch the kids play.

Later that year, she took a bad fall in the kitchen and broke her hip. She recovered from that, but she would never be the same again.

I started spending two weeks a month at Mom's home. Her condition worsened, and she needed a wheelchair and oxygen tank. The woman who had fought all those battles for me off the court was losing her own fight, and all I could do was sit there and watch her slip away.

You can't be in two places at one time, no matter how much you want to. Just over a year after Mom's fall, I was sitting on a plane at the Santa Barbara airport, about to take off for Belleville, when Patti called my cell to say that one of Aubree's best friends, Colleen Kennedy, who had been fighting leukemia for years, had passed away. Aubree had been driving to the hospital, hoping she would be able to say goodbye, but Colleen died before she could get there. I called Aubree immediately. When she heard my voice, she burst into tears.

"It's OK, Aubree. Pull over and take a deep breath. Calm down. I'm so sorry."

My mother needs me, my daughter needs me, and it's tearing me up. What's the right thing to do? There isn't one.

I flew to Belleville, leaving Patti to piece Aubree back together. Soon after I got home, I underwent the first of three hip-replacement surgeries in LA. I had been dealing with the discomfort and restricted movement for several years, but the constant travel between California and Belleville had started to make the pain unbearable. I'd put it off long enough, and if I didn't want to spend the rest of my life crippled, I had to overcome my fear of going under the knife and just get it done.

I'd been on Vicodin and Percodan for pain for a while leading up to my hip replacement. There's something to be said for getting through a day without pain and not knowing where you are, but I'd come to see that the amount of pills I was taking was becoming a problem.

Patti and Aubree were there in my room when I came out of the anesthesia. The operation had gone well, and after visiting for an hour or so they left and headed back to their hotel to pack and make arrangements for transferring me home the following day, October 22, 2005.

Aubree was driving when Patti took a call on her cell phone. It was her Aunt Nita but she couldn't get any words out before the line went dead. Patti knew something terrible had happened and asked Aubree to pull over. Moments later, her cousin called back with the news.

Patti's mom had been killed in a car accident. A huge part of my wife's life had been brutally ripped away from her—and I was in a hospital bed, barely able to move, incapable of supporting her. Aubree stayed home to look after me while Patti attended her mother's funeral without me.

Then, on November 12, 2006, Patti's stepfather, one of the most easygoing, coolest, wonderful men I've ever met—Gramps, we called him—died of a brain tumor.

It was as though some terrible curse had swept through our lives and left us wondering what disaster would happen next. I was never more aware of the importance of telling my family every day how much I loved them.

Not long after Gramps passed, tennis came back into my life again. I wasn't consciously looking for it, but maybe with all the loss and pain, I was searching for something I could control, something I understood.

At Wimbledon in 2005, I was being interviewed by 1976 French Open champion Sue Barker for the BBC when I mentioned I might be able to help out Andy Roddick with a few aspects of his game. Nothing major, just the small things that can make a difference, like playing more aggressively or taking his backhand a little earlier to generate more power. Andy's biggest weapon was his serve, plus he had a great forehand, but I thought if he could mix things up a little, he could continue to be a real force on the tour.

Wimbledon 2006 was a disappointment for Andy. He'd made it to two finals in a row (losing to Federer both times), but this time he lost in straight sets to Andy Murray in the third round, dropping his world ranking to 10th. Roddick and I spoke later that month about maybe working together, and on July 24 we made a formal announcement that I would be coaching him. Andy was the US Open champion in 2003 and the success that he'd already had was tremendous, so the changes I would be suggesting for his game would be small. Tinkering.

He spent four days in Santa Barbara with me, where we broke down some of the fundamentals of his game in preparation for a tournament in Indianapolis. He made it through to the finals there, and a month later he won his first title in over a year by beating Spain's Juan Carlos Ferrero in Cincinnati. At the US Open in September, he defeated Lleyton Hewitt in straight sets and had a great opportunity to beat Federer in the finals. Federer went on to win the title, but given where Andy had been, we were making good progress.

After the Open, I told Andy that the guys on the circuit were picking up on the changes we'd made to his game and to keep moving forward we had to work harder.

In practice he played brilliant tennis. He took the ball early, moved well, volleyed precisely, made the big shots, and fired serves that seemed impossible for anyone to return.

Our focal point became: Practice like you play your matches and play your matches like you practice. He had it in him, we knew that, but he wasn't taking the progress he had shown in practice into his tournament play, and that was frustrating to both of us.

In November, he played Federer again, at the Masters Cup in Shanghai, where he came within one serve of winning the second-set tiebreak and the match, which would have been tremendous for his confidence. But he walked off with a 4-6, 7-6, 6-4 loss. Both of us were emotionally drained and frustrated.

Andy worked hard and gave it his all every time he went out there, and in the end, that's all you can really ask of a man.

After almost 20 months of working together, it became clear that we'd gone as far as we could. When we should have been spending time, developing different aspects of his game, it wasn't happening. I wrote to him at the beginning of March 2008 to let him know I thought it was better that we part company and wished him the very best of luck. It was a great experience for me to be a part of Andy's career for that period of time and I hope that he feels the same.

I guess I needed to be back in tennis, even if it was just for twenty minutes.

It's spring 2006, a few months after Patti's mother's passing. My mother is in constant pain from the osteoporosis and becoming weaker every day. One evening during dinner, Mom just comes out and says, "Jimmy, I want to go home."

"What do you mean, Mom? You want me to take you down to 48th Street? See where you grew up?"

That wasn't the home she was talking about. Deep down I knew that.

Over the last couple of years I'd been spending two weeks in Santa Barbara, then two weeks in Belleville, and I had been watching my mother move slowly toward the end of her life.

From California I spoke to Mom 10 times a day.

"Hey Mom, you up?"

"Had your lunch, Mom?"

"Been outside?"

Most of the time she'd reply, "Nah. Not today, Jimmy."

I tried to keep her involved in my life by telling her about my coaching Roddick, about what the family was up to. I wanted her telephone to ring. I wanted her to interact. She'd been so active, so involved in everything for years that, when it all disappeared, I knew she would be missing it.

That day, when she said she wanted to go home, I said to her, "Mom, you've never given up on anything in your life. Why start now?"

Her answer was to look at me with an expression that said, "What's the point of living like this?"

In December she had her gallbladder removed. Because of her emphysema and other complications, they couldn't knock my mother out; instead they used "twilight sleep." How much more could her little body take? And for the first time I too felt, "Enough already."

I couldn't stand the thought of her being in the hospital over Christmas, and I managed to get her safely released just in time for the holidays. I went home to celebrate Christmas with my family then immediately returned to Belleville to make sure Mom was doing OK. One evening she turned to me and said, "I've had it, Jimmy." She repeated over and over again, "I've had it."

"I know, Mom. If you don't want to fight anymore, I get it. I do. It's OK."

I had to return to California for a few days to prepare for a trip to Australia with Roddick. Before I flew out, I stopped off in Belleville again, arriving at quarter to seven in the evening, Sunday, January 7, 2007. Mom was awake, and at the suggestion of her nurse, Hattie, I had brought her fried chicken for dinner. We sat together and ate. Afterward, Mom gave me a list of things she wanted from the drugstore, and I went to get them. When I walked back into her room I knew something bad had happened. Mom could barely talk.

"I think I just had a stroke," she managed to say. I can't be sure, but she sounded almost happy.

We called my doctor friend Curtis Jones, whom I'd gone to high school with and who had been taking care of Mom, looking in on her almost every day. He arrived within minutes. "Call the paramedics, Jimmy," he told me. "We've got to get your mom to the hospital right now."

I didn't want people buzzing round her, sticking tubes in her, scaring her. It was too late for that. With Curtis there, I asked Mom whether she wanted me to call an ambulance. "No," she managed to whisper. "No, Jimmy, not now."

I called Johnny. "You'd better come over right away, because Mom is failing quickly." I then called Patti and told her to come to Belleville.

Johnny arrived. We sat on either side of Mom's bed and held her hands, just the way we had done with Dad. She had a fixed gaze almost like she was staring at a light.

My buddy Lelly showed up and remembered that Mom had

said she wanted to have the priest there with her. At 12:30 a.m., Lelly pounded on Monsignor McKevely's door, woke him up, and brought him back to Mom.

After Monsignor McKevely administered the last rites, Mom took her final breath and died peacefully.

Mom was gone, but I knew that, wherever she was, she was going to be working on her backhand and enjoying a martini with Dad, Two-Mom, Pop, and my puppies.

After Mom passed, I wanted to bring her back with us to California to be near the family. I knew she would have left me instructions on how she wanted her funeral service conducted, and I had a good idea where I would find it.

Patti and I were leafing through her Bible, maybe her most precious possession. Mom used to put letters in there, things that mattered to her, and I thought maybe she would have left one for me. We read through all of her treasured notes and checked the backs of photographs and prayer cards, looking for a message, but there was nothing there.

I go through the pages one more time. Something catches my eye, a scribbled message in the margins of a page, Mom's handwriting.

"Jimbo, when the time comes, make sure I am buried next to your dad."

Next to it is a small slip of paper that we missed the first time around. I open the folded note, read it, and hand it to Patti. She studies Mom's words for a moment, then shows it to me.

"Stay with Patti, Jimbo," it reads. "She genuinely loves you."

23

MY VISIT TO THE BIG HOUSE

After Mom's passing, my life was relatively quiet. I wasn't hanging around the game much, and I'd finished coaching Andy Roddick. I was staying at home, laying low and playing golf with my buddies.

In November of 2008, Jerry, one of my golfing friends and a local commentator for the University of California at Santa Barbara college basketball team, invited Brett and me to the UCSB Thunderdome to watch the game with top-ranked North Carolina. Brett, who was living in LA at the time, got caught in the evening rush-hour traffic after a late start, and it took him a good four hours to get to the house. Running late, we decided to take a taxi to the game to avoid the hassle of parking.

At the Thunderdome, we went to pick up our tickets. There was a guy in line behind us who didn't look happy to see me. Maybe he lost some wagers on me in the past. All I know is that suddenly he bumps me and gets right in my face.

"Excuse me," I say and turn back around and don't think anything else about it. As Brett and I are walking toward the entrance, the guy follows and bumps me again. I turn around.

"What the hell?"

"You're a fucking loser," the guy tells me.

"I'm not denying that, but that's not what your wife said when I was on top of her," I fire back. I know, I know, lay off the wives, but not bad under the circumstances, huh?

Of course, one thing leads to another and finally Brett, who stands 6'4" and weighs about 210 pounds, has had enough and steps in to confront the guy.

"C'mon, Brett, let's just go watch the game," I tell him.

The guy's first mistake is that he's tubby. The second is that he reaches out and shoves me in the chest. You know enough about me at this point to know that I don't go looking for trouble, but sometimes it just finds me. Pop always told me, "Don't touch 'em first," so I figure the guy is fair game. I grab him by the throat to keep him off of me. (How are those anger-management classes working out for you, Jimmy?) The guy is making those "ack-ack" sounds and spitting all over me. I let go, push him away, and Brett and I head over to the stadium entrance.

I thought the whole incident was over until we start to hand over our tickets at the front door. That's when five UCSB campus cops approach me. Apparently, after I walked away from the guy, he went running to the campus cops and told them I had assaulted him.

"I'm sorry, you can't go into the game. You'll have to leave now," says the largest of the cops.

"Why?" I ask. "I've got a ticket."

"Doesn't matter. You have to leave the campus."

"Why?" I ask again, still not getting it. "You mean it's fine for the other guy to go in but I can't? Sorry, but I can't leave. I came here in a cab."

"You still have to leave the campus immediately," he insists. OK, now the guy is just showing off for his buddies.

I can't seem to make him understand that leaving would be no problem if I had a car. I have no way to leave unless they want me to hoof it off that large campus with my bum hip.

After the fourth time he asks me to get off the campus, I have only one answer.

"Look, I have no way to get home right now unless you want to take me, so fuck it, just arrest me." And he did! All 320 brave pounds of him and his four friends. I didn't know I could still command such an audience.

They put me in handcuffs.

"Dad," asks Brett, "what should I do?"

"Enjoy your evening, son. I'll see you later."

At some point, the campus cops have called the Santa Barbara County Sheriff, and they arrive, search me, and put me in the squad car, taking me to the Santa Barbara County Jail, where I'm finger-printed and mug-shot (quite a good photo, by the way, better than Nick Nolte's, that's for sure). Then it's off to my single cell for the night. All I need is a harmonica. Although the UCSB campus cops are not my favorite, the Santa Barbara County Sheriffs are good guys and take it easy on me.

After an hour in my cell, I'm taken to make my one phone call. I have to ask one of the guys for a quarter to drop in the box.

At home, the phone rings and Patti sees SANTA BARBARA SHERIFF on the caller ID.

She picks up the phone, laughing, and doesn't even bother to say hello.

"You've got to be kidding me," she says. "It's about time you called." I start to explain the situation to her, but she cuts me off. "I already heard. Brett called me."

"Will you pick me up?" I ask.

After Brett's call, she had phoned the jail and asked what the charge was.

"Failure to leave campus," they said.

Patti couldn't help herself: "Wow, you guys have got to be joking. If that's all we've got to worry about in this county, I feel really safe."

I was out in a couple of hours, but not before my arrest had hit the news wires and gone viral. "Tennis Great Jimmy Connors Arrested." Nice.

When Patti picked me up, she was still laughing.

"Are you hungry?" she asked.

"Yeah," I said, "they don't feed you too well in the big house."

We stopped at In-N-Out Burger and then, on our way home, we drove by our local restaurant and saw some of my friends I was supposed to have met at the game. We stopped and had a few drinks.

Let me tell you, getting arrested is instant celebrity. By the next morning, the media was banging on my door and blowing up my phone. I had friends calling me from all over the world, wanting to know what had happened. Jeez, if I'd known all it took to get famous was getting arrested, I might not have wasted my time winning 109 titles.

The case never went to court. The guy didn't press charges (but he got to see the game), and the whole thing ended up being a big waste of time. But for a moment I thought I might get to be on the Investigation Discovery channel. It never happened, just like my singing career.

24

PASSION PLAY

Writing this book almost pisses me off, because I have to go back and remember how I spent my life doing something that I genuinely loved, and now it's over. But I will tell you this: The desire to play and compete has NEVER left me, but when your body says stop, what can you do? You stop. If I could have my 25-year-old body with my 60-year-old mind, would I still want to play again?

Hell, yes!

In fact, if my body would cooperate, I'd be out on the court competing right now. But that's just not the way life worked out for me.

As I sit here today, almost back to normal after my third hip replacement, I'm thinking that maybe tennis should have come with the warning label MAY BE HAZARDOUS TO YOUR HEALTH. But if it had, would I have listened? Would I have done something else?

Hell, no!

I make no apologies for the way I played tennis. I wasn't out there to win a popularity contest—I was out there to win—and entertain at the same time. The thing is, I was good at being a bad boy, a real one. Not like some of the pretend bad boys who said sorry after every little incident. Face up to it or don't do it. I always accepted the fines, suspensions, and screaming headlines that followed my spontaneous assholery. That is a word, right? Well, it is now.

Did I step over the line a few times? Well, yeah, but that just made my job more exciting. I was letting the 25,000 people in the stands and millions more watching on TV into my office, to see, feel, and be touched by the pressures I experienced. (How many CEOs of big companies would allow that to happen? Bill Gates? Anyone? Raise your hand.) Did I make it harder on myself? Yeah, I could be a prick. I *had* to be one. Because when I was good, I was merely good, but when I was bad, I was great.

My grandmother Two-Mom understood the reality. She said to me, "You can get away with almost anything if you win." No one was going to fault a winner. I listened to Two-Mom, only I ignored the "almost." I honestly don't believe the guys today could carry the same load, whereas for me it was all part of the game; I craved the responsibility, loved it, and fed off it.

But I have to say that if I had come along on my own, it would have been a tough sell. I stood out and I was good, but my co-stars were great. With the Open Era, tennis entered a new world, one that was already crammed with professional sports—football, baseball, basketball, hockey, soccer—all vying for attention. To survive, tennis had to drag itself out of its comfortable little corner. It needed a facelift. The guys of my generation provided it. Suddenly there we were, a group of rebellious bandits, shooting from the hip—and the lip—with different styles, personalities, and attitudes. We were our parents' children, not willing to settle for the life we had been given. We were ready to break out, make some noise, and pay the price—good and bad. And we knew exactly what we were doing. None of it happened by accident. We recognized the show we had to provide, and we understood why we were doing it. Fighting, always fighting—for more than a column inch of coverage, for recognition, and, sure, for money.

What was the result? We moved tennis from those gated country clubs to the streets. We sparked the revolution that opened the doors to the people who loved sports, drank beer, ate hot dogs, and wanted to be a part of the spectacle—to see it, smell it, and, most important, let their feelings be known loud and clear. Back then, you could reach out and touch the players; that's how close the stands were. I didn't need to try hard to be heard, because they caught it all.

I appealed to a different crowd. The old-school fans hated what I was doing, of course; they were horrified by what they saw as a crude upstart trampling their precious traditions. But the new breed of fan, those who before had never considered watching a tennis match, suddenly had someone they could relate to. They saw themselves in what we were doing and liked what they saw.

If it weren't for the fans, we'd have played anyway, but I have to tell you, the fans made every broken bone, every knee operation, every wrist operation, every torn muscle, every aching back, and all three hip operations worth it. The fans won me more matches than I won myself. I fed off their energy, and I never for a moment took them for granted. I knew who I was playing for, and what I miss most is the appreciation and applause from the fans. It was my healthiest addiction.

How did the media react? Well, they sure wrote about me enough, so I must have been doing something right. Like me or not, I was good copy. They weren't afraid to hook onto me to further their careers. I even let one of them into my house. After that, the media and I had trust issues. They weren't all bad. There were some that I wouldn't mind sitting down with today for a beer.

The more the media criticized, the more I gave them to write about. They motivated me—that's the thing they never got—even though I knew the ongoing battle with the press was one I was ultimately going to lose. You can't stay at the top forever, and when you slip, they will always be there to have the last word.

I'd say there are plenty of players out there who have regrets over not achieving everything they wanted to in their career. I'm not one of them. I'm one of those fortunate people who got to spend his life doing what he loved to do and came away without even one "What If."

I just hope that if you take anything at all away from this book, it's that it's possible to keep doing what you love to do far beyond the age when others may be telling you to quit. That was a big motivation behind my run in 1991—all of a sudden age became irrelevant, 40 became the new 30.

Something still drove me to push even when I was past my prime. I played injured, dehydrated, hallucinating, and delusional. It's not what you accomplish; it's what you overcome to accomplish it that sets you apart. I wanted the responsibility of being the best and every pressure that went along with it. I walked away from the game not once, not twice, but three times. When I had no more to offer, I moved over and made room for a new era of tennis players.

What has the game done for me? Everything. I've played for royalty, for presidents, and for millions of people. I won and lost against some of the most talented athletes in the world. Me, a kid from East St. Louis.

I was lucky enough to be in a generation of guys who gave it their all. I don't have time for the other guys, the half-assed athletes who coast along with their eyes on nothing but the paycheck. I respect guys like Larry Byrd, Magic Johnson, Wayne Gretzky, Muhammad Ali, and Joe Montana, guys who laid it on the line, no excuses. For them, what mattered were the old-school values of pride and performance. Like Pancho said, "It's not your bank balance but what you feel about yourself."

One of the questions I hear most now is "What are you doing these days?"

I've got a lot of of projects that interest me, and some of them are in areas that you wouldn't expect. One thing that won't surprise you is that, even though I'm 60 and have been retired from the game for 12 years, I think it's time to get back to work. My hips are feeling pretty good, as long as I use a little WD-40 on them every morning, and I'm wondering if tennis *is* in my future.

Come on. Admit it. You'd love to see me come back . . . Wouldn't you?

ACKNOWLEDGMENTS

To my wife, Patti, without whose love, encouragement, patience, and forgiveness I don't think I could have made it. You allowed me to be who I was, not who I became. You've kept me aware of what is important, what is lasting, and what, in reality, life is all about.

To my son, Brett, and my daughter, Aubree. You have shown me that there is more to life than just playing tennis; the pleasures one has don't always have to be on a grand stage, and being a dad is the greatest gift I've ever been given.

To Mom, Dad, Two-Mom, Pop, Gramps, Grandma Mary: I owe you everything and I miss you every day.

To my brother, Johnny, for the life we had and the lessons we learned that were taught to us in a most unusual way. Thanks for helping me remember and for adding your feelings to my book. We've been through it all, good times and tough times, and in the end you are and will always be my big brother.

To my co-conspirator, Casey DeFranco. In the 30 years we've been friends, I had no idea your knowledge of sports was so deep. If I'd known that, I'd have been coming to you for my bets. Thanks for filling me in and coming out of the tennis closet for me, Casey. Your friendship and understanding of me, and all that I'm about, made it easy for me to express my feelings. You made the hard work fun, to say the least.

To David Hirshey, my brilliant editor. You covered me back in the day as a sportswriter for the New York *Daily News*, and, as far as I can remember, you didn't write anything that pissed me off, which is more than I can say for 99 percent of the press corps. Five years ago you said to me, "I will chase you to the ends of the earth to get your book." And you did, tearing your meniscus along the way and putting off your knee surgery until you were screaming from a different kind of pain. Thank you for your tenacity in convincing me to write my story and for allowing me the freedom of expression.

Also, I need to thank Richard Rosen at HarperCollins for his help polishing the final draft, William Ruoto for making me look so young in the photo sections, and Barry Harbaugh for making sure David didn't leap off the ledge before the book was finished.

To my UK publisher, Giles Elliott at Transworld, thanks for staying the course and not making me sound too British.

To my agents, Maggie Hanbury and Robin Straus, thanks for your patience, understanding, and support. It's been a real pleasure and an experience I'll never forget.

To Pancho Segura, whose wisdom and guidance gave me so much more. Your attitude fit my mold, and you were able to bring out the best in me. Your passion for tennis was infectious, and I couldn't help grabbing onto what you had to offer. Hard work, tenacity, pride, and personality. Lessons learned, Pancho.

To all my buddies: Spencer Segura, Ilie Nastase, David Schneider, Gerry Goldberg, John Lloyd, Bob Adler, Joel Pashcow, Lornie Kuhle, Bill Lelly (if I've forgotten anybody, I told you I've got amnesia). You guys have run me ragged, boggled my mind, and helped break down my body. But through it all, I wouldn't have missed one minute. Thanks for keeping me grounded (some of you) when it was needed, lifting my spirits when necessary, and throwing me under the bus . . . again, when required. Hopefully, we have a long life ahead of us to continue our friendships. But maybe we can tone it down a little. Nah!

To Billie Jean King and Ilana Kloss. Your love, friendship, and loyalty during tough times meant more to me than you'll ever know.

To my "twin sister" Brenda Richie, thank you for always being supportive and loving me.

To Dr. Bob Dean and everyone at Santa Ynez Pet Hospital, thank you for all the TLC you gave my pups when they needed it and for looking after them as if they were your own. Your compassion and caring will never be forgotten.

To Chrissy Lombardi, my physical therapist, and all those who took care of me at Elite Performance, thank you for keeping me motivated and mobile and putting up with my attitude during all three hip rehabs. I really can't thank you enough.

To Dr. Brad Penenberg, my hip doctor, thanks for easing my mind and making me feel as if it were no big deal. Oh, yeah, and for helping me be able to walk again.

To Dr. Rick Scheinberg, who gave me a new wrist and helped make my run at the 1991 US Open possible.

To Lloyd Greig, thank you for your care, understanding, and friendship.

If I've left any of my doctors out, that's just part of being old.

To my golfing buddies in Montecito, Barry, Chris, and the rest of you mutts, thanks for dipping in my pocket, so I guess more shots are in order. "I press."

To the fans. It didn't matter who you were rooting for; your passion for the game of tennis helped take our sport to a new level. Thanks for always being there. You made an incredible journey that much more exciting. You made it all worth it.

INDEX

Jimmy Connors was born in 1952 and grew up in East St Louis, Illinois, learning his tennis under the tutelage of his mother Gloria. He became Under-16 national champion and won a scholarship to UCLA, but after winning the Inter-Collegiate Singles title, quit his studies in January 1972 to turn pro.

He won his first major title in the men's doubles with Ilie Nastase at Wimbledon in 1973 and the following year won not only his first Wimbledon singles title but the Australian and US Open too. He went on to win eight Grand Slam singles titles in total, including Wimbledon again in 1982, beating John McEnroe in an epic final. He was the first player to win Grand Slams on all three surfaces (grass, clay and hard), won a record 109 tournaments in his career, was world number one for 268 weeks – over five years – and was still playing at the highest level in his forties.